Praise for *The Real Madrid Revolution*

"This book, like the first, will be one of the most influential books on sports ever written. It doesn't matter if you are a soccer or Real Madrid fan, you will look at sports and business in a different way after reading this book."

—**Billy Beane, former executive vice president of baseball operations and minority owner of the Oakland Athletics**

"With unprecedented behind-the-scenes access, this book is the most complete study of Real Madrid and football ever done, analyzing them both on and off the pitch."

—**David Hopkinson, former president and COO of Madison Square Garden Sports (New York Knicks and New York Rangers)**

"I thoroughly enjoyed *The Real Madrid Way* and implemented many ideas inspired by the book to help improve the NHL Florida Panthers. This new book will do the same."

—**Matthew Caldwell, president and CEO of the Florida Panthers**

"What sets this book apart from other books written about Real Madrid is the thorough research and incredible information from Steven's complete access to the club."

—**Kiyan Sobhani, host of the *Managing Madrid* podcast**

"The untold story of Real Madrid's journey to winning six European Cups in ten years and their transformative impact on football."

—**Stewart Wolfenson, president of Peña Madridista Los Angeles, and Dương Nhật Nguyên, president of Peña Madridista Vietnam**

THE
REAL MADRID
REVOLUTION

Also by Steven G. Mandis:

*The Real Madrid Way: How Values Created the Most
Successful Sports Team on the Planet*

THE
REAL MADRID
REVOLUTION

How the World's Most Successful Club
Is Changing the Game—
for Their Team and for Football

STEVEN G. MANDIS

BenBella Books, Inc.
Dallas, TX

BenBella Books, Inc.
10440 N. Central Expressway
Suite 800
Dallas, TX 75231
benbellabooks.com
Send feedback to feedback@benbellabooks.com

BenBella is a federally registered trademark.

Printed in the United States of America
10 9 8 7 6 5 4 3 2 1

Library of Congress Control Number: 2024022705
ISBN 9781637745311 (trade paperback)
ISBN 9781637745328 (electronic)

Editing by Rick Chillot
Copyediting by Michael Fedison
Proofreading by Sarah Vostock and Cape Cod Compositors, Inc.
Indexing by WordCo Indexing Services, Inc.
Text design and composition by PerfecType, Nashville, TN
Cover design by Sarah Avinger
Cover photo and logo courtesy of Real Madrid
Printed by Lake Book Manufacturing

This book is dedicated to the fans of football.

CONTENTS

PREFACE

LA DECIMOQUINTA (THE FIFTEENTH)

ON JUNE 1, 2024, the 2023-24 UEFA Champions League Final ends in a 2–0 Real Madrid victory over Borussia Dortmund at Wembley Stadium in London, secured by goals from Dani Carvajal (assist by Toni Kroos) and Vinícius Júnior (assist by Jude Bellingham). Vinícius became the youngest player to score in two Champions League finals, surpassing Lionel Messi. He also completed eight dribbles in the match, which is the most by any player since Lionel Messi (10) against Juventus in 2015.

It is Real Madrid's 15th—*fifteenth*—European Champions trophy. Almost as remarkable, for Real Madrid it is their sixth triumph in the competition in ten years: from Lisbon 2014 to London 2024. In their last nine finals in the competition, Real Madrid achieved a perfect 9-0. Since 2014, Real Madrid have won more Champions League titles (six) than the rest of the competing teams combined (Barcelona, Liverpool, Bayern Munich, Chelsea, and Man City—one title each). Real Madrid have won as many European Cups as the entire Premier League combined.

It is Florentino Pérez's seventh European Cup (in nineteen years as president of Real Madrid), more than Santiago Bernabéu's six (in his thirty-five years as president of Real Madrid). To put seven European Cups into perspective, AC Milan have seven in their entire history, and Liverpool and Barcelona have six and five, respectively.

Dani Carvajal, Nacho Fernández, Toni Kroos, and Luka Modrić tied Real Madrid legend Paco Gento to be the only players to win the European Cup six times. Real Madrid academy graduate Dani Carvajal is the only one of this generation to have started all six finals that he won. For manager Carlo Ancelotti, it is a record fifth success as a manager (he also won two as a player).

Real Madrid and Florentino Pérez aren't going to get complacent. They always want and demand more because of the expectations of their fans. The titles they just won are extra motivation going forward—on and off the pitch. Real Madrid define themselves by their values and results, and in particular by their performance in the European Champions League. The pride of the community at the team's wins is matched only by Real Madrid's passion for doing it in their own unique way. In London, the team's players felt the full weight of the community's expectations, which went beyond simply winning—those expectations include never giving up. There is an intense sense of responsibility and pride that comes with representing what the community is and the values they stand for. Real Madrid's secret to dominance on and off the pitch is the passion and values of their community members—which is where the club's culture and sustainable economic-sport model starts and finishes.

With a crowd chanting in the background "Campeones, campeones olé, olé, olé", Florentino said, "This legendary team has won six Champions League titles in ten years. This is the proof that nobody ever gives up with this crest and that we are capable of achieving magical things that seem impossible and that are difficult to explain. It has been an impressive season: the 15th European Cup, 36th La Liga title, and 13th Spanish Super Cup. This team has given everything and has shown that it continues to be hungry for victories and trophies. That's why I'm already telling you that this club is working right now to fulfil a new dream, which is the 16th European Cup."

After Cristiano Ronaldo was sold in 2018, many pundits said Real Madrid's great era cycle was over. In 2021, many pundits said Real Madrid needed to sign Mbappé. However, Real Madrid won the 2022 and 2024 European Cups without them.

And on June 3, 2024, Real Madrid announced the signing of Mbappé. One of the best players in the world is joining the reigning champions, who have won two out of the last three European Champions League competitions and have several young leading contenders (Jude Bellingham, Vinícius Júnior) for the 2024 Ballon d'Or.

In 2024, Real Madrid also had the highest revenues on the Deloitte Football Money League rankings and were named the world's most valuable football club in Forbes' ranking. In addition, Real Madrid successfully completed the massive restoration of their stadium to generate the emotions and revenues which will leave their mark on Real Madrid's future: hosting a Taylor Swift concert in May 2024, and being selected to host a NFL game in 2025. Lastly, in May 2024 a Spanish court ruled that UEFA and FIFA were practicing anti-competitive behavior, and were wrong to ban clubs from joining the European Super League—a similar decision was made by the European Court of Justice in December 2023.

Real Madrid was voted by FIFA as the Best Football Club of the twentieth century. Real Madrid will relentlessly pursue being recognized as the Best Football Club of the twenty-first century.

In many ways, 2024, on and off the pitch, was The Real Madrid Way, continued. But the period also highlights The Real Madrid Revolution.

POSTMORTEM

On May 8, 2024, as I watched in the Santiago Bernabéu Stadium, a part of me rationally thought Real Madrid couldn't come back again to win in a semi-final of the European Champions League with just minutes remaining in the match. But somehow, I remarkably believed Real Madrid would. I sensed that the players, coaches, and everyone in attendance believed it too. I didn't fully understand this special belief until I was lucky enough to experience it in person. Real Madrid substitute Joselu (a Real Madrid academy graduate) scored twice late ('88 and '90+1) to seal a stunning comeback victory in the second leg of the semi-final against Bayern Munich. Now I really understand what "Así, Así, Así gana el Madrid" truly means: "This is how Madrid wins."

Real Madrid, the 2024 UEFA Champions League Winners.

Dani Carvajal's header in 74th minute to take the lead 1-0 in the Finals of the 2024 Champions League at Wembley.

Toni Kroos, Luka Modrić, Nacho Fernández, and Dani Carvajal (from left to right)tied Real Madrid legend Paco Gento as the only players to win the European Cup six times.

Real Madrid's 15th European Cup is Florentino Pérez's 7th (in 19 years as president of Real Madrid), more than Santiago Bernabéu's 6 (in his 35 years as president). Here he's placing the trophy next to the 14 others in the Board Room. In the background, the FIFA Club of the 20th Century Award can be seen.

Any money that I receive for writing this book has been, and will be, donated to charity. This is true for any book that I have ever written. I did not, and do not, receive any compensation whatsoever from Real Madrid. They have not authorized or approved this book or anything that I have ever said or produced. They only provide me with access to the Real Madrid community and information. Opinions expressed are solely my own and do not express the views or opinions of Real Madrid.

I was an adjunct associate professor in the finance and economics department at Columbia University Business School and taught at Columbia University Sports Management master's degree program. After I published several books and articles about football and advised several professional sports clubs and leagues around the world, FIFA contacted me to help them in 2020. I stopped teaching at Columbia and became a Senior Academic Advisor to FIFA. For FIFA, I primarily teach club and federation executives about strategic plans, financial business models, and corporate governance; present and perform academic research; write "business school cases"; and perform data analysis. Typically, I work for FIFA a few days per month. This book has nothing to do with my work for FIFA, and I have worked on the book during my own time. FIFA have not authorized or approved this book. *Opinions expressed are solely my own and do not express the views or opinions of FIFA.*

I anticipate that I will take criticism from many sides for this book. Many people have very passionate opinions regarding Real Madrid, their own favorite and rival football clubs and leagues, the sport of football, and sports generally. Even though I didn't grow up a Real Madrid fan or even a football fan, I realize that I have biases, sympathies, and prejudices. However, I did take steps to challenge them as best I could, including research, data analysis, and actively seeking critical feedback.

I am not trying to say Real Madrid or their executives are perfect, or better or worse than any club or organization or their executives—I am providing perspective to help explain. I admire and respect many clubs and organizations and their executives. Some have read parts of the book to give me constructive feedback and respectfully disagree with some or most of my conclusions, but most admit that the book is well researched and that I raise several interesting facts (and history) that they didn't know.

Hopefully, at least, readers will learn something new, and this book will make them think more broadly about football. As you read, keep in mind that I am using my best efforts to draw on my academic training to shed light on a fascinating topic via a scholarly framework. Readers may agree or disagree, or even feel like other aspects should be mentioned or examined further. I genuinely welcome constructive feedback. As an academic and curious person, I am always learning and trying to get to the most reasonable conclusion.

There are sections or chapters of the book that are not specifically about Real Madrid and mention other clubs, organizations, businesses, and executives. However, they are necessary information and background to put topics into context. In addition, there are sidebars throughout most of the sections. The sidebars are related topics that don't fit the narrative but shed light on the topic discussed in the chapter. Often the sidebars relate to historical context, or an analysis of data or academic theories to illuminate an idea or help readers better understand the discussion. Lastly, I sometimes include postmortems at the end of sections or chapters to bring readers up to date.

If you have any thoughts or comments about the book, please feel free to email me at my Columbia University email: sgm2130@columbia.edu. I can't promise that I will respond to every message, but I can promise you that I will read each one.

INTRODUCTION

S OME PEOPLE DISMISS my views about football because I didn't grow up in a town like Liverpool or Marseille or Napoli, going to every home match with my father, or because I am not a member of a football club like Borussia Mönchengladbach or Club Atlético Osasuna. To them, I can't understand football culture, or the hope and threat of promotion/relegation, or the true meaning of domestic leagues and cups, or how a club is interwoven into the fabric of a town. To them, I am not an authentic "fan."

But I pay around a thousand dollars a year in subscriptions to watch my favorite clubs and competitions on TV or a device, hundreds of dollars per year to watch football clubs play in stadiums in America during the summer, and hundreds of dollars more per year on shirts and merchandise. If I'm not a fan, *what am I?*

And for big matches that I know will attract a raucous crowd, I often put on a team shirt and go drink, cheer, sing, and watch football at a bar (often at unusual hours in the morning in America) with other like-minded people. If we're not fans, *what are we?*

Meanwhile, my friends' Gen Z children who are passionate about their favorite clubs (but more passionate about their favorite players—whom they became attached to by playing FIFA video games) rarely watch an entire match, preferring to do other things online instead, like watch YouTube. When they do watch an entire match, it's usually a marquee match. And they always have another device open and are doing other things (possibly viewing TikTok), waiting for the commentator's voice to grab their attention that a goal or something dramatic happened. Then they start to share and discuss the highlight with their friends via social media. If they're not fans, *what are they?*

The value of the Premier League's international TV rights now eclipses that of the domestic TV rights. The Premier League's U.K. and overseas TV rights for 2016–2019 were £5.34 billion and £3.1 billion, respectively. For 2022–2025, the U.K. and overseas rights are £5 billion and £5.05 billion, respectively.[*] This is because there are more global fans of the Premier League than fans in the U.K. The Merseyside derby between Everton and Liverpool in June 2020, in the penultimate match in the Premier League's first full round of fixtures since its COVID restart, set a domestic football TV audience record in the U.K.—5.5 million people watched with Sky Sports, which has around 12 million subscribers (out of a country of 67 million people) for the Premier League.[†] Meanwhile, Premier League matches are viewed by 200 million subscribers around the world[‡] and are broadcast into 880 million households in 188 countries.[§] If those viewers outside the U.K. are not fans, *what are they?*

FANDOM AND OWNERSHIP

Since I am an academic and a researcher, I do like history and data, because they can explain or challenge conventional wisdom and folklore. So let's apply that to the concept of fandom.

When Liverpool fans, for example, challenge my "authenticity" as a fan or share their opinions about the European Super League—while I sip Liverpool's "official sponsor" beer, Carlsberg (from Denmark), and a "die-hard," "multi-generation" Liverpool season ticket holder tries to sell me their ticket for three times face value (and I was told American fans were greedy)—I ask them if they even know how and why Liverpool or the Premier League were founded. Most don't.

---

[*] https://theathletic.com/4240951/2023/03/08/premier-league-tv-rights-how-work-cost/#?access _token=12484233&redirected=1.

[†] https://www.sportingindex.com/spread-betting-blog/premier-league-viewing-figures. The match was made free-to-air by Sky Sports. The match finished 0–0. The previous record was the Manchester derby in April 2012, with four million watching Man City's 1–0 victory over Man U.

[‡] https://theathletic.com/1588394/2020/02/08/premier-league-tv-streaming-netflix-rights/.

[§] https://www.digicelpacific.com/mobile/ws/en/news/2022/may/6th/premier-league-partnership.html.

Before reading the answers that will probably surprise you, think about this: Liverpool have hundreds of millions of fans around the world who are passionate about the "authentic" values, culture, traditions, and history of Liverpool (the club and city are intertwined and synonymous). Most people would probably believe Liverpool are best understood by their season ticket holders. Yet in December 2020 only 5,832 of Liverpool's 27,000 season ticket holders (out of a total capacity of around 54,000) have Liverpool postcodes (22 percent of season ticket holders, 11 percent of capacity).*

The over 19,000 season ticket holders who are not from Liverpool . . . if they're not authentic fans, *what are they?*

For context, 25,647 of Everton's 30,500 season ticket holders (out of a total capacity of around 53,000) have Liverpool postcodes (84 percent of season ticket holders, 48 percent of total capacity). *Are Everton's season ticket holders more "authentic" Liverpool than Liverpool's?*†

Liverpool and Everton Are Not Comparable

While Liverpool and Everton both play football in the Premier League in the city of Liverpool (with both stadiums less than one mile apart and being within sight of each other), Liverpool are a global brand and a global sports, marketing, media, entertainment, and content company. And, respectfully, Everton really aren't. Everton generated €214 million in revenue during 2021–22. In comparison, Liverpool's revenues were €702 million. In November 2023, the Premier League determined that Everton lost £124.5 million in the three-year period up to 2021–22, which exceeded the permitted threshold of £105 million, and deducted ten points from their standing. Liverpool spent over two times (2x) the player wages than Everton—and relative financial strength correlates to relative performance. Since January 2011, Everton has beaten Liverpool . . . once. In 2022–23, Liverpool finished fifth in the

---

* https://classicfootballshirtscollection.com/what-percentage-liverpool-fans-from-liverpool/.

† In September 2023, Everton announced their sale to a U.S.-based private equity firm with a multiclub ownership model approach.

Premier League, and Everton finished seventeenth, one position from relegation. In many ways, Everton and Liverpool are not really comparable.

As for Real Madrid . . . Real Madrid have 60,127 season ticket holders (around 75 percent of 81,044 total stadium capacity), and 100 percent of them are socios, members who own the club and can vote on matters such as election of the club president every four years.[*]

So when pundits in Europe, for example, say "football belongs to the fans"—*who exactly do they mean?* Because I mean fans in the most inclusive way possible.

IN CASE YOU FORGOT

To illuminate all this further, let's take a closer look at some truths about football that fans tend to overlook.

Super League

The headline: "Sunderland Chairman Has Concerns over Plans for New 'Super League.'"[†]

Then-Sunderland chairman Bob Murray said: "That wouldn't be good for the long-term future of football."

The headline and quote were from June 1991 . . . about the English Premier League.

At the press conference in June 1991 to launch the Football Association's "Blueprint for the Future of Football," which backed an eighteen-club breakaway Premier League, supposedly to help England be more competitive in international competitions, Graham Taylor, then the England manager, said he had not even been consulted. At the time, he said, "I'm not totally convinced this [the Premier League] is for the betterment of the England team. I think a lot of this is based on greed."[‡]

---

[*] 26,687 have a Madrid postcode (45 percent).

[†] https://rokerreport.sbnation.com/2022/6/20/23175012/on-this-day-20-june-1991-sunderland-chairman-has-concerns-over-plans-for-new-super-league.

[‡] https://www.theguardian.com/football/2004/nov/14/sport.comment.

(England still hasn't won a major international competition since the 1966 World Cup, and the English Premier League has the highest percentage of foreign players than any of the Top 5 Leagues. Since the formation of the EPL, not a single English manager has won the title.)

Football author and investigations correspondent at *The Guardian* David Conn wrote: "This was the truth that got lost in the furor. The Premier League was a breakaway, and its purpose was to keep all the money about to flow into football."*

While the FA and media pitched that the new breakaway league was for the good of England, representatives of the Big Five clubs (Arsenal, Everton, Liverpool, Man U, and Tottenham) were holding secret meetings with BSkyB and ITV to learn how much money the broadcasters would give them if the clubs broke away from the Football League.

In addition to being the catalyst for England to win the World Cup, the FA and media helped sell the breakaway league with the idea that the big clubs could be relegated. Conn wrote: "Nobody believes that can happen today, because everyone knows any semblance of equality has been ripped away." Conn wrote that in . . . 2004!

In 2008–09, the gap between the sixth and seventh highest revenue earning clubs in the Premier League was just £2 million. In 2019, the revenue gap was a "record" £191 million. The gap in revenues is more than Chelsea or Liverpool or Man City spend on annual player wages! In addition, the gap between the Big Six (now Big Seven with Newcastle . . . and growing) and the rest of the Premier League clubs will only increase with the changes in the division of international TV rights revenues between clubs.

Liverpool Ownership: Who Owns Football?

In April 2021, in reaction to the announced European Super League, a Liverpool fan said, "[the owners have] ignored fans in their relentless and greedy pursuit of money. Football is ours, not theirs. Our football club is

---

* There were many reasons for the creation of the English Premier League, beyond helping the England national team and TV rights money, including hooliganism, outdated stadiums, the Bradford fire disaster, the Hillsborough disaster, lack of vision, and bureaucracy.

ours, not theirs. It is purely financial, cynically, greedily driven without any thoughts for the football fan, and that's the challenge that we have."[*]

Once again, respectfully, I have to ask:

Who exactly do they mean? Who does "ours" refer to, and who exactly do they mean is "the football fan"?

To put this quote into context, one needs to understand how and why Liverpool were even created. Liverpool were founded as a breakaway club (actually a for-profit company) specifically for financial reasons (some would go further and say Liverpool were founded because of "greed," not for the "fans").[†]

Wealthy beer baron and landowner John Houlding wanted to raise the rent that football club Everton FC, founded in 1878, paid to use his football pitch, called Anfield. Houlding also wanted to exclusively sell his beer on his own pitch during games. At the time, Everton were a member's club (which Houlding belonged to), and the members thought Houlding was trying to financially exploit the club. So Houlding resigned from Everton and started his own club, Liverpool FC, to play at Anfield and sell his own beer at games.[‡]

In 1892, Liverpool were founded as a for-profit company, instead of a member's club, with specific rules in its Articles of Association. In fact, Liverpool were one of the first for-profit football companies in England. The idea of a major shareholder owning and controlling his own club for commercial and financial purposes was a novel concept in 1892. English members football clubs didn't start to convert into joint-stock companies until 1888.

One Liverpool corporate rule established that: "The office of director shall not be vacated by his being concerned or participating in the profits

* https://scroll.in/field/992716/in-photos-stolen-by-the-rich-how-fans-are-reacting-to-european-super-league-announcement.

† *The Man Who Created Merseyside Football: John Houlding, Founding Father of Liverpool and Everton* (2020) by David Kennedy.

‡ Everton moved to Goodison Park and have been there ever since.

of supplying the company with any goods or stock," clearly so Houlding could sell his beer.*

When English Football Stopped Being "Owned" by Fans; Spain and German Ownership Rules

The first English members football club to convert into a joint-stock company were Birmingham City in 1888. The English football clubs primarily converted to for-profit private companies to raise capital to buy land, build and improve stands and stadiums, and fund losses due to paying more in players' salaries than revenues generated (the FA legalized paying players in 1885). Once players started legally getting paid, football started a transition in search of more and more money and revenues to help fund getting better players who cost more money.

After Birmingham City converted in 1888, more English clubs converted, and by 1921, eighty-four of the eighty-six Football League's clubs had converted to private companies. The average share price and valuation was often too high for the average working-class supporter, and most clubs lost money (primarily because player wages were higher than revenues) and required capital calls. Therefore, typically, shares were concentrated with a few wealthy local businessmen, many of whom had businesses that benefited from the club and/or were involved in club and/or local politics.†

Over time, the owners kept looking for more and more money, and even kept changing the rules accordingly. For example, in 1983, the Big Five (Arsenal, Everton, Liverpool, Man U, and Tottenham) got the league rules changed so that home clubs got to keep all gate money instead of sharing it with the visitors—and from that moment clubs who regularly filled big stadiums got more money. But it wasn't enough. The football club owners eventually changed from a few wealthy local businessmen to foreign billionaires.‡

---

* https://www.thisisanfield.com/2020/10/the-forgotten-legacy-of-john-houlding-the-man-who-created-merseyside-football/.

† https://footballpink.net/in-the-beginning-the-rise-of-fan-ownership-in-english-football/.

‡ Arsenal, Liverpool, and Man U are controlled by Americans who also own American professional sports clubs. In September 2023, Everton announced the sale to an American PE firm with a multi-club ownership model. Tottenham announced a willingness to sell at least a stake in the club. Tottenham Hotspur Stadium is the first purpose-built NFL stadium outside of the U.S. and hosts at least two NFL games per year.

The arrival of foreign owners, together with the growing interest in football, led to higher ticket prices as both demand and the cost of football matches (player salaries) increased and often the supply of seats decreased with new stadium safety regulations. Some of the local fans were unable to afford the higher ticket prices, and this negatively impacted their sense of belonging. Their marginalization increased as stadiums were remodeled into new "consumer cathedrals," and terraces and standing tiers with discounted tickets were removed—an unintended consequence of safety protocols in the 1990s.

Recently, as we'll examine in depth in chapter four, ownership has been changing to closely government-related, private equity, and multi-club ownership models. The transition happened because of the amounts of money required and at risk. Football became a big business and more about entertainment and brands than just sport—especially for the top clubs.

Spain

Fans "owned" their football clubs for much longer in Spain than in England, and some fans there still do own their club. In Spain, before 1990, Spanish football clubs were structured as mutual organizations owned by, and run for, the benefit of their members. By the 1980s, poor financial management, such as spending too much money on players and having too much debt, threatened the financial viability of almost every club. With uncertainty about who was accountable in the event of default of debt by a club (many members thought a local government entity would bail out their club), in 1990, the Spanish government intervened and created Sports Law 10/1990 to regulate the legal structures of the clubs. The regulation required all clubs that could not prove they were financially viable, with a positive balance in their accounts during the 1985–86 season, to convert into what is called a Sociedad Anónima Deportiva (SAD), which is like a limited liability company (LLC), to increase financial accountability.

The SAD structure still did not prevent the clubs from being financially irresponsible and borrowing too much money, but now most people recognize that it is the SAD entity that is accountable. Initially, the ownerships of the SADs were very diverse, but over time ownership became concentrated, so that today most SADs are controlled by high net worth individuals.

Of the forty-two professional clubs in Spain, only Real Madrid, Barcelona, Athletic Bilbao, and Osasuna were able to prove they were financially viable, and therefore stay as not-for-profit member-owned clubs. These clubs had to develop sustainable economic-sport models, since they didn't have wealthy owners to support them.

According to the Sports Law 10/1990, the elected president and board of directors of not-for-profit member-owned clubs must personally pledge 15 percent of total expenses and assume 100 percent of losses. This legal provision was added to increase the financial accountability and responsibility of the member-owned clubs. One of the unintended consequences of the regulation, combined with Real Madrid's incredible financial success, is that only a very wealthy individual, thus someone from a very limited pool of candidates, can meet the personal guarantee to run for president of the club.*

Germany

Prior to 1998, football clubs in Germany were owned exclusively by members' associations. This meant that clubs were run as not-for-profit organizations, and private ownership was not allowed. This changed following a ruling by the German Football Association (DFB) in October 1998, which allowed clubs to convert their football teams into public or private limited companies. However, the parent club's members had to own at least 50 percent plus one additional share of the football company ("50+1 rule"), ensuring that the club's members still hold a majority of voting rights.† For example, Audi,

---

* On December 22, 2022, the Congress of Deputies approved the Law 39/2022, simultaneously repealing the law that until then governed Spanish sport, Law 10/1990. Among many changes, the law was amended so that each member's club has the capacity to decide the percentage or amount of the pledge, if any, that should be registered in the corporate bylaws. Real Madrid decided to maintain the provision and not change the corporate bylaws of the club, and leave the provision as it is at 15 percent of the club's annual budget to specifically provide long-term stability for the club.

† There are some exceptions to the rule. In cases where a person or company has substantially funded a club for a continuous period of twenty years, it is possible for that person or company to own a controlling stake in the club. This exception most notably applies to Bayer 04 Leverkusen (owned by pharmaceuticals company Bayer), and VfL Wolfsburg (owned by automobile manufacturer Volkswagen), because they have been owned by their parent companies since their inception, predating the Bundesliga, and had more recently allowed SAP co-founder Dietmar Hopp to gain control of his former youth club of 1899 Hoffenheim. In 2023, Hopp announced he intended to transfer the majority of his voting rights to the club, waiving his exemption. RasenBallsport Leipzig e.V., better known as RB Leipzig or Red Bull Leipzig, got around 50+1 by exploiting a loophole. The Rassen-Ballsport verein – the team wasn't permitted to call it "Red Bull" – was formed in 2009. That year, it purchased the license to participate in the fifth division of German soccer from a small verein called SSV Markranstädt. Red Bull, the energy drink company, then pumped millions into the team, much as Hopp did for Hoffenheim. The difference between the two is that Red Bull controls its verein via limiting membership to just 21 people, making it by far the smallest club in the Bundesliga. The identities of some RB Leipzig members remain unknown, but all are thought to have links to the company, allowing Red Bull to theoretically control the club by proxy.

Adidas, and Allianz each own an 8.33 percent stake in Bayern Munich, with the remaining 75 percent owned by the fans. While Borussia Dortmund are listed on the German stock exchange and 67 percent of the club's shares are freely floated and theoretically can be purchased by anyone, the members still have control of the club.* Borussia Mönchengladbach (Gladbach) is 100 percent owned by members.†

The 50+1 rule is not without its detractors in Germany, with critics pointing out that it discourages major investment on a scale that would perhaps help German clubs better compete with Premier League sides. Honorary Bayern Munich president Uli Hoeness (a former player, general manager, and president of Bayern Munich) said he wished Germany would relax its 50+1 regulation because he believes Bayern Munich risk falling behind internationally.‡

On March 7, 2023, Chelsea beat Borussia Dortmund 2–1 on aggregate in the Round of 16 in the Champions League. According to transfermarkt .com, Chelsea's squad had a value of €1.03 billion and Borussia Dortmund's was €522 million. Chelsea spent around £323 million on new players in the January 2023 transfer window. Ironically, some fans in England want the Premier League to adopt a 50+1 rule to have more control over their clubs— one potential consequence could be lower squad values and a competitive disadvantage to clubs not subject to the rule (note this would place Premier League clubs on more of a comparable organizational structure footing to Real Madrid, Barcelona, and Bayern Munich).

Houlding also socially engineered the identity of early Liverpool FC. He wanted active Conservatives and freemasons from masonic lodges to be shareholders.

---

* German specialty chemicals company Evonik Industries owns around 8 percent (they are also Dortmund's main advertising partner), Bernd Geske (founder of Geske Lean Communication and previously marketing manager at advertising agency BBDO Group) around 8 percent, and German sportswear manufacturer Puma around 5 percent. https://aktie.bvb.de/eng/BVB-Share/Shareholder -Structure.

† Bayern and Borussia Dortmund have global brands. RB Leipzig (Red Bull), VfL Wolfsburg (Volkswagen), and Bayer Leverkusen (Bayer) have strong corporate company backing. TSG Hoffenheim (Dietmar Hopp), FC Augsburg (David Blitzer), and Hertha BSC (777 Partners) have access to capital markets.

‡ https://keepup.com.au/news/hoeness-claims-bayern-want-germanys-501-ownership-rule-scrapped/.

Another rule Houlding put in the Liverpool Articles of Association was that "The Executive Committee should have sole control over the ground and finances, power to engage players, arrange fixtures and of all matters including the election of members during its year in office." Obviously, Houlding specifically didn't want "members" or "fans" to have a vote like at Everton FC, which was then a member's club where each member had a vote.

The *Athletic News* described the shareholders of Liverpool FC as "a few private gentlemen, who will meet when it pleases them, and let the public know just as much of their affairs as they may choose to communicate."—in May 1899!

Liverpool were *never* a members' club, or "owned" by the fans. So, when a Liverpool fan, for example, tells me "Liverpool belongs to the fans," I must ask, "Since when?" And who exactly do they mean when they say "fans," especially since the vast majority live outside Liverpool and the U.K.?

In 2022, in response to fan protests over their involvement in the European Super League, Liverpool announced changes in their Articles of Association providing a role for "fans" in the club's decision-making processes.

The history and tradition of all big football leagues and clubs were built with many motivations—including money and power.

THE REAL MADRID WAY

Real Madrid have always been owned by socios (members) who vote to elect their president every four years and on other key matters, including the budget. Real Madrid talk about fans owning football because, steeped into their history, ethos, *and legal organizational structure* . . . they do.

Real Madrid need a sustainable economic-sport model because they are owned by socios—not a billionaire or a state-sponsored entity. Real Madrid were the only club in the Top 5 Leagues to report profits each year during the pandemic. As of June 30th 2023, Real Madrid have negative net debt (meaning more cash than debt), excluding financing of the stadium remodeling project.

Real Madrid have been in all twenty-four European Champions League tournaments since reforms were implemented in 1999–2000 to include up to four clubs per country. And Real Madrid won seven of them (2000, '02, '14, '16, '17, '18, '22, '24). Liverpool have been in fourteen tournaments (won two), and Everton have been in one (reached the third qualifying round in 2005–06 before losing to Villarreal).*

In 2014, I was granted unprecedented behind-the-scenes access to Real Madrid to write a book that revealed their fascinating secrets to success, which I titled *The Real Madrid Way: How Values Created the Most Successful Team on the Planet*. At the time, I was a complete outsider. I grew up and lived in the United States, had worked in finance and consulting, had a PhD in sociology, taught in the finance and economics department at a business school, didn't speak Spanish, and knew very little about European professional football and Real Madrid.† I, and almost everyone else I met in sports, was surprised that Real Madrid gave me, of all people, such access.‡ Fortunately, sports executive icons Billy Beane, Sir Alex Ferguson, and David Stern provided comments and feedback on my book to help me.

My primary reasons for writing the book were intellectual curiosity and academic contribution. After reading Michael Lewis's *Moneyball*, and watching the film based on it, I wanted to answer the question: *What are the secrets to building a successful sports team?*

I became the first researcher to be given access to rigorously analyze both the on-the-field and business aspects of such a big and successful

---

* Mikel Arteta, Tim Cahill, Duncan Ferguson, Phil Neville, and David Weir played for Everton. Villarreal won 4–2 on aggregate. Villarreal lost in the semifinals of the Champions League to Arsenal, 0–1, on aggregate, beating Rangers in the Round of 16 and Inter Milan in the quarterfinals. Arsenal keeper Jens Lehmann saved a last-minute Juan Román Riquelme penalty, in the second leg, that would have taken the tie to extra time in front of Villarreal's home support.

† I use the word *football* and not *soccer*, and use other "global football terms," because the book is for a global audience. I sincerely apologize in advance if this causes any annoyance or confusion for readers in the United States. I also refer to a club in the plural sense (as they) to distinguish them from a city.

‡ When I started my first book about Real Madrid, I was such an outsider that I had never even heard of Emilio Butragueño or Raúl González. After I revealed this to my good friend Borja Arteaga in Madrid, he politely suggested that maybe I should stop working on the project so as to not risk further embarrassing myself! Fortunately, instead, Borja and many others (including the Managing Madrid community) were tremendously helpful.

sports team. What I learned was completely unexpected, and challenged the conventional wisdom that moneyball-fueled data analytics are the primary instruments of success in sports. Instead, Real Madrid's winning formula, both on and off the pitch, from player selection to financial management, is based on aligning strategy with the culture and values of its fan base.

Chasing the most talented (and most expensive) players can be a recipe for a winning record, but also financial disaster, as it was for Real Madrid in the late 1990s. Real Madrid's current executives believe that the club exists to serve the Real Madrid community. They discovered that their fans care more about *why* the team exists, *how* their club wins, and *whom* it wins with versus *just winning.* The why, how, and who create a community brand and identity, and inspire extraordinary passion and loyalty, which has led to amazing marketing and commercial success—in turn, attracting and paying for the best players in the world, with the values the fans expect. The club's values and culture also provide a powerful environment for these best players to work together to win trophies.

Since I started my research for the original book, Real Madrid won the UEFA European Champions League six times (2014, 2016, 2017, 2018, 2022, and 2024).* I reflected on the last eight years and asked myself if enough things had changed to merit a sequel to the book.

While many players were no longer with the club (Bale, Ramos, Ronaldo) when I started my research for this book, many new players had joined (Bellingham, Rodrygo, Valverde, Vinícius Júnior), and some remained (Carvajal, Kroos, Modrić, and Nacho). The on-the-pitch results didn't seem to change that much. Real Madrid won more trophies.† Real Madrid players won more Ballon d'Or trophies (Benzema, Modrić, and Ronaldo).

---

* Real Madrid have won fifteen UEFA Champions League titles. AC Milan have won seven. Liverpool and Bayern Munich have won six. Barcelona have won five.

† Throughout the book, I provide selected examples in parentheses to help explain. I don't necessarily provide complete lists. Since I started my research, Benzema left and Bellingham joined in the summer of 2023.

Real Madrid were still owned by approximately 94,000 socios (members), and still elected the club's president and board of directors every four years.* Florentino Pérez was still president.

Most senior executives (José Ángel Sánchez, Manuel Redondo, Emilio Butragueño, Carlos Ocaña) and board members (Eduardo Fernández, Pedro López, Enrique Sánchez) were still at the club, and the off-the-pitch results didn't seem to change that much either. In 2021–22, Real Madrid still had a very strong financial position, and one of the best balance sheets in football.[†] They were profitable, even during COVID, and had a negative net debt (debt minus cash), meaning Real Madrid had more cash than debt, excluding financing of the stadium remodeling project.[‡]

Real Madrid still had the highest number of football shirts sold on Amazon and the highest number of social media followers (over 550 million).[§] In 2014–15, Real Madrid were #1 in the Deloitte Football Money League Rankings, with €577 million in revenues. (The Deloitte Football Money League is an annual ranking of football clubs by revenue generated from football operations by the accountancy firm Deloitte.)

And in 2020–21, they were #2 with €641 million in revenues, just €4 million shy of Manchester . . . City. (Real Madrid ranked #1 in Deloitte Football Money League 2022/23.)

---

* Member-owned clubs (Real Madrid, Barcelona, Athletic Bilbao, and Osasuna in Spain) are not-for-profit organizations, although they pay taxes, and do not provide financial distributions to members. The profits, if any, are reinvested for the benefit of the members and provide for internal financing to sustain and grow the organization. While not-for-profit entities in Spain are taxed at 25 percent versus 30 percent, they are only able to deduct 7 percent of reinvestments from pre-tax income for tax purposes, versus 12 percent for corporations. The net result is Real Madrid pays *more* in taxes than if it were a corporation.

† For those who believe that Real Madrid received €18.4 million in illegal state aid from Madrid City Hall in a series of transactions involving municipal land to pay off their debts, in 2019 the European Union's General Court ruled that Real Madrid got no such state aid. In addition, in 2019, the European Court of Justice ruled that Real Madrid, as well as three other member-owned Spanish clubs, did not receive state aid as it relates to taxes. https://www.reuters.com/article/uk-soccer-spain-rma-idUKKCN1SS1T5.

‡ Excluding the stadium renovation project loan of €800 million. https://www.realmadrid.com/en-US/news/club/latest-news/real-madrid-close-the-2021-22-financial-year-with-a-13-million-profit-.

§ https://sportsbrief.com/facts/top-listicles/20934-real-madrid-claims-top-spot-10-football-clubs-social-media-revealed/.

That is right: not Manchester United (Man U), but Man City.*

In 2008–09, Man City were ranked #19 in the Deloitte Football Money League Rankings. In 2008, the Abu Dhabi United Group, controlled by Sheikh Mansour, the deputy prime minister of the United Arab Emirates (UAE), acquired a controlling stake in Man City.† Man City's parent, City Football Group (CFG), has become a multi-club owner, owning stakes in over a dozen football clubs around the world. In twelve years, Man City became #1 in revenues. In 2022, the CIES Football Observatory added up the transfer fees paid by the "Cityzens" over the last ten years and arrived at a total of €1.7 billion.‡

Table 0.1: Deloitte Football Money League Rankings

2008–09			2020–21			
Rank	Club	Euros (m)	Rank	Club	Euros (m)	Change 08–09
#1	Real Madrid	401	#1	Man City	645	543%
#2	Barcelona	366	#2	Real Madrid	641	239%
#3	Man U	327	#3	Bayern Munich	611	322%
#4	Bayern Munich	290	#4	Barcelona	582	216%
#5	Arsenal	263	#5	Man U	558	231%
#6	Chelsea	242	#6	PSG	556	455%
#7	Liverpool	217	#7	Liverpool	550	333%
#19	Man City	102				
#21	PSG	101				

In addition, in 2008–09 Paris Saint-Germain (PSG) were ranked #21. In 2011, Qatar Sports Investments (QSI), a sports fund of the Qatar government (note QSI is separate from Qatar Investment Authority [QIA], which is the state-run sovereign-wealth fund of Qatar), purchased

* In this book, I am not arguing if Man City being #1, or any particular ownership, is good or bad or better or worse. I am explaining the changes and why/how the changes happened, and then why/how Real Madrid are adapting to the changes.

† Abu Dhabi United Group has publicly stated that it is separate from the Abu Dhabi government.

‡ https://twitter.com/post_liberal/status/1483512776849080328.

a controlling stake in PSG.* By 2020–21, PSG had moved up to #6. And PSG also are pursuing a multi-club ownership model.

IMPACT OF THE ENGLISH PREMIER LEAGUE

The Premier League is by far the most successful football league in selling TV rights—both domestically and internationally. The Top 5 Leagues in football are England's Premier League, Germany's Bundesliga, Spain's LaLiga, Italy's Serie A, and France's Ligue 1.[†] According to Deloitte, in 2020–21, the Premier League had €5.5 billion in revenue, the Bundesliga €3.0 billion, LaLiga €2.95 billion, Serie A €2.5 billion, and Ligue 1 €1.6 billion.[‡]

Table 0.2: Deloitte League Revenues in 2020–2021

Rank	Club	Euros (bn)	% of #1
#1	Premier League	5.50	
#2	Bundesliga	3.00	55%
#3	LaLiga	2.95	54%
#4	Serie A	2.50	45%
#5	Ligue 1	1.60	29%

* QIA is completely separate, and a completely different kind of company—QIA is worth hundreds of billions and invests across sectors. QSI only own PSG, 21.67 percent of Braga, and Premier Padel. It is a private investment company, not the sovereign wealth fund.

† Unsurprisingly, the "Top 5" Leagues are played in the most economically powerful and populated countries in Europe. Clubs in those countries have large fan bases and their domestic league broadcasting rights can be sold at significantly higher amounts than those of other European countries. These economic circumstances give the most prominent clubs in those leagues the opportunity to generate comparatively higher revenues, which in turn allows them to invest and sign the best players. By signing better players, clubs are then able to enhance their sporting performance, leading to improved UEFA nation coefficients, maintaining the superior number of places available to the top countries to take part in the competition, and hence a vicious cycle perpetuates itself.

‡ https://www2.deloitte.com/uk/en/pages/sports-business-group/articles/deloitte-football-money -league.html. According to LaLiga, they grew their domestic broadcasting revenues by 15 percent from €1.39 billion since 2016–17, faster growth than the Premier League, whose broadcast rights income grew by 5 percent over the same period, from €2.4 billion to €2.5 billion. The league noted that "the number of subscribers to OTT platforms is also more than twice as high in the UK as in Spain (36 million subscribers compared to 14 million in Spain), as well as having a higher population, a higher number of households and a higher per capita income level than in Spain." https://www.laliga.com /es-GB/noticias/nota-informativa-reparto-derechos.

Domestically, Sky has around twelve million subscribers for the Premier League. People in Spain don't watch as much TV as people in the U.K., so they don't subscribe or pay as much for TV subscriptions.* In addition, the average annual income in the U.K. is around $49,000 compared to around $32,000 in Spain (and $76,000 in the U.S.).† In Spain, Movistar, which has the rights to LaLiga, has only about three million subscribers (one-third of England's), even though Spain has 70 percent of England's population (forty-seven million in Spain and sixty-seven million in the U.K.).‡

Internationally, the Premier League dominates. The Premier League's annual international TV rights revenues are €1.6 billion, LaLiga's €897 million, Bundesliga's €240 million, and Ligue 1's only €80 million.§ In contrast to the recent increase of the overall English broadcast deals (driven by international growth), the French, German, and Italian leagues have all seen a drop.¶

In *The Real Madrid Way*, I mentioned a key challenge to Real Madrid and professional domestic football leagues: the Premier League was developing into the NBA of football, and would or could make the other professional leagues (as well as their domestic clubs) less relevant. In 2015, LaLiga president Javier Tebas said, "We run the risk of having the Premier League become the NBA of football in the next five years, with the rest of European leagues turning into secondary tournaments."** The sig-

---

* An Ofcom study shows 70 percent of British adults watch free-to-air catch-up services such as iPlayer or All4, ahead of France and Spain, on 52 percent. https://www.theguardian.com/media/2015/dec/10/uk-most-advanced-tv-watching-country-in-world-says-media-regulator.

† https://www.worlddata.info/average-income.php.

‡ In Spain, Movistar have a 50/50 rights split with DAZN, where Sky has around 80 percent of the EPL rights in the U.K. (TNT Sport have one match per week, Amazon two full matchdays). Sky also holds many of the second-tier sports rights, which are very popular in the U.K. (international football, cricket, and rugby). In Spain, besides basketball and Formula 1 (both DAZN), viewing figures are very low on other sports.

§ https://www.footballbenchmark.com/library/broadcasting_revenue_landscape_big_money_in_the_big_five_leagues.

¶ https://brandequity.economictimes.indiatimes.com/news/media/tv-revenue-epl-earns-more-from-overseas-rights-for-1st-time/89504991.

** "LaLiga Goes Abroad to Try to Keep Pace with Premier League." *USA Today.* http://www.usatoday.com/story/sports/soccer/2015/11/01/la-liga-goes-abroad-to-try-to-keep-pace-with-premierleague/75018236/.

nificant difference in revenues has led to a significant difference in player salaries (and presumably talent), with the Premier League having total salaries of €3.9 billion, almost double that of Bundesliga's €1.95 billion.

According to Off The Pitch's player salaries database, the median Premier League basic guaranteed player salary among 530 players in the twenty first-team squads was €3.1 million, in mid-November 2022. The second best–paid league was Serie A with €1.1 million (35 percent of the Premier League's).* The data for LaLiga—which finished fourth— shows a median salary of €837,520 for 498 first-team players (27 percent of the Premier League's).†

Table 0.3: Top 5 Median Player Salaries by League in Mid-November 2022

Rank	Club	Euros (m)	% of #1
#1	Premier League	3.1	
#2	Serie A	1.1	35%
#3	Bundesliga	.9	29%
#4	LaLigue	.8	27%
#5	Ligue 1	.5	16%

SOURCE: Off The Pitch Player Salary Data

Beyond player salaries, as the following chart shows, Premier League clubs spent almost four times the next highest league in player transfer fees. In terms of net spending (transfer revenue minus spending), the Premier League, with its negative net transfer balance of €2.1 billion, is significantly higher than rival leagues—none of which had a collective net spend of more than negative €52 million. The massive spending difference highlights a dangerous imbalance in European football. If sustained,

---

* https://offthepitch.com/a/new-salary-database-premier-league-players-now-earn-twice-much-laliga -players?wv_email=sgmandis%40me.com&wv_id=0b33e863-2b87-44e3-82bb-a46dd11bfd0d&wv _name=&check_logged_in=1.

† https://offthepitch.com/a/new-salary-database-premier-league-players-now-earn-twice-much-laliga -players?wv_email=sgmandis%40me.com&wv_id=0b33e863-2b87-44e3-82bb-a46dd11bfd0d&wv _name=&check_logged_in=1.

all other leagues could eventually become "farm leagues" for the Premier League, and the integrity of European competitions will inevitably suffer.

Table: 0.4 Transfer Spending and Revenue of Clubs
from the Top 5 Leagues in 2022–23

Rank	League	Spending On Players in Euros (m)	% of #1	Revenue from Selling Players (m)	Net (m)
#1	Premier League	-3075		1,000	-2075
#2	Serie A	-798	26%	824	26
#3	Ligue 1	-699	23%	797	98
#4	LaLiga	-558	18%	506	-52
#5	Bundesliga	-559	18%	600	44

SOURCE: Transfermarkt.com

With such a disparity, one must wonder, "How can a club in another league compete against a Premier League club in a European competition—especially if the Premier League club has closely government-related ownership with almost unlimited resources?"* In 2023, Daniel Levy, chairman of Tottenham, addressed this issue: "The landscape of the Premier League has changed significantly in the last decade. It is understandable that some fans call for more spending, much of which is unsustainable for many clubs. We are competing in a league in which we have seen increased sovereign wealth ownership and consortia finance; and in a league where the spending power is now vested in the hands of a few who dominate and have the ability to distort the market."† And Levy was just talking about within the Premier League—what about the clubs outside the league?

---

* The gap causes clubs not in the Premier League to typically spend a higher percentage of revenues to keep up with the Premier League. According to Off The Pitch, in LaLiga, around 85 percent of a club's total wage bill (all employees) will be spent on players (all levels from first team to youth academy), with a large majority of total player pay being spent on first-team wages—while in the Premier League it is around 75 percent.

† https://www.express.co.uk/sport/football/1733436/Tottenham-Man-City-Pep-Guardiola-Daniel-Levy-Premier-League-news.

While PSG have been able to rise quickly in the Deloitte Football Money League Rankings even with France's Ligue 1 TV contract being the lowest, what are the consequences? In a January 2023 interview with Off The Pitch, Tebas said he "doesn't mind that the [Qatari] state owns PSG . . . What I do care about is that they keep running the club at a loss and injecting money that has nothing to do with football into it . . . This generates massive inflation in terms of salaries and players, which generates a domino effect and result in losses in other clubs."* Many suspect that some clubs are artificially inflating the values of the contracts with sponsors (especially those they directly or indirectly control or influence) to boost revenues to circumvent Financial Fair Play rules and enable them to spend more on players, hence inflating the player salaries.

Overall player wages are growing faster than overall revenues. According to a 2023 report, UEFA president Aleksander Čeferin wrote: "Despite the unprecedented turmoil of recent years, wages have continued to grow, rising on average by 16 per cent compared to pre-pandemic standards. Top-division players' salaries, for example, have more than doubled during the past decade. And while this is not a negative trend per se, it is clear that many are compromising their economic sustainability in their reckless pursuit of success." One must wonder if this would be as true if Financial Fair Play (FFP) were consistently applied and rigorously enforced.

Continuing the trend of closely government-related ownership, in 2021, Saudi Arabia's sovereign wealth fund, PIF, bought control of Premier League club Newcastle United (Newcastle). Saudi Arabia's GDP is around twice as much as UAE's and four times as much as Qatar's.

---

* In fairness, many clubs have been accused of distorting the market and circumventing FFP. For example, Barcelona and Real Madrid have been scrutinized for selling future revenue streams. UEFA have deemed that certain transactions must now be declared as debt and not revenue for FFP calculations. In another example, UEFA closed the loophole that Chelsea allegedly used to circumvent FFP by utilizing longer-term contracts than typical to amortize the value of players over a longer time to reduce the negative financial impact each year. Lastly, some clubs have expressed concerns that transfer prices of players between clubs with shared ownership can be inflated to comply with FFP regulations (including transfers between Newcastle and PIF-owned clubs). In addition, in 2021, LaLiga president Javier Tebas criticized the RFEF for agreeing to hold the Supercopa de España in Saudi Arabia, then in 2023 Tevas and LaLiga agreed on a global partnership with Visit Saudi, the tourism board of Saudi Arabia. According to Spanish outlet 2Playbook, the deal is worth more than $20 million annually.

Newcastle fans celebrated wildly outside St James's Park after the £305 million Saudi fund takeover was confirmed.* The Saudi fund takeover means Newcastle now boast the richest owners in football. Legendary Newcastle striker Alan Shearer led the celebrations on social media. He tweeted: "Yessssssss. We can dare to hope again."

But not all were celebrating and heralding news of the takeover. BBC *Match of the Day* host and former top player Gary Lineker tweeted: "Football fans want their clubs to succeed, but at what price? The dilemma facing @NUFC supporters." It's a dilemma that goes well beyond a club's, and their supporters', values. It can go to the integrity of competition.

On November 18, 2022, around the time I started my research for this book, Off The Pitch wrote: "Manchester City have climbed to the top: Highest revenue-generating football club in the world . . . Well-established giants like Real Madrid, FC Barcelona, and Manchester United have been surpassed in just a few years by the Abu Dhabi-owned club. Could Newcastle United be the next?"† Based on Man City and PSG's rise, I thought to myself, "Probably." I looked at the Premier League standings, and Newcastle had already broken into the "Big Six."‡ And then I wondered, "How can a Premier League club compete with a Premier League club that has closely government-related ownership with almost unlimited resources?"

In his January 2023 interview with Off The Pitch, Tebas expressed his continued concerns about the Premier League. He said, "What I'm worried about is the Premier League, and I've been worried for many years now . . . But now it's converted into a competition that has losses all year. All clubs lose money. There is no sustainability in the Premier League. The Premier League is not a financially sustainable model." Leicester City are often referred to as one of the best-run clubs in the

---

* https://www.dailymail.co.uk/sport/sportsnews/article-10069899/Party-time-Newcastle-fans-celebrate-takeover-wildly-outside-St-James-Park.html

† https://offthepitch.com/a/manchester-city-have-climbed-top-highest-revenue-generating-football-club-world?wv_email=sgmandis%40me.com&wv_id=0b33e863-2b87-44e3-82bb-a46dd11bfd0d&wv_name=.

‡ The "Big Six" are London clubs Arsenal, Chelsea, and Tottenham; Manchester clubs Man City and Man U; and Liverpool. Since 2000, the vast majority of Premier League qualifications for the European Champions League have come from the Big Six.

Premier League. Everyone wants to talk about how Leicester City overcame 5,000-to-1 odds to win the Premier League trophy in 2015–16. No one wants to talk about this: Leicester City have reported a record loss of £92.5 million for the 2021–22 financial year, following deficits of £31.2 million in 2020–21, £67.3 million in 2019–20, and £20 million in 2018–19. And after the 2022–23 season, Leicester City were relegated—winning just nine of their thirty-eight league matches. But it's not just the clubs in the Premier League that don't have a financially sustainable model. Most clubs in most leagues don't.

SATURATION

Putting aside financial sustainability, on Wednesday, February 15, 2023, I looked at the possible football matches to watch on TV: Borussia Dortmund versus Chelsea in the UEFA Champions League Round of 16, Club Brugge versus Benfica in the UEFA Champions League Round of 16, Arsenal versus Man City in the Premier League, and Real Madrid versus Elche in LaLiga.* A Premier League regular season match's global viewer ratings easily beat the UEFA Champions League Round of 16 matches!!—and the LaLiga match with Real Madrid came in dead last. So UEFA, LaLiga, Real Madrid, and other leagues, competitions, and clubs should be very concerned about the Premier League. In addition, the sport of football should also be concerned with the saturation of matches . . . on a Wednesday.

---

* The Arsenal versus Man City match was originally due to take place on Wednesday, October 19, 2022, but due to a fixture pile-up, the teams were forced to fit the crucial game into their schedules in midweek. UEFA is normally against the idea of having a Premier League game on the same day as the Champions League. However, UEFA made an exception this time after the Premier League did the European governing body a favor earlier this season with scheduling after their Europa League game against PSV had to be rearranged. Due to the crammed footballing calendar in the 2022–23 season, leagues and teams are finding it harder and harder to find spots in the packed calendar following the 2022 World Cup. Real Madrid announced that their match against Elche, which was scheduled to be held in the twenty-first round of the Spanish League competition, was postponed due to Real Madrid's participation in the FIFA Club World Cup.

OWNERSHIP CHANGES

Back to ownership. Changes in the types of owners hasn't been restricted to closely government-related entities—private equity giants (Arctos, Ares, Clearlake, CVC, Eldridge, Oaktree, RedBird, Silver Lake, Sixth Street, 777 Partners) are among those that have recently purchased stakes in European football clubs or their future rights to revenues or European football leagues. In 2018, private equity investment in European football's Top 5 Leagues amounted to €66.7 million.

In 2022, investment firm Eldridge's Todd Boehly and Clearlake Capital, a U.S.-based private equity firm, purchased Chelsea for a commitment of up to £4.25 billion, after they were put up for sale by Roman Abramovich.* It was the highest price ever paid for a sports team at the time. The transfer of Chelsea from a Russian oligarch to a U.S. institutional investor group highlights a wider shift in the market for football clubs: (1) assets that were once the loss-making trophies of tycoons are increasingly being seen as financial opportunities with the potential for attractive investment returns and (2) the prices are so high, and investments required so large, that fewer individual tycoons could afford them (it even took at least two private equity funds to buy Chelsea).

Intriguingly, government-related entities, sovereign wealth funds, and PE (private equity) funds are not allowed to buy control of major sports franchises in the U.S. (NFL, NBA, MLB, NHL) but could do as they liked in Europe. And there is a fundamental difference between U.S. and European sports ownership—if the team is in last place in the middle of the season in a major U.S. sport, the owner doesn't have to worry about relegation and the significant negative financial consequences. A European football club owner in that situation feels intense pressure—and one way to solve that pressure is through the transfer market. A PE fund, as a manager of money, will be under even more pressure with the prospect of lost revenues due to relegation—which can lead to irrational transfer prices. And it's not just relegation risk—it can be missing the qualification and money of the European Champions League.

---

* https://www.buyoutsinsider.com/theyre-in-the-big-leagues-now/.

Chelsea's January 2023 spending alone amounted to £323 million—more than the *combined* spending by clubs in Serie A, LaLiga, Bundesliga, and Ligue 1 during the winter transfer window. (Chelsea have now spent more than €1.1 billion in the last three transfer windows—so it's not as simple as saying it's Man City, PSG, and the Middle East that are distorting the market.) Chelsea and Liverpool are going to miss out on at least £50 million of prize money and participation fees because of their twelfth and fifth place Premier League finishes in 2022–23, respectively (Saudi Arabia PIF's Newcastle finished fourth).[*] In addition, there could be significant commercial consequences because many sponsors include performance-related add-ons. Chelsea's and Liverpool's budgets for their squads will be affected as FFP relates to revenues.

After the price of the Chelsea sale was announced, Liverpool and Man U confirmed reports that they were talking to potential buyers. Closely government-related entities and big private equity firms are among the most interested potential buyers—even if they own stakes in other clubs. Gary Neville, an English football pundit who spent his entire playing career with Man U, was asked for his stance on a potential Qatari-led takeover of Man U on his podcast with Sky Sports, and he said, "The horse has bolted in that respect . . . We can talk about state ownership at Man United but we have already got two state-funded clubs in Newcastle and Man City. They've been allowed to come in already, so I find it difficult to say Man United shouldn't, on the other hand, have a Qatari ownership . . . There's a feeling they want an ownership that can compete with the Middle East estates we have in this league . . . which is Saudi Arabia at Newcastle and Abu Dhabi at Man City." I couldn't help but think there are a limited number of countries in the Middle East, so what about those Premier League clubs (or other clubs in Europe) that don't have closely government-related ownership—what about the integrity of competition?

---

[*] But the real difference will come from UEFA payments. Liverpool were knocked out of the Champions League at the Round of 16 by Real Madrid in 2022–23 but still earned a total of €67.7 million (£58.9 million). The figures are much lower in the Europa League. Man U, for example, made €15 million (£13 million) for reaching the quarterfinals of that competition only to be beaten by Sevilla. A Europa League participation fee is only €3.6 million, with group stage wins earning €360,000 and progressing into the knockout stages worth an initial €500,000 (£435,000).

Closely government-related and big private equity firms can have two different primary motivations. Private equity firms have the primary financial incentive to generate an attractive return for their investors. (Remarkably, Financial Fair Play made it safer for those with financial incentives, like American owners, to buy clubs. According to the rules, competing billionaires couldn't just spend whatever they wanted anymore. There were limits. Also, theoretically, the clubs with already established global brands and revenue sources were more protected from free-spending new entrants.) Closely government-related entities often have political and/or other purposes in addition to generating investment returns. (This is not to say they are mutually exclusive.)[*]

FIFA executives have argued that private equity investors may, over time, gain enough commercial power to force a future breakaway, akin to the Super League project.[†] And while some closely government-related entities may have political and/or other motivations, some are selling stakes to private equity owners. Private equity firm Silver Lake owns a stake in Man City's parent group. In 2023, PSG sold an up to 12.5 percent stake to U.S. private equity group Arctos Partners. Saudi Arabia's PIF fund owns a 5 percent stake in Clearlake, one of the owners of Chelsea.[‡] Private equity's purchases of minority stakes in clubs controlled by closely government-related entities or vice versa will impact the dynamics and motivations.

And it's not just government-related or private equity ownership. When I looked at the Premier League table, another club was trying to crash the Big Six (now Big Seven with Newcastle) party—the Wolverhampton Wanderers (Wolves). Essentially, there already is a breakaway

---

[*] An analogy: closely government-related entities are more like the local wealthy superfans in the old days who bought their local club for prestige and political purposes. The financial goal was not losing too much money—which is a relative term depending on how much money the owner had. The difference is that closely government-related entities have unlimited resources while the local wealthy superfans usually reach a point where they can't sustain the losses anymore—even Berlusconi reached that point with AC Milan. Private equity firms are more like American owners—it's a business investment—but with more money pooled from many wealthy investors.

[†] https://www.ft.com/content/268989a1-5299-473e-adc4-ed02d247cd3c.

[‡] Reportedly, Arctos Partners are looking to buy between 5 to 15 percent, and PSG have another U.S. bidder and an Asia bidder. All bidders value PSG above 4.25 billion Euros, compared to a 70 million Euros value in 2011. Even after the 1.5-billion-euro investment by QSI since 2011, this is an enormous growth and capital return.

league within the Premier League of the Big Six clubs and Newcastle . . . and it's growing. In 2016, the Wolves were taken over by a large Chinese conglomerate, Fosun. But there is an interesting twist. Fosun also owns a stake in the football agency of super-agent Jorge Mendes (Cristiano Ronaldo's agent). Many of the Wolves' managers and players have a close connection with Mendes. As we'll see in chapter five, super-agents have a lot more money, power, influence . . . and potential and/or perceived conflicts. In another example, in 2017, LaLiga's Girona became 44.3 percent owned by super-agent Pere Guardiola (Man City manager Pep Guardiola's brother) and 44.3 percent owned by Man City's parent. Man City's parent, City Football Group, has a multi-club ownership model, of which Girona is now a member. In the 2023–24 season, Girona was ahead of Barcelona in the tables. Today, City Football Group is the world's leading private owner and operator of football clubs, with total or partial ownership of thirteen football clubs in major cities across the world (at the time, Girona was its sixth club).

Multi-club ownership has proliferated, in part, due to a key decision by UEFA. At the end of the 2016–2017 season, both Red Bull Leipzig (Germany) and FC Red Bull Salzburg (Austria) qualified on merit from their respective leagues for the UEFA Champions League 2017–18 season. Since both clubs are ultimately funded in some manner by Red Bull, many believed UEFA would exclude one of the clubs from the Champions League to maintain the integrity of the competition. However, UEFA allowed both clubs to participate. Since the decision, multi-club ownership has grown significantly. Man City and several private equity firms own stakes in multiple clubs (and Chelsea announced they will pursue a multi-club model).* I then started to wonder, what if people or entities closely connected to the same Middle Eastern governments or private equity firms purchased clubs? For example, could two princes from the same Middle East royal family own stakes in two Big Six clubs in the

---

* In fairness, PSG have not yet been an active MCO player beyond their 21.67 percent of Braga. There are many active MCO clubs, PSG/QSI have barely done anything—but because it's a "Gulf" club, they are often labeled, grouped, and scrutinized like Man City.

Premier League and compete in the Champions League?* The broth-ers could claim they are technically independent, like the two Red Bull clubs, and that at least they don't have the same direct brand association as Red Bull. What if the princes or funds they were associated with also were major investors in private equity firms that controlled other football clubs? Over time, a few closely government-related entities and people could gain enough control over the biggest clubs, providing them with much more power and influence over football.

Private equity ownership has many consequences and likely will lead to changes in football. The investment firms need to generate attractive returns, and that means they need to increase cash flows.† Boehly sug-gested the Premier League introduce an all-star game like those featured in a variety of major sports in the United States. When a reporter put the idea to Liverpool's Jürgen Klopp for his reaction, the manager said, "He [Boehly] doesn't wait long. Great. When he finds a date for that, he can call me . . . Does he want to bring the Harlem Globetrotters as well and let them play against a football team?" The congested calendar Klopp raised is an important issue as clubs, leagues, and federations try to generate more TV revenues . . . which typically means more matches to sell to broadcasters. Meanwhile, the quality of matches and players' performance can suffer with so many matches.

Boehly admitted that there's a cultural aspect in football that's real that will resist change, though he predicted "there's going to be an evo-lution."‡ The owners of the Big Five in England in the 1990s came to

---

* This is just one illustrative example. There are many potential examples, including with private equity firms. U.S. private equity firms are much more pervasive in European football club ownership than Middle Eastern people/countries/entities.

† Global credit-rating firm Fitch Ratings believes private equity owners will have a positive impact through a combination of developing revenues and stricter cost-control and spending discipline from the ownership side.

‡ In *Calling the Shots*, David Dein wrote: "You have to understand how Dickensian English football was in 1989, and how profoundly it resisted change. Three years previously, shortly after I joined the Football League Management Committee, I proposed there should be two substitutes instead of one. One chairman put up his hand. 'You can't have that.' 'Why not?' 'It's an extra hotel room, extra meal, and extra appearance fee.' Others nodded, the notion was rejected, and I came home and felt like putting my head in the microwave. 'How backward are we?' I said to myself . . . I remember at one Management Committee meeting, I proposed that we should put names on the back of the shirts, as they did in America. This was not just to make it easier for fans in the stadium to follow

the same conclusion, which led to the breakaway Premier League. And those owners didn't have the pressure of paying such high prices for their clubs with capital from institutional investors who have attractive financial return expectations. They also were not competing with closely government-related entities and multi-club owners.

Keep in mind, in the midst of new closely government-related entity and private equity and multi-club owners, Real Madrid are still a members-owned club. Currently, Real Madrid can't sell a stake or raise equity to fund player signings. And it would be challenging for Real Madrid to pursue a multi-club ownership model for financial and other reasons, including the fact that most of the members that I interviewed don't believe in having different tiers of clubs, i.e., a parent club and feeder club. If you are a fan of a parent club then you may feel you are lucky, but you probably do not feel as lucky if you are a fan of a feeder club, as you watch your best players moved to the parent club.*

The changes in ownership (not to mention the announcement of the European Super League and subsequent reactions and opinions) led me to believe some things really have changed and deserved further investigation. What I learned is completely unexpected.

In this book we'll consider the serious systemic changes going on in football:

- Football is starting to lose the global entertainment battle against other sports and platforms.
- Closely government-related, private equity, and multi-club ownership models have proliferated (including how commercial revenues from closely affiliated sponsors can be inflated to circumvent Financial Fair Play and how people/entities with many roles can have at least perceived conflicts of interest).

---

the game but also for a global TV audience . . . One owner of a big club said, 'I'll vote against that.' 'Why?' 'We don't have a big enough laundry room.' That's what I had to contend with." Dein even had challenges extending halftime from ten minutes to fifteen minutes to be more fan-friendly and increase commercial opportunities (FIFA made this change in 1995).

* Not all fans of "feeder clubs" feel unlucky. For example, Girona (City Football Group) have done very well. Antwerp have reached European competition with players on loan from Chelsea, likewise Vitesse Arnhem in Holland. RB Salzburg have benefited being a feeder club to Leipzig.

- While broadcasting revenues have grown in the past but may have peaked, player salaries and infrastructure costs have grown even faster, making the economic model for the majority of clubs even more unsustainable and riskier.
- The Premier League is becoming "the NBA of football" (and the Big Six and Newcastle *and growing* are already effectively in their own breakaway league, from the other Premier League clubs).
- The few dominant clubs with global brands in the other (non–Premier League) Top 5 Leagues have further separated themselves, both financially and in performance, from the domestic clubs who primarily rely on league broadcasting revenues and from most others in the Champions League. Which makes matches less exciting and league winners / Champions League qualifiers more predictable.
- There is pushback from local, multi-generation, hard-core, season-ticket-holder club fans against global capitalism and newer, much larger-in-numbers, global club fans (and new young fans) who are not as tethered to local rivalries and have never been to the stadium.*
- Calendars and competitions seem more congested, while the physical intensity required by players has increased, driven in part by FIFA and UEFA continually expanding tournaments. This results in more player injuries because of the correlation between number of matches, play intensity, and injuries.
- Football's regulation system has been exposed as a patchwork of rules that often differ by jurisdiction, are inconsistently enforced, and are often challenged in courts. FIFA, UEFA, leagues, clubs, and players often have conflicting interests.
- FIFA and UEFA have been exposed as controlling the multibillion-dollar transnational activity of football (including the regulatory function over clubs, the moneymaking hosting

---

* In 2018, Liverpool CEO Peter Moore said, "Our pulse is global, our heart is local." https://leaders insport.com/sport-business/videos/liverpool-fc-local-heart-global-pulse/.

of tournaments function utilizing clubs, and the judiciary and discipline function over clubs) but being subject to limited regulation or oversight (including over potential conflicts).

- Super-agents are making more money with increasing player transfer fees and salaries and have more power than ever, as well as more influence with clubs.
- Players have essentially become global brands, and many make more money than the profits of their clubs. This trend includes video games leading to more player recognition and more educated fans.
- Football media has become immediate news, with limited editorial oversight (including fans' fascination with transfers and individual players' money and lives, and more people getting their sports news via YouTube, Instagram, and TikTok).
- A spending spree thrust Saudi Arabia football onto the global stage. This led to the Saudi Pro League signing superstar players; an SPL club reaching the 2022 FIFA Club World Cup final; Saudi Arabia beating Argentina in the 2022 World Cup; and Newcastle, controlled by Saudi's Public Investment Fund, finishing fourth in the 2022–23 Premier League standings and qualifying for the European Champions League.

In addition, there are serious systemic changes going on more broadly in sports, entertainment, and content:

- Consumers have new and over-the-top platforms to watch entertainment.
- An increasing use of data capture, analytics, and management, both on and off the pitch, is leading to questions over who owns player data, and an increasingly more educated fan base.
- The way that fans engage with the sport is changing under the influence of factors like storytelling, social media, video games, and fan tokens. Fan experiences are planned based on key ingredients of participation, community and togetherness, gamification and rewards, and real-time data visualization.

- Viewership is changing, not only in terms of demographics, but with viewing behaviors like having multiple screens active at one time and snippet consumption.
- Changing experience expectations among fans, including better stadium experiences, has led more sports teams to recognize the value in building and owning and/or modernizing their own stadiums and arenas rather than leasing them.
- Sports organizations are becoming increasingly uncomfortable with their association with, and revenues from, betting companies.
- Women's sports and women athletes are increasing in popularity and influence.

Some of these systemic changes, which we'll look at in chapters five and six, may put football at risk of no longer being the world's most popular sport to watch—unless football adapts and innovates.

Do you think the idea that one day football couldn't be the most popular sport in the world to watch is crazy? It wasn't too long ago that baseball was the most popular sport in the United States to watch (baseball was referred to as "America's pastime"). Today, baseball is *third* behind American football and basketball.[*] Technology, sports viewership, and experience expectations changed rapidly. Baseball didn't modernize or innovate enough (or fast enough).

There are rapid changes in technology, viewership, and experience expectations. Gen Z's overall interest in attending live sports games and watching them on TV is significantly lower than that of older generations.[†] The future of football depends on its fans, so as fans change their behaviors, it is essential that football adapts. Will football modernize or innovate enough (or fast enough) for the reality of today's world and for future generations?

---

* In a 1937 Gallup Poll, 34 percent of those polled stated baseball was their favorite sport, 23 percent stated (American) football, and 8 percent stated basketball. In 2017, those numbers were 9 percent, 37 percent, and 11 percent, respectively. https://news.gallup.com/poll/224864/football-americans -favorite-sport-watch.aspx

† https://morningconsult.com/2022/12/13/gen-z-interest-in-watching-sports/.

This book is an invaluable inside look at the systemic changes going on in football, and more broadly, sports, entertainment, and content and how Real Madrid are trying to innovate for football—and themselves—to stay ahead. I discovered the two are more intertwined than you think.

REAL MADRID: BACKGROUND

In my background research, I learned that Real Madrid have always been a leader in innovation. Real Madrid helped create Fédération Internationale de Football Association (FIFA), the European Cup, and later the UEFA Champions League to help football—and themselves. Both football and Real Madrid benefited tremendously.

On May 21, 1904, FIFA was founded by the football federations of Belgium, Denmark, France, the Netherlands, Sweden, Switzerland, and—Real Madrid (England was not a founding federation).* Real Madrid were the only club to help create FIFA; the other founders were federations of countries.[†] Carlos Padrós, the president of Madrid Football Club (which later became Real Madrid), was a key driving force behind the creation of FIFA.[‡] The Royal Spanish Football Federation (RFEF) was not founded until 1913, and therefore Spain only became an official member of FIFA at that time. Padrós and the other founders wanted to protect, develop, and grow football around the world. They believed sports governance was required to oversee international competition among national associations. FIFA then introduced the World Cup in 1930.[§]

---

* On the same day, the German Football Association sent a telegram expressing their desire to join. England, Scotland, Wales, and Ireland wanted to remain independent, but in 1905 the English Football Association became the first British entity to join.

† England did not participate in the World Cup until 1950.

‡ Padrós also helped create the Spanish Championship (later became the Copa del Rey).

§ Spain (nicknamed *La Roja* or *La Furia Roja*, "the red one" or "the red fury") would win the World Cup in 2010 with Vicente del Bosque as manager (former Real Madrid manager, Real Madrid player, Real Madrid academy graduate) and Iker Casillas as captain (Real Madrid captain and Real Madrid academy graduate). Of the twenty-three-player squad, seven played for Barcelona (and two more attended Barcelona academy) and five played for Real Madrid. The Spanish Fury (or Spanish Terror) refers to a number of violent sackings of the cities of the Netherlands, mostly by Spanish Habsburg armies, that occurred during the Dutch Revolt (1568–1648). The most notorious Spanish Fury was the sacking of Antwerp in 1576.

In the mid-1950s, Santiago Bernabéu, the president of Real Madrid, supported and helped create the European Cup (which later became the UEFA Champions League) with the owner of and journalists from French newspaper *L'Équipe*. Bernabéu wanted to showcase his club (with star players such as Alfredo Di Stéfano) and their then 124,000-capacity stadium in a European competition (back then most stadiums had large standing sections). He also wanted to build the Real Madrid brand beyond Spain—which would generate more revenues and allow the club to attract and retain the best players from around the world.[*] The idea for a sixteen-team European tournament was taken to FIFA, who liked it but asked UEFA (which was just founded in 1954) to take the reins.[†] UEFA initially refused because they couldn't see why federations should organize club competitions, and so for a while Bernabéu helped lead the European Cup Organizing Committee—and both football and Real Madrid benefited greatly.[‡] However, at the behest of FIFA, UEFA finally decided to take over the European Cup. England's Football League ruled that their clubs should not participate, but in 1956–57 Man U ignored the ruling and participated. Real Madrid would go on to win the first five European Cups (1955–1960) and have won fifteen in total so far.[§]

In the late 1980s and early 1990s, Real Madrid's president Ramón Mendoza, AC Milan's owner Silvio Berlusconi, and Glasgow Rangers'

---

[*] The participating clubs in the first five seasons of the European Cup were selected by *L'Équipe* on the basis that they were representative and prestigious clubs in Europe.

[†] The sixteen teams being: AGF Aarhus (Denmark), RSC Anderlecht (Belgium), Djurgardens IF (Sweden), SC Rot-Weiss Essen (Germany), Gwardia Warszawa (Poland), Hibernian (Scotland), AC Milan (Italy), MTK Budapest (Hungary), FK Partizan (Yugoslavia), PSV Eindhoven (Netherlands), SK Rapid Wien (Austria), Real Madrid (Spain), Stade de Reims (France), 1. FC Saarbrücken (Saarland), Servette (Switzerland), and Sporting CP (Portugal). England didn't participate the first year as the FA believed it could distract from the domestic game. Man U became the first English club to play in 1956–57. https://www.uefa.com/MultimediaFiles/Download/uefaorg/General/02/59/07/69/2590769_DOWNLOAD.pdf https://nutmegassist.com/why-the-esl-owners-were-wrong-a-brief-history-of-european-football/.

[‡] Gusztáv Sebes (Hungary's undersecretary of sport and manager of the Hungarian football team) and Ernest Bedrignans (deputy chairman of the association of French football clubs) were also on the committee.

[§] In the 1950s, Spain and Italy allowed foreign players to play for clubs. Real Madrid had an unusually large number of foreign players. In the rest of Europe, there were strict limitations on foreign players. However, in the early 1960s, Spain and Italy placed restrictions on the number of foreign players. In 1966, Real Madrid won the European Cup with a Spanish-only squad.

secretary Campbell Ogilvie proposed a new competition with a single round-robin format, called "the Super League," to UEFA. They believed that the competition would be more attractive for international television broadcasters, would allow the contestant teams to earn more guaranteed income, and would give the contestant teams more possibilities to progress through the competition. That didn't happen, but the idea—and the threat—directly led to the evolution of the European Cup to the Champions League in 1992–93.

In 1998, Real Madrid led a push by big clubs for UEFA to reform the Champions League, including an increase from twenty-four to thirty-two teams and more Champions League places going to the continent's strongest leagues. Revenues and viewership increased significantly—and again both football and Real Madrid benefited greatly.

In 1998, Real Madrid were also a key founder of the G-14, fourteen leading clubs to provide a unified voice in negotiations with UEFA and FIFA, which led to clubs finally being compensated when their players played international matches.*

In my previous book about Real Madrid, I explain how Bernabéu developed in the 1950s what I believe was the first sustainable economic-sport model. However, after winning the first five European Cups (1955–1960), Real Madrid won only one European Cup in the next thirty-eight years. Many European football clubs copied and improved upon Real Madrid's economic-sport model, and Real Madrid didn't continue to innovate to stay ahead. The current senior executives of Real Madrid have not made that mistake.

Of all the football clubs, Real Madrid have made the most consistent and significant contributions to football. Presidents of Real Madrid have been visionaries and key drivers of improvements and innovations in football—which have also benefited Real Madrid.

. . . which leads us to today (and the elephant in the room).

---

* The G-14 disbanded in 2008 and became the European Club Association (ECA).

THE EUROPEAN SUPER LEAGUE

In late 2020, rumors began about a European Super League project. Real Madrid president Florentino Pérez had discussions with other clubs in Europe about new reforms for the Champions League or the idea of a breakaway competition. The talks became more serious as the COVID-19 pandemic made football's structural problems worse (which was essentially the title of a 2021 article published by the World Economic Forum). JPMorgan allegedly pledged €3.5 billion toward its formation.

In April 2021, leaks about the potential formation of a European Super League prematurely forced a rushed press release by twelve clubs who had agreed to be involved, including six English clubs (Arsenal, Chelsea, Liverpool, Man City, Man U, and Tottenham), three Italian clubs (AC Milan, Inter Milan, and Juventus), and three Spanish clubs (Atlético Madrid, Barcelona, and Real Madrid).* The leadership was Florentino Pérez as chairman, and two vice chairmen (Juventus chairman Andrea Agnelli and Man U co-chairman Joel Glazer). Within the press release, Pérez expressed hope that the new competition would provide (i) higher-quality matches and additional financial resources for the overall football pyramid, (ii) significantly greater economic growth and support for European football via a long-term commitment to uncapped solidarity payments that would grow in line with league revenues, (iii) more appeal to a younger generation of football fans, and (iv) strict and fair Financial Fair Play regulation.

Inspired by European basketball's EuroLeague, the proposed competition was to feature twenty clubs who would take part in matches against each other; fifteen of these would be permanent members, dubbed "founding clubs," who would govern the competition's operation. It was not a "closed" league: five places (25 percent) would be given to clubs through a qualifying mechanism focused on the teams who performed best in their country's most recent domestic season. Each year, the competition would

---

* In an interview, UEFA president Aleksander Čeferin said that Chelsea and Man City were least convinced by the project and that one of them called him. Both clubs are in the Premier League, and the owners of both clubs may have political and/or other purposes in addition to generating investment returns. https://www.football-espana.net/2023/03/16/uefa-president-reveals-two-english -clubs-leaked-superleague-plans-to-them.

see the teams split into two groups of ten, playing home-and-away in a double round-robin format for eighteen group matches per team, with fixtures set to take place midweek to avoid disrupting the clubs' involvement in their domestic leagues, and a playoff over four weeks at the end of the season.

Within days of the announcement, most of the clubs withdrew their support for the European Super League project. (While Real Madrid are still committed to the project, Barcelona and Juventus's statuses are unclear.)* In a June 20, 2021, article titled "Football Super League Is Not Dead Just Resting," *The Times* reported that the six English clubs, which remained co-owners and shareholders of the Spanish holding company that is the European Super League, have not formally left it, and the project's leaders believe that the competition would "eventually relaunch in modified form." Reportedly, there is "no mechanism" for the clubs to formally withdraw, as only unanimous consensus among the twelve founding clubs can dissolve the holding company, and any club leaving unilaterally faced significant fines.†

For Florentino, the European Super League is not a breakaway league, but an evolution. At Real Madrid's annual general meeting in October 2022, Florentino said that football is "sick":

> To fix a problem, you have to first recognize that you have a problem . . . Our sport is sick. It's losing its leadership as a global sport . . . We must not be confused by the impact of Real Madrid's European Cup run [in the Champions League in 2021–22] when we were involved in seven games of the highest intensity and interest . . . That was the result of the draw, and of the quality and

---

* In July 2023, Juventus reported that they initiated the discussion and procedure to pull out of the European Super League project. Juventus said that their exit would only be completed and effective if authorized by Real Madrid and Barcelona. Reportedly, Juventus received pressure to initiate the process or potentially be sanctioned as a part of open cases with UEFA. Juventus and UEFA deny this. In June 2023, *Forbes* and *Marca* reported Barcelona suggested abandoning the European Super League project as a gesture of goodwill for not being handed a suspension from the Champions League by UEFA for potential violations related to making payments to the Technical Committee of Referees' ex–vice president. Barcelona and UEFA deny this. Barcelona also pulled out of a lawsuit with Real Madrid and Athletic Club against LaLiga over a deal with CVC.

† https://www.thetimes.co.uk/article/football-super-league-is-not-dead-just-resting-gbrp00dpv.

greatness of our team. It was a spectacle that helped bring excitement back to the viewers. That's why we believe European competitions must change, to offer fans top-level games year-round between the strongest teams, with the best players competing.

Florentino compared the number of times that big European clubs compete against each other to the number of top-level meetings in other sports:

In tennis, [Rafa] Nadal and [Roger] Federer have played forty times in fifteen years. Nadal and [Novak] Djokovic have played fifty-nine matches in sixteen years . . . In football we've only played Liverpool nine times in sixty-seven years. We've played Chelsea four times in the history of the European Cup. What sense does it make to deprive fans of all these games?

Need for More Blockbuster Matches

Regarding the proposed European Super League, UEFA president Aleksander Čeferin said, "Why should we create a system where Liverpool faces Real Madrid for ten straight years? Who wants to see that every year?" Umm . . . ask the global broadcasters and sponsors who must satisfy global fans' preferences and expectations.*

Until the 2021–22 Champions League, remarkably, Real Madrid had never played Chelsea. Bayern Munich and Liverpool, who each have six European Cups, have only played each other twice in sixty-five years.

The data shows that the Champions League has more "unequal" and "boring" matches than ever before. The following table shows the number of matches won by four or more goals in each Champions League season. In the ten years before the 2013–14 season, there were never more than ten

---

* Badia reflected that "the pressure exerted by the large media groups for the big European clubs to leave their domestic league and concentrate on a European Super League has become more present than ever and is gaining ever greater purpose, more based on the notion that the model of such a Super League would provide the participants and owners with significant negotiating capacity to increase their ordinary income (broadcasting, marketing and matchday)." Badia J. "La superlliga europea. Pressions mediàtiques, necessitats econòmiques i esportives." *RUTA Comun* (2013) 5:1–25. Available at: https://www.raco.cat/index.php/Ruta/article/view/275933 (Accessed: 14 May 2021).

matches won by four or more goals. In nine out of the last ten seasons, there have been ten or more matches with a four-or-more-goal difference. This is because the financial and talent gap between the big global clubs and the others is increasing.

Table 0.5: Champions League Seasons with Matches Won by Four or More Goals

Season	Matches Won by Four or More Goals
2001/02	Competition changes from two "group stages" to just one group stage
2002–03	7
2003–04	5
2004–05	8
2005–06	5
2006–07	4
2007–08	5
2008–09	4
2009–10	4
2010–11	8
2011–12	9
2012–13	4
2013–14	11
2014–15	15
2015–16	11
2016–17	14
2017–18	12
2018–19	9
2019–20	10
2020–21	11
2021–22	13
2022–23	15

The idea behind the European Super League is a global product with "blockbuster" competitive matches each week to capture global audiences.

In fact, Stefan Szymanski, co-author of *Soccernomics* and professor at the University of Michigan, co-authored an academic paper about the need for the top clubs to play each other more often . . . over twenty years ago![*]

Florentino referenced a 2022 *Forbes* ranking that suggested football clubs are falling behind United States teams:[†]

We were top in all sports, and now we've fallen to 13th . . . We've been overtaken by 12 clubs from American sports. They must be doing something very well in the United States and very badly in Europe . . . Football is losing the global entertainment battle against other sports and other platforms.

To be fair, most fans aren't concerned about the valuations of clubs. However, the valuations can help indicate the popularity of a sport and its value to fans, sponsors, and broadcasters.

Lastly, Florentino mentioned the football governance structure, saying: "We need professional, modern, transparent management . . . not based on old structures designed in the last century."

Seemingly continual investigations; accusations of conflicts, bribery, corruption, and breaches of rules; and questions about accountability, consistent enforcement, good governance, and ethics have cast a cloud over football.[‡] Will the cloud negatively impact the belief in the integrity of competition in the sport?

In February 2023, Bernd Reichart, the chief executive of the A22 Sports Management Group, which is behind the European Super League, said that a revamped Super League would be based on sporting

---

[*] Hoehn, T. & Szymanski, S. (1999). "The Americanization of European Football." *Economic Policy*, 14(28), 204–240. Szymanski believes the preservation of entry into competition by merit is crucial to the European football model, and while also the cause of the financial instability, does not affect the sustainability of the clubs. Szymanski, S. (2017). "Entry into Exit: Insolvency in English Professional Football." *Scottish Journal of Political Economy*, 64(4), 419–444.

[†] https://www.forbes.com/sites/mikeozanian/2022/09/08/the-worlds-50-most-valuable-sports-teams-2022/?sh=5f0e2f63385c.

[‡] It is important to note that many people and organizations have never been formally charged or were ultimately cleared.

performance and not contain any permanent membership from any clubs—which would see sixty to eighty teams competing in a "multi-divisional competition." Reichart added that A22 had consulted with nearly fifty European clubs and developed ten principles based on that consultation that underpin its plans for the new-look league.

In the end, Florentino and Real Madrid want football to prosper and remain the most universal sport in the world. As you'll see in the subsequent chapters, what's good for football—and Real Madrid—are more intertwined than you think.

With that background in mind, let's start by recounting LA DECIMOCUARTA (the fourteenth). This 2022 finals match against Liverpool provides an opportunity to explain some important on-and-off-the-pitch elements about Real Madrid and football.

In many ways 2021–22, on and off the pitch, captures the Real Madrid revolution.

Real Madrid, 2022 UEFA Champions League winners.

Chapter 1

LA DECIMOCUARTA
(THE FOURTEENTH)

ON SATURDAY, MAY 28, 2022, Real Madrid's football players walk onto the pitch for the 2022 UEFA Champions League final in Paris, France's Stade de France. The world's most-watched annual sporting game is about to air in more than 200 countries, drawing an estimated global audience of 400 million viewers, around 13 million in England, 8 million in Spain, and 3 million in the United States. (To put this into perspective, around 140 million people worldwide watched the 2021 Super Bowl, around 100 million of them in the United States and 1 million in England. Also, around 1.5 billion people watched the 2022 World Cup final, around 25 million in the United States, 19 million in England, and 11 million in Spain.* However, views don't necessarily mean more money. Some media executives estimate the value of the broadcasting rights of the Champions League final is around half of the estimated rights for the Super Bowl.†)

The global brands of the two big clubs, the global appeal of football, and the diversity of nationalities of the players on the two teams transcends the national identity of the clubs. Of Real Madrid's starting eleven players, eight different countries are represented—Austria, Belgium,

---

* https://en.as.com/nfl/super-bowl-vs-champions-league-final-which-is-the-most-watched-sporting-event-n/. https://www.goal.com/en-us/news/super-bowl-vs-world-cup-champions-league-viewing-figures-soccer-nfl-compare/blte47db8809dbd0a6d.

† https://franchisesports.co.uk/super-bowl-versus-champions-league-final-which-event-is-bigger/.

Brazil, Croatia, France, Germany, Spain, and Uruguay. In addition, their manager, Carlo Ancelotti, is Italian.

Real Madrid's players are dressed in their traditional gleaming white jerseys, which led to their nicknames—*Los Blancos* (the Whites) and *Los Merengues* (the Meringues). The front of the shirts are adorned with "Fly Emirates," a Real Madrid sponsor's logo.[*] On the upper-left front of their shirts, over their hearts, is the club's famous emblem with a royal crown on top. On the upper-right front is the logo of Adidas, another Real Madrid sponsor. The crest on the left sleeve shows the number of European trophies won by Real Madrid, thirteen. Their opponent in the final are Premier League's Liverpool, wearing their traditional red shirts.[†] (Outside the stadium, fans are paying €140 for an official replica team jersey and €30 for an official UEFA Champions League 2022 final T-shirt. A 500 ml bottle of water is €5 and an official program costs €10.)

It's the third time the two sides are meeting in the European Cup final—Real Madrid beat Liverpool in 2018, and Liverpool beat Real Madrid in 1981. Incredibly, in the sixty-seven years of the tournament, the two storied clubs had only met eight times, with Real Madrid holding a slight edge—four wins, three losses, and one draw.

Real Madrid's Champions League run to the finals has been legendary. Real Madrid overcame aggregate deficits in stunning fashion in each of the knockout stages against powerhouses PSG, Chelsea, and Man City, respectively. To stay alive against Man City in the semifinals, Real Madrid needed two goals after eighty-nine minutes had passed on the clock, and out of nowhere the team wrote another magical chapter in the club's history books. Rodrygo pulled one goal back in the ninetieth minute and equalized in stoppage time to force extra time, and Karim

---

[*] Emirates is one of two flag carriers of the United Arab Emirates (the other being Etihad—sponsor of Man City). Based in Garhoud, Dubai, the airline is a subsidiary of The Emirates Group, which is owned by the government of Dubai's Investment Corporation of Dubai. Emirates sponsor AC Milan, Arsenal, Asian Football Confederation, Olympiacos, Olympique Lyonnais, Real Madrid, Benfica, and The Emirates FA Cup.

[†] Under management by Bill Shankly, in 1964 the club changed from red shirts and white shorts to all-red home strips.

Benzema converted a penalty to win the tie.* Benzema has been the star of the tournament thus far with ten goals in seven knockout games, including two hat tricks. What makes this remarkable run so special to Real Madrid's management is that the players lived up to the community's expectations of never giving up—reflecting the ideal that whether on the pitch or in the daily lives of their fans, there is always hope.

Spectators are told the kickoff is pushed back by fifteen minutes due to fans arriving late and crowd congestion issues. UEFA's initial fan ballot gave supporters a range of ticketing options between €70 (£60) and €690 (£586). But with those tickets long sold, fans without one have desperately turned to resale websites in the hope of landing a precious seat for the final at the Stade de France, which can hold up to seventy thousand people. A top-tier VIP hospitality package is being offered at £12,500. Of the non-VIP tickets, fans face paying just under £9,000 for a category one ticket, while the cheapest restricted-view seat has been made available at just over £1,880, £1,190 more than UEFA's most expensive offering in the fan ballot.†

The delay is extended another fifteen minutes to 9:30 PM as social media posts and the news display chaos at the entrances to the stadium and police using pepper spray and tear gas to control crowds.‡ UEFA, organizers of the tournament, claim turnstiles became blocked by thousands of Liverpool fans who had purchased counterfeit tickets that did not work. The match eventually starts at 9:37.

---

* In the extra time against Man City, vice-captain and leading scorer Benzema, who had won the penalty kick, asked Rodrygo if Rodrygo would like to take the kick—deferring to the etiquette of helping a teammate complete a hat trick. Rodrygo declined as Benzema was typically designated to take the penalty kicks. The respect to etiquette over ego by Benzema is an example of Real Madrid's culture—veterans lead by example.

† https://www.dailymail.co.uk/sport/sportsnews/article-10860487/Champions-League-final-tickets-soar-9-000-eve-Liverpools-showdown-Real-Madrid.html.

‡ The actions were later defended by organizers UEFA and several French political figures who accused the supporters of Liverpool of disorderly conduct, including to gain access to the stadium with counterfeit tickets. Later, UEFA issued an apology. On May 30, 2022, UEFA announced they were commissioning an independent report into the events to be made public upon its completion. An independent panel, led by Professor Phil Scraton who previously led a report into the 1989 Hillsborough stadium disaster, concluded the organization and management of the event was "an abject failure." A French inquiry found the chaos was caused by administrative errors and that authorities had unfairly blamed Liverpool fans.

In 2022, Real Madrid had the highest number of social media followers in football, 277 million, and Liverpool were #7 with 103 million.* Real Madrid and Liverpool are global brands, and two of the most valuable and widely supported clubs in the world. While Real Madrid have been a not-for-profit club owned by members (today over 94,000) since their founding in 1902, Liverpool have been a for-profit corporation owned by few wealthy individuals since their founding in 1892. Today, Liverpool is owned by U.S.-based Fenway Sports Group (FSG), which has a multi-club ownership model. FSG is a global sports, marketing, media, entertainment, and real estate company anchored by three iconic clubs, Premier League's Liverpool, MLB's Boston Red Sox, and NHL's Pittsburgh Penguins.† U.S.-based private equity firm RedBird, owner of both AC Milan and Toulouse, have been the third biggest shareholders in FSG with 11 percent since they closed a $750 million deal with FSG in 2021.‡

In the 2020–21 Deloitte Football Money League, Real Madrid ranked #2 with €641 million in revenues, and Liverpool ranked #7 with €550 million—most of the €91 million difference due to commercial revenues (sponsors)—reflected by the difference in social media followers above.§ (Real Madrid ranked #1 in Deloitte Football Money League 2022/23.) While Liverpool had won the 2019 Champions League trophy, they have fallen two spots in the revenue rankings due to Man City's and PSG's rise. PSG ranked #4 in social media followers with 136 million and Man City ranked #9 with 89 million.

Real Madrid had announced their financial results for the financial year ending June 2022 with a €13 million profit. This result means that the club had managed to remain in profit over the three financial years

---

* https://www.totalsportal.com/list/football-clubs-with-highest-social-media-followers/.

† Basketball star LeBron James has been a part owner of Liverpool since 2011 and had around a 2 percent stake, which cost £4.7 million. He has since exchanged the stake and owns around 1 percent of FSG, worth an estimated £40 million.

‡ In September 2023, Dynasty Equity purchased a minority stake in Fenway Sports Group. In November 2023, according to a report from Bloomberg, RedBird is considering a potential sale of Toulouse.

§ While theoretically they should correspond, there is not a clear, linear correlation between revenues and social media followers.

affected by the pandemic, making a profit in both 2019–20 (€313,000 after tax) and 2020–21 (€874,000 after tax). They were one of the few big clubs in Europe that did not incur losses over those two financial years.

Based on a study by UEFA, the accumulated operating losses of European clubs between 2019–20 and 2020–21 are close to €6 billion.* Liverpool had announced their financial results for the financial year ending in May 2021, with the Merseyside club posting a pre-tax loss of £4.8 million. Their pre-tax loss improved from a £46.3 million loss the previous financial year.[†]

Squad Value Correlates to Winning

In a November 2022 Off The Pitch article, Anton Drasbaek demonstrated football performance is highly corelated with squad valuation.[‡] Previously, several studies focused on showing football performance is highly corelated with salaries.[§]

According to the Football Player Benchmark Tool, as of April 1, 2022, the values of the semifinalists of the Champions League in order of team valuations were: Man City (€1,119 million), Liverpool (€988 million), Real Madrid (€816 million), and Villareal (€430 million).[¶]

---

* https://www.realmadrid.com/en-US/news/club/latest-news/real-madrid-close-the-2021-22-financial-year-with-a-13-million-profit.

† Owing to the COVID-19 pandemic, these financial results include the period in which Liverpool won the Premier League. It primarily covers the 2020–21 season, where the majority of matches were played behind closed doors. That had a significant impact on match-day revenue, which fell by almost 95 percent. https://www.liverpoolfc.com/news/lfc-announces-financial-results-year-may-31-2021.

‡ In many propriety player valuation models, players whose contract is set to expire before the next transfer window (or July 1, 2022) are assigned zero value (Luka Modrić). And those who have only a short time left on their contract may also have artificially low values.

§ Salaries can be misleading. The highest paid player in the final was Gareth Bale. Closely behind Bale was his teammate Eden Hazard. Liverpool's starting eleven payroll was estimated at $95 million compared to Real Madrid's $148 million, with Karim Benzema making an estimated $25 million compared to Mohamed Salah's $13 million. https://www.sportscasting.com/who-is-the-highest-paid-player-in-the-2022-uefa-champions-league-final-between-liverpool-and-real-madrid/.

¶ https://www.insideworldfootball.com/2022/05/10/liverpool-vs-real-madrid-e998m-vs-e816m-e276m-defense-vs-e242m-attack/.

According to Football Benchmark, Trent Alexander-Arnold was Liverpool's most valuable player (€115 million, the highest defender in the world) and Vinícius Júnior was Real Madrid's most valuable player (€129 million).

The total for the Champions League final four clubs was €3,353 million. In comparison, the total for the Europa League semifinalists was €1,363 million. The aggregate value of the Champions League final four clubs was 2.5 times the semifinalists in the Europa League. The UCL's final stages are essentially a closed shop for Europe's big clubs—even a Top 5 League club such as Villarreal are more of a surprise participant, also reflected by their squad value, which is around half of the other three sides. In addition, in the past five seasons ending 2022, the only club outside the Top 5 Leagues to reach the Champions League semifinals were Ajax. The last time Ajax, four-time winners of the European Cup / Champions League, reached the semifinals was 1996–97.

The few dominant clubs with global brands in the other Top 5 Leagues have further separated themselves, both financially and in performance, from the domestic clubs who primarily rely on league broadcasting revenues and from most others in the Champions League.

Think about this . . . According to Off The Pitch in February 2023, the Brazilian Serie A is the only non–Top 5 League where the collective value of all teams surpasses that of Man City alone. Despite a large pool of over four hundred players with valuations in each non–Top 5 League, they are still overshadowed by the staggering €1.5 billion valuation of Man City's thirty-eight-man roster.[*]

Table 1.1: Squad Values in February 2023

Rank	League and Man City	Euros (bn)
#1	Brazilian Serie A (League)	1.6
#2	Man City	1.5
#3	Portuguese Primera (League)	1.4
#4	Dutch Eredivisie (League)	1.1
#5	Belgian Pro (League)	.9

Source: Off The Pitch Data Analytics Tools

---

[*] https://offthepitch.com/a/valuation-analysis-fc-porto-boast-highest-valued-squad-outside-big-five-still-worth-less-90?wv_email=sgmandis%40me.com&wv_id=0b33e863-2b87-44e3-82bb-a46dd11bfd0d&wv_name=.

Even mid-to-low-tier Top 5 League clubs have separated themselves from others in the Champions League. According to Off The Pitch, rather than other Champions League sides, the likes of FC Porto have squad valuations that are more comparable to mid-to-low-tier Top 5 League clubs such as Rennes (€344 million), Real Betis (€287 million), and Sassuolo (€285 million). Eighteen out of twenty Premier League squad values are higher than any teams in leagues outside the Top 5. Only Fulham (€296 million squad value) and Bournemouth (€264 million) are topped by FC Porto, Ajax, and Benfica in terms of value.

Both clubs are going for their third trophies of the season. Real Madrid had won LaLiga and the Supercopa de España. Liverpool had won the EFL Cup and FA Cup (and finished second in the Premier League, behind Man City). The final is Real Madrid's fifty-sixth match of the season and Liverpool's sixty-third.* Most of their players also star on their national teams and participated in an additional four to eight international matches (2022 FIFA World Cup qualification, continental tournaments, and international friendly matches). At this point, at the end of the season, the players are more focused on rest and recovery than practice.

The game ends in a 1–0 Real Madrid victory, secured by Vinícius Júnior's fifty-ninth-minute winner (for more details, see "Play by Play of La Decimocuarta" later in this chapter). Real Madrid receive a total of €83 million in payouts by winning the tournament. Each Real Madrid player receives around €2.6 million gross (before tax) in performance bonuses for winning the Champions League, LaLiga, and the Spanish Cup.†

---

* In spite of fixture congestion, Liverpool participated in every game they were eligible to play throughout the 2021–22 season.

† https://www.besoccer.com/new/madrid-s-double-has-a-prize-1-3-million-for-each-player-1146153.

Social Media Impact

Real Madrid amassed 1.7 million followers on X (then Twitter), Facebook, Instagram, and YouTube over the weekend of the club's fourteenth Champions League title, according to Blinkfire Analytics. This figure was the highest ever achieved by any previous winners of the competition—more than double any previous champion. Real Madrid's 136 million engagements (on X, Facebook, Instagram, and YouTube) in the Paris final is also the highest ever recorded—again more than double any previous champion. Across all their social media channels, Real Madrid gained 3.1 million new followers on May 27, 28, and 29, with TikTok (1.4 million) and Instagram (1.2 million) making up more than 80 percent of the total. Real Madrid's TikTok account exceeds ten million views per post. According to social measurement platform MVPindex, Real Madrid have such a strong presence on Facebook, Instagram, and X, their social index value was worth about $1.7 billion in 2017 (roughly half of the club's then estimated $3.6 billion value), the highest in pro sports. At the time, Real Madrid had a total of 182 million followers; at the end of 2022, the total was 295 million (62 percent higher).

Amongst the players, Benzema had the biggest increase in new followers on Instagram. He received a total of 3 million new followers from right before the semifinal to 12 hours after the final—50.6 million to 53.6 million, a 6 percent increase.[*] For players that have a lot of followers on social media, it can lead to big amounts of money. For example, Cristiano Ronaldo had around 446 million followers on Instagram when he played at Man U in 2021–22. Experts estimate that Cristiano Ronaldo is the world's top Instagram earner, making about $2 million for a "one-off" sponsored Instagram post, *and he made a total of $55 million in 2021 from sponsorships* (sponsorship deals often require a certain number of social media posts).[†] Experts estimate players with approximately 50 million followers, like Benzema, could make around $200,000 per every "one-off" sponsored Instagram post.

---

[*] https://finance.yahoo.com/news/social-media-winners-champions-league-070000680.html.

[†] https://www.insider.com/cristiano-ronaldo-net-worth-how-soccer-star-makes-spends-money-2022-8#the-other-55-million-was-earned-off-the-field-2.

Incredibly, for Real Madrid it is their fifth triumph in the competition in nine seasons and, for Carlo Ancelotti, a record fourth success
as a manager (he also won two as a player). It was Florentino Pérez's
sixth European Cup (in eighteen years as president), equal to Santiago
Bernabéu's six (in thirty-five years as president of Real Madrid) and Paco
Gento's six as a player for Real Madrid. To put six European Cups into
perspective, Liverpool have six in their entire history and Barcelona have
five. Fifteen players have won at least five European Cups at Real Madrid,
including nine players that night—Bale, Benzema, Carvajal, Casemiro,
Isco, Kroos, Marcelo, Modrić, and Nacho.

On their way to winning the trophy, Real Madrid beat several teams
that many experts argued were better on paper. There was no argument
that several of the teams were more expensive to assemble. However,
Real Madrid's culture and DNA make them especially lethal in Europe,
beyond any individual player.*

When in 2018 Cristiano Ronaldo (thirty-three years old) reportedly
asked Real Madrid for another pay raise to match Lionel Messi's salary
at Barcelona† less than a year after Ronaldo's last contract renegotiation,
Florentino Pérez sold Ronaldo to Juventus for €100 million.‡ (Later, Barcelona would have financial difficulties, even with receiving €222 million for Neymar from PSG, and Messi would leave for PSG. Juventus
would also have financial challenges.) In addition, when legend and captain Sergio Ramos (thirty-five years old) reportedly asked for a two-year
extension without a pay cut during the pandemic in 2021, Real Madrid
weren't willing to make an exception to their policy of not offering more
than a one-year extension to a player whose contract expires after he is
over thirty years old. (Later, Ramos would sign a two-year contract with
PSG. He only played twelve matches in 2021–22.) Florentino Pérez wasn't

---

* https://gameofthepeople.com/2022/04/24/real-madrids-dna-makes-them-so-lethal-in-europe/.

† Messi would receive a maximum of €555,237,619 (US$673,919,105) over four seasons, including
a signing-on bonus of €115,225,000 for accepting the renewal and a "loyalty" bonus of €77,929,955.

‡ https://www.transfermarkt.com/cristiano-ronaldo/transfers/spieler/8198; https://www.espn.com/soccer
/barcelona/story/4302791/lionel-messis-leaked-barcelona-contract-the-biggest-in-sports-history
-report.

willing to risk Real Madrid's sustainable economic-sport model and go against one of the club's stated values of financial responsibility.

"How do you explain the Real DNA in the Champions League?" Former defender Manolo Sanchís, who captained Madrid to the title against Juventus in 1998, rhetorically asks. He answers, "It's something that new investors in this sport—people being very successful in other business activities—do not understand properly. They are used to being able to buy practically everything with money. But not this. You cannot buy the 116 years of history that Real Madrid has, nor the legacy that so many superb players have left in the locker room, nor the genetic line that reaches [Sergio] Ramos and Cristiano [Ronaldo] since the time of [Alfredo] Di Stefano and [Raymond] Kopa. And it also makes the man who is on the other side with the checkbook ask himself: 'How could I buy it?' Well, you cannot. I'm sorry."* In my previous book, *The Real Madrid Way*, I explained that money, talent, and data analytics were very important to winning—but the most important element was a club's culture, and it can't be copied (it's authentic from decades of history and traditions).

However, these days it's no longer just a local wealthy superfan's club on the other side of the pitch. Frequently Real Madrid are contesting against closely government-related, private equity, and multi-club ownership model clubs.

On Sunday, the day after the final, the team arrive at Madrid's Plaza de Cibeles with the trophy. There are tens of thousands of Real Madrid fans in the square celebrating. The banners on the I of Madrid's city hall read: "¡Gracias Madridistas!" and "Ch14mpions." The players get off the bus and take their places on the stage placed on the fountain, as they dance and sing along with the fans. Captain Marcelo, wearing five Super Bowl winner–styled rings (he won five European Cups with Real Madrid) and a number 14 jersey (for the fourteenth Champions League trophy; his normal jersey number is 12), puts a Real Madrid scarf and flag on the statue of the goddess and holds the Champions League trophy aloft from

---

* https://www.goal.com/en-us/news/what-is-the-secret-behind-real-madrids-champions-league-winning-machine/1e6nvllklypat10pyxupxp2v3m.

the top of the fountain. The Real Madrid fans revel in yet another historic moment to celebrate the fact that the team are the European Cup's most successful side.

Recalling this, I can't help but pause at the images, and smile as I remember what Carlos Martínez de Albornoz, Real Madrid's former finance director and a key member of the executive team responsible for turning Real Madrid into an international powerhouse, once told me: "They don't celebrate balance sheets at Cibeles Fountain." He was right, but without their sustainable economic-sport model and financial strength, a socios-owned club like Real Madrid would not be able to celebrate their fifth trophy in nine years—off the pitch and on the pitch are codependent.

Florentino Pérez says, "It's time to start working hard towards the fifteenth. Hala Madrid!" Difficult to translate exactly, *Hala Madrid* means something like "Go, Madrid, Go!" or "Forward, Madrid!" Real Madrid and Florentino Pérez aren't going to get complacent. They always want and demand more because of the expectations of their fans. The titles they just won are extra motivation going forward—on and off the pitch.

Real Madrid define themselves by their values and results, and in particular by their performance in the Champions League. The pride of the community at the team's wins are matched only by their passion for doing it in their own unique way. In Paris, the team's players felt the full weight of the community's expectations, which went beyond simply winning. There is an intense sense of responsibility and pride that comes with representing what the community is and the values they stand for. Real Madrid's secret to dominance on and off the pitch is the passion and values of their community members—which is where the club's culture and sustainable economic-sport model starts and finishes.

PLAY BY PLAY OF LA DECIMOCUARTA

The thirty-seven-minute delayed start is unsettling. The Reds kick off to start. Three minutes in and an early opportunity for Liverpool. Liverpool's Trent Alexander-Arnold puts in a free kick, which is cleared by Real Madrid's Karim Benzema. As expected, Liverpool are pressing high.

Liverpool seem to have settled in. The Reds are controlling the ball and pushing Real Madrid deep into their own half. Real Madrid seem to be content sitting deep and waiting for the right time to spring on the counter.

In the sixteenth minute, Liverpool's Mohamed Salah shoots on target but Real Madrid's goalkeeper Thibaut Courtois gets down well and makes the save. It was a warning for Real Madrid. A few minutes later Liverpool get another shot on goal. Liverpool's Sadio Mané finds Salah inside the box and Salah hits it first time, but it's straight at Courtois. In the twenty-first minute, from the edge of the box, Mané strikes the ball with pace, but an outstretched Courtois tips the shot with his right hand onto the post and then gathers the ball. Courtois saves Real Madrid once again.

Mané and Salah appear dangerous as they float along the front line. The Real Madrid defenders don't seem quite certain how to deal with them yet.

In the thirty-first minute, Toni Kroos plays a ball through toward Vinícius Júnior. Trent-Alexander makes a saving intercepting block because Vinícius would have been in on goal. The attempted pass highlights a key matchup. Vinícius (the impossibly quick Real Madrid left winger and team's most important counterattacker) versus Trent Alexander-Arnold (Liverpool's crucial attacking weapon and right back but who at times can struggle defending). Play is starting to open up and the action is end-to-end.

In the forty-third minute . . . after a little chaos in the box, Benzema finds the ball at his feet and kicks it into the back of the net, but the assistant has his flag up. Benzema appears offside, but the ball was off the knee of Liverpool's Fabinho, which could make Benzema eligible to play the ball. The question seems to be, did Fabinho play the ball or was his touch inadvertent? After a VAR check, Benzema is ruled offside. The goal is disallowed. However, Liverpool have been reminded that Real Madrid are old masters. Real Madrid can clinically take advantage of the smallest opportunities.

Halftime. 0–0. It was pretty much all Liverpool until the end of the half with Salah and Mané both testing Courtois on multiple occasions. But it was Liverpool who were saved by the ruling that Benzema was offside.

The second half starts with brilliant defending from Real Madrid. Dani Carvajal and Ferland Mendy break up what could have been promising chances. Liverpool are putting Real Madrid under pressure high up the pitch, but Los Blancos have been up to the task. In the fifty-fifth minute, Alexander-Arnold fires a ball in from the right and Thiago can't get on the end of it, but Courtois is forced to acrobatically punch the ball away.

In the fifty-ninth minute, Valverde rushes down the right side. The recognizable voice of TV commentator Ray Hudson, known for his emotional, hyperbolic, off-the-cuff color commentary, rises in excitement to reveal in his North East England Geordie accent that he thinks something special is happening: "Watch out . . . Liverpool's defense are stretched out like spandex on Miami Beach!" (Full disclosure, there isn't any Ray Hudson commentary available for this match. So, since he's my favorite commentator, I'm having some fun by imagining what he would say.)

Valverde fires a low ball into the box.* It finds its way to the back post and Vinícius side-foots it into the empty net. Hudson reacts, "Vini . . . Vidi . . . Vici . . . Vinícius arrived like ghost. There ain't any tracking him . . . even the Ghostbuster meter can't find this guy." Vinícius fractionally caught out Alexander-Arnold.

Goal. Real Madrid. Real Madrid take the lead against the run of play.

Liverpool start to push harder. In the sixty-fourth minute, Salah is denied by another excellent save by Courtois. In the sixty-ninth minute, he makes another remarkable save, denying Salah again at the back post. The Real Madrid players are making brilliant interceptions and blocks and quickly closing on players, but Courtois pulls off a few more incredible saves. Hudson tries to explain: "Look at these saves, man. Catlike quick . . . and mix in a bit of octopus and gladiator."

---

* Some fans and analysts were arguing about whether or not Valverde was aiming for a shot or a pass, but the midfielder ended the controversy and owned the fact that he wasn't trying to deliver that assist, which is a very humble and honest thing to admit.

Valverde's pass to Vinícius Júnior in the 2022 Champions League final.

Vinícius Júnior after scoring the winning, and only, goal in the 2022 Champions League final.

With every jaw-dropping Courtois save, the inevitability of a Madrid win seems to grow. Three times in the tournament, Los Blancos were staring defeat in the face, and three times they somehow came out victorious.

In the eighty-seventh minute, Real Madrid get another chance. Vinícius gets on the end of a magical ball from Luka Modrić, and he runs toward goal before back-heeling to Benzema, but the Frenchman is defended by Alexander-Arnold.

Five minutes of time added on. Real Madrid's Dani Ceballos, who had only just come on, is through but tries to pass to Vinícius instead of going for the goal. Liverpool make a final push, but Real Madrid show their experience, belief, and composure. Full time.

Real Madrid are the UEFA Champions League Winners, 1–0.

Hudson sums it up: "Magesteeeeerial! Beautiful big-ears is coming home! Kids, don't let stats fool you. Don Carlo's game plan was a masterpiece . . . much better than Michael Corleone's . . . because Don Carlo didn't need an alibi."

Liverpool had 55 percent possession and nine shots on target. Real Madrid only had one shot on target. Chances were few and far between for Los Blancos, but they only needed one. Real Madrid proved once again—doubt the old masters at your peril.

Courtois was named "man of the match." Real Madrid had a plan and perfectly executed it. They could risk absorbing pressure, conceding chances, and daring their opponent closer, believing the defense and Courtois would make the necessary saves, and when an opening presented itself, Benzema or Vinícius or Rodrygo would score on the counter.[*]

In 2018, Real Madrid beat PSG (champions of France), Juventus (champions of Italy), Bayern Munich (champions of Germany), and Liverpool in the Champions League final. However, most likely, no team have ever had a harder route to winning a Champions League final than Real Madrid in 2022. Real Madrid beat PSG (champions of France), Chelsea (reigning European champions), Man City (champions of England), and Liverpool in the final (Liverpool finished in second place in the Premier

---

[*] https://www.nytimes.com/live/2022/05/28/sports/champions-league-final.

League, won two trophies, and had only lost three of sixty-two matches all season before the final).

In many ways, 2021–22, on and off the pitch, was The Real Madrid Way, continued. But the period also highlights The Real Madrid Revolution.

The next chapter will provide background on how and why professional football became entertainment and content, which led to discussions over the years of a European Super League. This is necessary to then understand why the changes in football are happening and how and why Real Madrid are addressing them. The idea of viewing matches as content and entertainment (and the subsequent explosion of the value of TV rights) started before Florentino Pérez won the election in 2000 to become president of Real Madrid. However, Florentino and Real Madrid helped take the idea to another level. They had to, in order to compete against billionaire owners changing the dynamics of football. Now, Real Madrid are competing against closely government-related, private equity, and multi-club ownership models.

After the background in chapter two, the chapter that follows will describe The Real Madrid Way. This will provide a baseline about how the club is managed, and why the club uses their approach. Much of this information is covered in more detail in my previous book, *The Real Madrid Way* (2016).

After the chapter focusing on Real Madrid's way of doing things, our discussion will turn to the systemic changes happening in football today, starting with changes in ownership models, and what Real Madrid are doing to address the changes—changes that go far beyond the European Super League.

Chapter 2

FOOTBALL BECOMES ENTERTAINMENT AND CONTENT, WHICH LEADS TO EUROPEAN SUPER LEAGUE PROPOSALS

TO BETTER UNDERSTAND how professional football became entertainment and content, I need to provide some historical background, which also inevitably provides some background on a "European Super League"—an idea that goes back to the creation of the European Cup.

In 1954, *L'Equipe*, a French daily newspaper devoted to sport, published an article proposing a European club competition between the champions of each domestic league in Europe, which would take place midweek alongside the national leagues throughout the season—a European league. The idea of the competition appealed to most of the big clubs in Europe, as it would help protect their positions and generate more revenues. However, some clubs preferred a cup competition that would require fewer matches and less travel than a league. As a compromise, the idea developed into a knockout cup tournament, but not with the traditional one-match knockout format. Each round of the competition was to be competed over two legs, home and away, like a domestic league. (The first year, some of the invited clubs were not national champions, but selected based on their prestige and attractiveness to fans. From the second year, the clubs were domestic champions and the reigning champion.)*

Until 1966–67, if there was no outright winner from the two legs, a third deciding leg was played at a neutral location. So, the European Cup was never structured along the same lines as the FA Cup, where there was only one game in each round, and a higher chance that a small club could upset a big club. One of the reasons the two-leg format was specifically used for the European Cup was to tip the scales to the big clubs and reduce the impact of luck. And it worked.

Real Madrid won the first five European Cups (1955–56 through 1959–60) and won their sixth in 1965–66.

During those first eleven years, as intended, the big clubs from the Top 5 Leagues dominated. Real Madrid and Barcelona were in the finals seven times (Real Madrid six and Barcelona once), Milan and Inter Milan twice each (Fiorentina once), Reims twice, and Frankfurt once. Benfica (essentially the sixth Top League) got to the finals three times.

Real Madrid had a big, imposing stadium that would intimidate smaller clubs. In table 2.1, notice that Real Madrid's stadium (124,000-capacity stadium renovated in 1955) in 1956–57 was much larger than all the other venues, except 1959–60 Hampden Park, Scotland—where a nineteen-year-old Queens Park striker named Alex Ferguson watched Real Madrid win their fifth European Cup with a style of play and skill he had never seen before.†

---

* Real Madrid did not win LaLiga in 1955–56. But there was a free domestic spot left by French protectorate Saar after its reunification with West Germany, and the additional place was awarded to Real Madrid as the competition's reigning champion.

† The city of Glasgow with Hampden Park, Celtic Park, and Ibrox possessed the three largest football stadia in the world at the time Hampden opened in 1903. Hampden Park was the biggest stadium in the world from the time of its opening until it was surpassed by the Maracanã in Rio de Janeiro in 1950.

Table 2.1: The First Eleven European Cup Finals

Season	Winners		Score	Runners-Up		Venue	Attendance
	Nation	Team		Nation	Team		
1955–56	Spain	Real Madrid	4–3	France	Reims	Parc des Princes, Paris, France	38,239
1956–57	Spain	Real Madrid	2–0	Italy	Fiorentina	Santiago Bernabéu, Madrid, Spain	124,000
1957–58	Spain	Real Madrid	3–2	Italy	Milan	Heysel Stadium, Brussels, Belgium	67,000
1958–59	Spain	Real Madrid	2–0	France	Reims	Neckarstadion, Stuttgart, West Germany	72,000
1959–60	Spain	Real Madrid	7–3	Germany	Eintracht Frankfurt	Hampden Park, Glasgow, Scotland	127,621
1960–61	Portugal	Benfica	3–2	Spain	Barcelona	Wankdorf Stadium, Bern, Switzerland	26,732
1961–62	Portugal	Benfica	5–3	Spain	Real Madrid	Olympisch Stadion, Amsterdam, Netherlands	61,257
1962–63	Italy	Milan	2–1	Portugal	Benfica	Wembley Stadium, London, England	45,715
1963–64	Italy	Inter Milan	3–1	Spain	Real Madrid	Praterstadion, Vienna, Austria	71,333
1964–65	Italy	Inter Milan	1–0	Portugal	Benfica	San Siro, Milan, Italy	89,000
1965–66	Spain	Benfica	2–1	Yugoslavia	Partizan	Heysel Stadium, Brussels, Belgium	46,745

Many European Cup matches were lopsided. It was not unusual to see 7–0 or 8–3 aggregate scores in the first round, quarterfinals, and even semifinals. For example, in the first three rounds of the 1959–60 European Cup, Real Madrid outscored their opponents 24 to 7, and they beat Eintracht Frankfurt 7-3 in the final in front of 127,621 people in Hampden Park (Ferenc Puskás and Alfredo Di Stefano both scored a hat trick in the final). Typically, Eintracht Frankfurt played in front of 55,000 people. In the 1959–60 tournament, Barcelona (Spanish champions with a 93,000-capacity stadium built in 1957) beat Wolverhampton (English champions with a 33,000-capacity stadium) 9–2 in the quarterfinals, then Real Madrid (reigning European Cup champions) beat Barcelona 6–2 in the semifinals.

After being introduced in 1967–68, aggregate goals decided the tie instead of a neutral third leg, with away goals having more meaning.* Once again, this rule was to favor the big clubs. The rationale was that a small club would be less likely to score at a big club's larger, more intimating stadium.†

At the time, matchday/stadium revenues were the largest sources of revenues for clubs. And the bigger the stadium capacity, the more money clubs could make, and then the more money they had to sign the best players. After World War II, the early years of public television in Europe coincided with the return of major international sporting events, especially the FIFA World Cup in 1954 in Switzerland—which led to greater TV interest in the European Cup.‡ Football helped fuel the rise of television. In 1948, there were only 48,000 TV sets in England. By 1965, there were over fifty-eight million TV sets in countries connected by the Eurovision network. Santiago Bernabéu lobbied Spanish dictator Francisco Franco for Spain to join Eurovision in 1956 to ensure Real Madrid's European Cup matches could be seen on TV in Spain—which Franco finally

---

* It was introduced in the 1965–66 Cup Winners' Cup and the 1967–1968 European Cup (but only for the first round of the competition, and extra time goals were not included in the rule).

† In 2021–22, the Champions League no longer uses away goals as an aggregate-goal series tiebreaker.

‡ The 1954 World Cup champions were West Germany, runners-up Hungary, third place Austria, and fourth place Uruguay.

authorized in March 1960.* In May 1960, an estimated seventy million television viewers around Europe watched Real Madrid beat Eintracht Frankfurt in the European Cup final—which is widely regarded as one of the greatest football matches ever played.

Since the start of the European Cup, different proposals for a European Super League with different variations of structure, eligibility, and competition have been made with one thing in mind—broadcasting rights, which slowly overtook matchday/stadium revenues.

In 2016–17 (selected because pre-pandemic), broadcasting represented 45 percent of the revenues of the top twenty clubs in the Deloitte Money League Rankings as compared to matchday's 17 percent of revenues. And smaller clubs without large, modern stadiums with VIP hospitality boxes to increase matchday revenues or global brands to attract big sponsors to increase commercial revenues rely much more on broadcasting revenues. For example, Everton, which ranked twenieth—broadcasting represented 76 percent of Everton revenues as compared to their matchday's 9 percent of revenues.†

---

* Broadcast matches enjoyed large audiences. However, during its first General Assembly held in Vienna in March 1955, UEFA asserted—against the clear desires of the public—that national federations had absolute discretion over televised broadcasts of football matches, with de facto control over whether to authorize a televised broadcast of a particular match. This controversial decision was never really challenged by European governments. Often, the national federations refused live football match broadcasts. The justification of the refusal to provide live coverage on the part of federations or professional football leagues was to protect the ticket sales of amateur clubs. This invariably sparked outrage, especially when the national team—supposed to represent the entire nation—could not be viewed by the public. For example, the Italy–Germany match played on December 18, 1955, was to be the "match of the year" on Eurovision, and the German federation refused to broadcast the match live "to protect the rare amateurs still playing one week before Christmas." The German public were outraged. In addition, the joint union for technicians for Italian television (RAI) took European football "hostage" by striking before the match to get higher wages. The strike lasted until halftime of the match, preventing live televised broadcast or radio coverage of the first half to Italy and the rest of Europe. https://ehne.fr/en/encyclopedia/themes/material-civilization/european -sports-circulations/televised-football-a-european-mass-spectacle-1950-1960.

† Most Serie A clubs don't own their own stadiums (AC Milan, Inter Milan, Napoli, Roma), so generally Serie A clubs are more reliant on broadcasting revenues.

Table 2.2: Revenue Split Between Real Madrid, the 2018
Deloitte Money League Top 20, and Everton

	Real Madrid		Top 20	Everton	
Revenue Stream	Euros (m)	%	%	Euros (m)	%
Matchday	136.4	20%	17%	16.8	8%
Broadcasting	236.8	35%	45%	151.9	76%
Commercial	301.4	45%	38%	30.5	15%
Total	674.6			199.2	
Stadium Capacity	81,044			52,888	

Source: Deloitte

Although broadcasting rights deals don't typically capture headlines, today they have become the lifeblood of football, and all major
sports. For global audiences, broadcasting allows them to follow the game
without boundaries, while for football clubs it has become a vital revenue source in their operations—much more than matchday revenues
for most clubs. Even more important, reaching and growing a passionate
global audience via broadcasting with "entertaining content" leads to big
commercial sponsor opportunities with global companies. The sponsors
want to tap into the passion and love fans have for their clubs by association. Eighty-one percent of consumers either completely or somewhat
trust advertisements or sponsorships from brands in a sporting context,
a significantly larger percentage than other channels and close to the
89 percent consumers apply to recommendations from friends and peers.[*]

The following are some key moments in the 1980s and 1990s in
sports and football, before Florentino won the 2000 election to be president of Real Madrid, that highlight the changes caused by the increasing
value of TV rights:

- 1982 and 1993: NFL's 1982 TV deal makes the Big Five envious,
  and Rupert Murdoch's success with Fox Sports is a game changer.

---

[*] https://sportfive.com/beyond-the-match/insights/sports-fans-as-consumers-loyal-vocal-and-priceless.

- 1992: The breakaway FA English Premier League is broadcasted by Rupert Murdoch's BSkyB.
- 1987 and 1992–93: Silvio Berlusconi buys AC Milan for content, and after a Real Madrid European Cup match and together with Real Madrid push UEFA to change the European Cup to the Champions League.
- 1997–2000: Rupert Murdoch and broadcasters want to own content (clubs), and the clubs want to own their own broadcasting.
- 1997–98: The G-14 with the help of Real Madrid push UEFA to expand the Champions League.

Looking at the list, you quickly see that Rupert Murdoch, Silvio Berlusconi, and Real Madrid were key drivers of change. They saw the power of sports as valuable entertainment content. To understand how football became entertainment and content, which led to European Super League proposals, one needs to understand some history. Let's examine each of those key moments in more detail.

1982 AND 1993: NFL'S 1982 TV DEAL MAKES THE BIG FIVE ENVIOUS, AND RUPERT MURDOCH'S SUCCESS WITH FOX SPORTS IS A GAME CHANGER

In 1982, the NFL agreed to a five-year, $2 billion TV deal with the established "Big Three" U.S. broadcast networks (ABC, CBS, and NBC), which was considered a watershed moment in sports broadcasting history. American football was no longer a sport, it was "entertainment and content." Each NFL team would average $14.2 million a year in broadcasting revenues for the duration of the agreement. The average was three times what each team received from the league's last deal. In 1980, the Denver Broncos were sold for $20 million.

In comparison, in the following year, 1983, English football signed a two-year deal worth £5.2 million. The primary difference was the approach: the English were broadcasting a sporting contest, while the Americans were broadcasting a compelling "entertainment show" (with lots of commercials) that appealed to advertisers.

In 1993, CBS (which had been home to NFL games for thirty-eight years) lost their TV rights to Rupert Murdoch's fledgling Fox Network. Murdoch and his team astutely calculated that, among the Big Three networks, CBS was the most focused on cutting costs—and therefore the most susceptible to an aggressive Fox bid. Fox offered a then-record $1.58 billion to the NFL over four years ($395 million per year), significantly more than the $290 million per year offered by CBS. Fox was only seven years old and at the time had no sports division.*

Murdoch's numbers were far beyond what any network had been prepared to pay at the time. Industry sources were estimating that Fox would lose $500 million to $700 million in the deal. However, what they missed was Fox's NFL rights ownership made the network a major player in American television by attracting many new viewers and provided a platform to advertise its other shows.

The NFL contract vaulted the young Fox network, then far behind the Big Three, to the very powerful role it now plays in media and entertainment. After winning the NFL bid, Rupert Murdoch said, "Like no other sport will do, the NFL will make us into a real network. In the future there will be 400 or 500 channels on cable, and ratings will be fragmented. But football on Sunday will have the same ratings, regardless of the number of channels. Football will not fragment."[†] A 2019 *New York Times* investigative series suggested just how accurate Murdoch was in his prediction.[‡]

The success of Fox is now the business model case study for technology companies such as Amazon, Apple, Netflix, and YouTube who want to attract subscribers.[§] It is one factor driving the value of sports franchises today.

For the 1994–97 seasons, many of the twenty-eight (or thirty, after the 1995 expansion) NFL owners thought they'd be fortunate just to

* By 1990, *before* the NFL bid or his purchase of the *Wall Street Journal*, Murdoch's holding company, News Corp, had acquired Britain's *News of the World*, *The Sun*, and *The Times*; had formed European media conglomerate BSkyB; and in the U.S. had acquired HarperCollins and 20th Century Fox.

† https://hbr.org/2019/04/rupert-murdoch-the-nfl-and-the-negotiation-that-remade-tv.

‡ https://www.nytimes.com/interactive/2019/04/03/magazine/rupert-murdoch-fox-news-trump.html.

§ https://www.nytimes.com/2022/07/24/technology/sports-streaming-rights.html?.

match the $3.6 billion of their last TV contract ($32.5 million per team per year for four years), but with the Fox deal, the league increased its TV rights fees to $4.4 billion. Now each team would get $39.2 million a year from Fox, NBC, and ABC and cable entities ESPN and TNT. As a result, sports broadcasting rights and team valuations had dramatically changed forever.

Postmortem

In 2021, the NFL signed media rights deals that are, combined, worth $112.6 billion for a period of ten years starting in 2023, which is an 82 percent average annual increase over the current deals. Therefore, the NFL will generate about $11 billion in broadcast revenue each year, over around 272 games ($40 million per game). Only around 3 percent of income from NFL media rights is international.

The Premier League generates around £1.6 billion ($2 billion) from domestic TV rights and around $1.8 billion for international rights (47 percent international), over around 380 matches per year ($10 million per match).*

Table 2.3: League 2021 Ranking Domestic TV Rights Value per Season

League	Country	Level	Value per Season (m)
Premier	England	1	£1,600
Bundesliga 1 & 2	Germany	1–2	€1,100
LaLiga	Spain, Andorra	1	€990
Serie A	Italy	1	€927.5
Ligue 1 & 2	France, Monaco	1	€582
Major League Soccer	USA, Canada	1	€259
Brasileirao	Brazil	1	£162
English Football League	England, Wales	2	£119

SOURCE: Wikipedia

* According to the *Financial Times* in October 2023, the Premier League was set to make significant changes to the sale of its TV rights in the U.K. One of the changes was extending the duration of the deal and eliminating some games offered to Amazon. This will reduce the risk to broadcasters who wanted more time to invest in production.

In 2018, the English Football League (the Championship, League One and Two—which consist of seventy-two clubs) sold domestic broadcast rights to Sky TV in a five-year deal worth £119 million per year. Ironically, as many as fifteen Championship clubs threatened a breakaway over the deal (reportedly led by Leeds United, Aston Villa, and Derby County) because they felt undervalued as the distribution of broadcasting revenues doesn't consider how many times clubs are on TV (a repeating theme!). The English Football League generates around £23 million per year from international broadcasters.

In May 2023, Sky signed a new five-year deal worth £935 million with the EFL starting from the 2024–25 season—around £187 million per year. Sky also committed to broadcast or stream around four times as many matches as are currently shown.

Many feared the English Football League would suffer after the Premier League breakaway. Instead, its broadcasting rights value currently ranks ahead of many first leagues including Japan, Turkey, Belgium, Russia, and the Netherlands. The EFL's new deal even puts it ahead of Portugal and Brazil's first leagues.

1992: THE BREAKAWAY FA ENGLISH PREMIER LEAGUE IS BROADCAST BY RUPERT MURDOCH'S BSKYB

The 1982 $2 billion NFL TV deal got owners of England's Big Five, the five football clubs with the most storied history and the biggest crowds in English football (Arsenal, Everton, Liverpool, Man U, and Tottenham Hotspur), thinking and dreaming. Remember that, in 1983, English football signed a broadcasting rights deal worth £5.2 million for two years.

In 1984, media owner Robert Maxwell reportedly offered to buy Man U for £10 million and withdrew the offer amid fan fury and not meeting then chairman Martin Edwards's asking price.

In their book *The Club*, Joshua Robinson and Jonathan Clegg of the *Wall Street Journal* describe in detail exactly what their book's subtitle states: "How the English Premier League Became the Wildest, Richest, Most Disruptive Force in Sports." In their extremely well-written and researched book, they explain that the distribution of broadcasting revenues for the Big Five was a key motivation behind the formation of the Premier League itself in the early 1990s.

In his book *Calling the Shots: How to Win at Football and Life*, David Dein, former deputy chairman and co-owner of Arsenal, explained in the 1980s he was fascinated by the entertainment value of American sport and frustrated by the bureaucracy of the English Football League, the competition to which English football clubs then belonged. (In full disclosure, David and I both serve on an academic board together at FIFA.)

In the late 1980s, Rupert Murdoch was planning on launching Sky in the U.K. and offered £47 million for the rights to First Division football to have content to attract subscribers. Greg Dyke, meanwhile, at that time both chief executive of London Weekend Television and the chairman of ITV Sport, wanted to show the Big Five's matches on ITV and offered to buy their rights separately from the rest of the twenty-two clubs who formed the League's elite First Division. It would have amounted to a breakaway competition, and they assumed English football fans would probably not like the idea, unless they could be persuaded there were good reasons.

The English Football League found out about the breakaway discussions happening in the late 1980s. They were so desperate to prevent a breakaway, the League made several changes, including increasing the percentage of the TV contract money to the elite First Division and decreasing the percentage to the lower league clubs. (Historically, the threat of a breakaway from big clubs often lead to changes and/or concessions.) Greg Dyke of ITV and David Dein negotiated the first major TV deal in English football. ITV paid £44 million over four years for all four leagues (ninety-two clubs).

In 1989, Sky launched in the U.K., but without football rights, it initially was a flop.

In 1989, English businessman Michael Knighton had an agreement with the Edwards family, which had controlled Man U for twenty-five years, to buy the club for £20 million—the biggest takeover in the history

of British football. Reportedly, the deal didn't close due to the buyer having insufficient funds.*

When the English Football League TV rights deal began to approach
its end, the representatives of the Big Five clubs—David Dein of Arsenal,
Philip Carter of Everton, Noel White of Liverpool, Martin Edwards of
Man U, and Irving Scholar of Tottenham Hotspur—wanted to form an
elite league, which could sell its own rights and share income only among
member clubs.

Dein was (and still is) a visionary. In his book, David Dein wrote:
"If football was a public company, what sector would we be in . . . We'd
be in the entertainment sector . . . You go there to be entertained. We
have to make football appealing." He concluded: "Forming the Premier
League was more about natural survival . . . We have to break away . . .
The Premier League will save the game [English football]."

That phrase, *save the game* . . . hmm . . . the same words Florentino
Pérez would later use and be criticized for. Ironically, there are many par-
allels between the rationale for the European Super League and English
Premier League.

In their book, Robinson and Clegg wrote: "For starters, the Big Five
were staring at a public-relations nightmare. While it was true that the
impetus behind the Premier League was a desire for greater control—of
their finances, their commercial arrangements, and the entire business of
English football—they couldn't possibly share that with the general public. It sounded a little too much like naked self-interest . . . They would
have to find a more palatable solution, something that England's football
going public could understand, even support."

One of the big differences between the European Super League and
the English Premier League is the public relations spin of nationalism.

The Big Five, through their ambassadors—Arsenal's Dein and Liverpool's White—approached the English football governing body, the FA,
with their intention to break away. They correctly calculated that the

---

* Man U made its original IPO in June 1991, seeking to raise £10 million to finance stadium
improvements. The float of 1.2 million shares on the London Stock Exchange was a disappointment,
however, because more than half of the available shares went unsold. Man U's share price was under
£2, down from an IPO price of about £8.33, by the late 1990s.

crucial element to their plan was getting the governing body on their side. They won the FA's support by justifying their breakaway on the grounds that it would raise the standard of the national team, which hadn't won a major football trophy since the 1966 World Cup. Genius! The general idea was that the Big Five would make more money and the clubs would reinvest the money into youth academies, and the Big Five would have more money to keep England's best talent from going to play abroad, especially to Italy and Spain. They and the complicit media astutely spun the narrative so that if a fan was against the new breakaway league, they were essentially against England winning the Euros or World Cup.* Even politicians representing areas with small football clubs that were initially excluded wouldn't dare stand in the way of "The Three Lions," especially with England hosting the 1996 Euros.†

As further background, every Sunday millions in England watched Serie A on Channel Four. AC Milan won back-to-back Champions League trophies in 1988–89 and 1989–90. The best English player of his generation, Paul Gascoigne, moved to Lazio from Tottenham in 1992 during the golden era of Serie A. He followed David Platt, who left Aston Villa for Bari in 1991.

A few years earlier, after winning the Golden Boot at the 1986 World Cup in Mexico, Gary Lineker left Everton to go to Barcelona. Barcelona were managed by former Queens Park Rangers manager Terry Venables who also brought in Man U and Wales striker Mark Hughes. Barcelona gave Lineker his first chance at European competition as Leicester had never qualified for the European Cup, and while he was at Everton, English clubs were banned from the European Cup following the Heysel disaster.‡ (Now, of course, generally many top managers and players go to England.)

---

* England failed to qualify for the 1994 World Cup, have not been to a World Cup final since 1966, and have never won the Euros.

† This was in stark contrast to English politicians threatening legislation to stop the European Super League. There was no compelling national interest narrative spun for England's football-going public. From the start, the idea of a "European" league was an uphill battle. After all, in 2016, a 51.9 percent majority of U.K. voters voted for "Brexit," leaving the European Union.

‡ The Heysel Stadium disaster was a crowd disaster that occurred on May 29, 1985, when mostly Juventus fans escaping from a breach by Liverpool fans were pressed against a collapsing wall in the

England created modern football, and in the 1980s and early 1990s they had the third best league in terms of revenues behind Italy and Spain. English players and managers were leaving for the continent. The 1992 European Cup final at Wembley Stadium in London featured Barcelona of Spain and Sampdoria of Italy. All of this seemed completely unacceptable to the average working-class football-loving Brit. The breakaway English Premier League had great timing and nationalism to gain fan support.

Utilizing English Nationalism and Hooliganism

The 2021 announcement of the European Super League came after the 2016 Brexit referendum for the U.K. to leave the European Union. In 2016, Fintan O'Toole of *The Guardian* wrote: "When you strip away the rhetoric, Brexit is an English nationalist movement . . . The passion that animates it is English self-assertion."* English nationalism was used to support the breakaway Premier League, and English nationalism was used to help stop a "European" league. The Premier League was also now the dominant league, and some English fans think they don't need continental Europe to make English football better.

In addition, there is growing tension in society about disparities in wealth and opportunities—also exasperated during the pandemic. The ideas of hope in promotion (best-ranking teams getting moved up to a higher division) and merit in relegation (worst-ranking teams moved to a lower division) in football is steeped in history and mythology—regardless, if the Big Six don't get relegated and the Big Six dominate Champions League spots—and defies a British social class system.

A similar tension in society also existed in the 1980s in England, when football hooliganism was at its worst. "Two Britain's emerged in the 1980s," writes Andrew Marr in his *A History of Modern Britain*. "The rich got richer but the bottom 10 percent saw their incomes fall by about 17 percent. A lot

---

Heysel Stadium in Brussels, Belgium, before the start of the 1985 European Cup final between the Italian and English clubs. Thirty-nine people—mostly Italians and Juventus fans—were killed and six hundred were injured in the confrontation.

* https://www.theguardian.com/commentisfree/2016/jun/18/england-eu-referendum-brexit.

of people fell through the cracks."* "Hooliganism" was often a way for people to express their frustrations about inequality and Prime Minister Thatcher's government's power in the 1980s. The proposed Premier League promised to clean up the game, which it wanted to resell and repackage as family entertainment. Therefore, politicians and club owners used combating hooliganism as another reason to support the Premier League. UEFA condemned hooliganism and banned English football clubs in European competition from 1985 to 1990 to send a message, which Thatcher controversially supported.

When the European Super League was announced in 2021, the local protests had many parallels to hooliganism—and many similar images.† Man U legend Bryan Robson described the fan protests as "hooliganism."‡ He said, "Look at the image of that injured policeman's face. I'm all for the passion of Manchester United supporters—no one loves it more than me— but I can't condone the aggressive behavior of those who throw around bottles, cameras, rip up seat covers, swing on crossbars and then break into the dressing rooms."

This time the frustrations were not against the British government's power; they often were directed against inequality and foreign power and wealth—many Premier League clubs are owned by rich foreigners. In addition, there was an emergence of protests and changes of behaviors and attitudes throughout the world during the COVID-19 pandemic due to numerous societal frustrations and movements.§ Ironically, "hooliganism" got the attention of British politicians who were facing questions about their own abuse of power and privilege at the time of the European Super League announcement. Opportunistic politicians then used the fortuitous timing to redirect working-class frustration, change the news cycle topic, and score political points by threatening a "legislative bomb" to stop the European Super League. The Eton- and Oxford-educated prime minister Boris Johnson positioned himself as the defender of working-class fans and the enemy of the foreign billionaire owners who now dominate English football. He also had won the majority by promising Brexit.

---

* https://www.fourfourtwo.com/features/worst-five-months-english-football-thatcher-fighting-and-fatalities-1985.

† https://punditarena.com/football/daniel-hussey/bryan-robson-united-hooligans/.

‡ https://punditarena.com/football/daniel-hussey/bryan-robson-united-hooligans/.

§ https://www.ncbi.nlm.nih.gov/pmc/articles/PMC9596683/. https://www.nature.com/articles/s41599-022-01082-y.

Ironically, this time UEFA didn't condemn the violent protests—it celebrated them as a message.* Yet, the following year, UEFA blamed and condemned many working-class Liverpool fans (some of whom were indiscriminately sprayed with tear gas or pepper spray) for the chaos at the 2022 Champions League final in Paris.† And while UEFA seemed to appreciate the idea of British government intervention to stop the European Super League in 2021, UEFA has not commented on the proposal of a U.K. government-appointed independent regulator in football (while FIFA expressed concern over it potentially breaching rules over political interference in football).‡

After meeting Dein and White in the late 1980s, the FA commissioned an executive from advertising firm Saatchi & Saatchi to imagine how a new league might be organized and calculate the revenues it might generate. They determined that substantial revenues were available from increased TV exposure with more "event" matches between the Big Five. They concluded that the England team would benefit (they never even consulted with the then-current England manager) and that the breakaway league would have more money to reinvest in the national and grassroots game.

There was a rival power-block within the old First Division, coordinated by Chelsea and Crystal Palace. They wanted to stop English Football being ruled by the Big Five.§ Dein also knew the league clubs outside the top division would be nervous. He explained: "What mattered to

---

* Contrast this to seven European countries abandoning the diversity gesture of wearing OneLove armbands during the 2022 FIFA World Cup in Qatar, fearing their captains would be exposed to "unlimited liability" and would have faced suspensions. England players did nothing. Germany players covered their mouths in protest before their game and the squad sported tops with rainbow colors on their sleeves in the warm-up.

† UEFA later apologized to Liverpool fans and promised "a special refund scheme for fans." Real Madrid have refused to accept UEFA's ticket refund scheme for fans who attended the final in Paris and have offered legal help to their fans who wish to sue UEFA for damages.

‡ On September 7, 2023, a policy paper was published by the Department for Culture, Media & Sport: "A Sustainable Future—Reforming Club Football Governance: Consultation Response." The U.K. government made a renewed commitment to introduce an independent regulator for English football "as soon as possible." There are still several details to be decided.

§ Bates and Noades recognized that it was the Big Five who delivered the largest TV audiences and eventually accepted that the clubs they represented needed to remain in alliance with the Big Five. No one in the old First Division voted to exclude themselves from the Premier League.

them was the prospect of promotion—three clubs going up and three going down—to keep the dream alive. We never even thought of taking that away . . . I passionately believe in the pyramid."

While the new league would have promotion and relegation, a key tenant for support for the breakaway league, the representatives of the Big Five knew that with their established advantages (greater history/ brands, larger stadiums, larger fan bases, bigger local markets), they really didn't risk relegation.* The Big Five believed the dream of promotion to the new league for the other clubs, or even winning it (as remote as that seemed), added to excitement and gave fans a reason to be interested in their teams all season long.† (While the European Super League had permanent "founding members," ironically that essentially is what the Big Five, Six, and now Seven and growing are. The big clubs aren't effectively at risk of being relegated.)

Everything in the Premier League would be voted on by the clubs (ultimately to be comprised of twenty teams instead of eighteen), every club would have one vote, and every vote would require a two-thirds majority to pass. By streamlining its governance, the breakaway league would be more agile than its predecessor and other European football leagues. (Later, the big clubs would still find that their interests often didn't align with the other clubs.)

In addition, all TV revenue would be split in a new way. The Premier League would not share its money with the lower divisions, but the Big Five would also not take a share directly commensurate to their size. All money would be divided 50/25/25. Fifty percent was to be split equally between the clubs, 25 percent according to the league position achieved

---

* Arsenal, Chelsea, Everton, Liverpool, Man U, and Tottenham have never been relegated since the Premier League started. Last time selected clubs had been relegated: Arsenal (1913), Everton (1951), Liverpool (1954), Man U (1974), Tottenham (1977), and Chelsea (1988). Manchester City have been relegated twice in the Premier League era, the last time in 2001. However, with their new ownership in 2008, it is highly unlikely. Newcastle were relegated in 2009 and 2016. However, with their new ownership in 2021, it is highly unlikely. A review of the history of promotion and relegation practices in England shows that a core group of clubs tend to dominate the Premier League—and this is true even before the Big Six. From 1888–89 to 2000–2001, eight teams—Liverpool (18), Man U (14), Arsenal (11), Everton (9), Aston Villa (7), Sunderland (6), Newcastle United (4), and Sheffield Wednesday (4)—account for over 70 percent of the top football division championships.

† There is an academic debate over whether this is actually true.

in the previous season, and only 25 percent dependent on the number of times a club appeared on TV. Any international TV revenues, which then were almost zero, were to be divided equally. (Later, the international TV revenues grew exponentially and the Big Six wanted a bigger percentage because their brands were the key drivers. And they succeeded.[*])

"The Premier League: A League Motivated by Greed, No Doubt, but Not the Sole Fault of One Mr. Murdoch"

In May 2020, Mark Dennis, who was deputy sports editor of the (London) *Evening Standard* during the formation of the Premier League, wrote an article for norwichcity.myfootballwriter.com about the start of the Premier League. He wrote that he was "actively courted" by Irving Scholar (Tottenham's chairman until 1991) and David Dein to support the breakaway Premier League, and provided some more background:[†]

> Norwich City, under Robert Chase, were among the clubs who quickly backed the new league. But there were plenty of other enthusiasts. Elton John, then chairman of Watford, told me he was flattered that his club were invited to regular meetings about the plot . . .
>
> The only real opposition came from clubs lower down the food-chain and from Gordon Taylor at the PFA (yes, really). And, although the new competition was supposed to help the England team, the England manager at that time, Graham Taylor, told

---

[*] In 2018, led by Manchester City and Liverpool, supported by Man U, Arsenal, Chelsea, and Spurs, the six successfully pressed their case that, as they are the prime attractions for global audiences and money paid by international broadcasters, they should receive more of the money. From 2019–20, the first season of TV deals being concluded now, the current level of revenue from international TV rights sales, £3.3 billion, will still be shared equally between all twenty clubs. Any increase on that level will then be distributed according to where a team finish in the league. So the six, confident of finishing in the higher places every season for the foreseeable future, will for the first time be paid more of the international TV rights revenues on that basis.

[†] https://norwichcity.myfootballwriter.com/2020/05/20/a-league-motivated-by-greed-no-doubt-but-not-the-sole-fault-of-one-mr-murdoch/.

me he had not been consulted and believed the scheme for a new league was motivated by greed.

It's impossible to quibble with that assessment. Dein and Scholar, the lead conspirators, are not bad people. I still get on well with Dein in particular. But they wanted their clubs to be among Europe's elite, were envious of the ease with which Italian clubs and the Spanish giants, Barcelona and Real Madrid, picked off the continent's best players and knew that the two monopolistic TV broadcasters in England—BBC and ITV—had been getting football on the cheap.

Where I took exception to Dein, Scholar and the rest—and told them so, regularly—was that they wanted not only to increase the TV cake, but to take much bigger slices and leave mere crumbs for lower division clubs.

Where I depart from the popular consensus is that I don't place Murdoch among the instigators of the rebellion, nor accept that his part in proceedings has been inherently malign. I have to declare that I worked for three organisations that were part of his empire. I learned that he is a ruthless despot who employs ruthless generals. He makes his products brand leaders, the best at what they do, yet I abhor much of what some of them have done and do. But the avarice of the Big Five football clubs was manifest long before Murdoch ever looked at the heavens and began thinking about satellites . . .

I was present in 1983 when Sir Norman announced the findings of another investigation into football, this time commissioned by the Football League. Again, he spoke of the unhappiness of the biggest clubs.

Later that year (1983) the elite forced a significant concession. Home clubs were to keep all gate money instead of sharing it with the visitors—and from that moment teams who regularly filled big stadiums grew richer and richer every fortnight.

It wasn't enough for them. Two years later they made the first overt threat of breaking away from the Football League if they were not given a bigger portion of TV money. They earned another concession—half of all TV money would go to the top division—but wanted still more . . .

As for the present mess, in which there is no good way forward for the Premier League, only a range of calamities, there is
only one certainty. We can't pin this one on Murdoch. He hasn't
owned Sky since September 2018.

When the FA announced plans for a breakaway league in April 1991,
the name FA *Premier League* was chosen as being less confrontational
than one of the original working names often used by the British press,
the "Super League."* By June 1991, sixteen clubs joined, and despite legal
challenges from the English Football League, it was a fait accompli.

The Premier League was to launch in August 1992. Now this
entertainment-broadcast-friendly creation needed a TV rights deal. Sky
was seen as an unproven, risky choice with few subscribers. The majority
of the Big Five wanted the established ITV (and be loyal to Greg Dyke).†

In a dramatic bidding war, Sky won the rights to the Premier League
in a £304 million five-year deal (ITV had offered £262 million). The BBC
won the highlights package and revived *Match of the Day*, essentially
freezing out ITV.

The final vote was 14–6 in favor of Sky and the BBC; in the end, the
non–Big Five clubs just wanted the most money. Unlike the Big Five, the
other clubs were worried that they may be relegated (which is the common
concern for the small clubs across most leagues and often leads to short-
term greed and division amongst big and small clubs)—so they wanted to
maximize near-term revenues. In the end, Sky paid just £190 million, after
the league failed to meet certain international sales metrics.

The Super League War

Coincidentally, in the mid-1990s, Murdoch and News Corp helped start what
the Australian press often referred to as "the Super League War" over control
of the top-level professional rugby league competition of Australasia. After

---

* The Phoenix League was another idea.
† Tottenham's Alan Sugar wanted Sky to win because his satellite business would benefit.

much legal action from the already-existing league, in 1997 Murdoch's Super League ran one season parallel to the existing league after signing enough clubs unhappy with the existing league. At the conclusion of that season, a peace deal was reached and both leagues united.

In 2020, Joe Frost of theroar.com.au wrote an article titled "Who Really Won the Super League War?" He concluded, "The way I see it, two winners emerged from the Super League war—and neither of them were the governing bodies. First, the players are infinitely better off . . . the other major winners of the Super League war: the TV-watching public . . . But when I think of the winner of the Super League war, I think of the athletes who can retire—if they're smart—well set for the second act of their lives, as well as the people like you and me, who get to watch every game live and for a relative pittance compared to the cost of a season ticket. The real winners of the Super League was? Us!"[*]

Postmortem

In 1996, Sky renewed the deal for £670 million over four years, beating a rival joint bid from the *Daily Mirror* and Carlton.

In 2019, vysyble, the financial analysts, released a report that showed almost three-fifths of all Premier League revenues are shared between the six biggest teams in the top flight by value—Arsenal, Chelsea, Liverpool, Man City, Man U, and Tottenham. Further demonstrating the "significant" disproportion between the Big Six and the remaining clubs, the report reveals the revenue gap between the sixth and seventh biggest clubs—Spurs and Everton respectively—was a "record" £191 million. In 2008–09, the gap between the sixth and seventh highest revenue earning clubs was just £1.88 million.

Vysyble highlighted the Big Six clubs' desire to reduce risk, which they did with a greater share of the Premier League's international broadcast rights revenue and concluded: "The downside is that the remaining group of 14 clubs, irrespective of the constituents, will fall

---

[*] https://www.theroar.com.au/2020/03/10/who-really-won-the-super-league-war/.

further behind the Big Six in terms of revenue, profitability and on-the-pitch performance."[*]

1987 AND 1992–93: SILVIO BERLUSCONI BUYS AC MILAN FOR CONTENT AND AFTER A REAL MADRID EUROPEAN CUP MATCH TOGETHER WITH REAL MADRID PUSH UEFA TO CHANGE THE EUROPEAN CUP TO THE CHAMPIONS LEAGUE

In 1986, Silvio Berlusconi, a then fifty-year-old Italian entrepreneur, acquired AC Milan and saved the club from near-certain bankruptcy. AC Milan had won the European Cup in 1962 and 1969, but they struggled in the years that preceded Berlusconi's purchase. The club benefited from his passion and significant investment, which in turn helped to usher in a new era of success and changed football, and more broadly sports, entertainment, and content—forever.

Berlusconi's business career began in construction. In the late 1960s, he built Milano Due (Italian for "Milan Two"), a development of four thousand residential apartments east of Milan, and convinced the Milanese, used to the city center, to consider living outside the city. Milano Due became popular because it has a system of walkways and bridges that connects the whole neighborhood so that it is possible to walk around without ever intersecting traffic. In 1973, Berlusconi set up a small cable television company, TeleMilano, to service units built on his properties. TeleMilano was the first Italian private television channel and later evolved into Canale 5, the first national private TV station. Berlusconi possessed an acute understanding of what the masses craved. His television stations would become a dreamland of entertainment, importing American shows such as *Baywatch*, *Dallas*, and *Dynasty*.

Having conquered the world of broadcasting, he turned his attention to Italy's *calcio* (Italian for "football"). At the time, Italian clubs could negotiate their own broadcasting rights with TV networks. Berlusconi realized that if he owned AC Milan, then he would control valuable

---

[*] https://talksport.com/football/561292/the-big-six-destroying-premier-league-new-study/.

entertainment content—and he could ensure their matches would only be available on his channel. At a press conference a few days after buying the club in 1986, Berlusconi declared: "Milan is a team, but it's also a product to sell; something to offer on the market."*

Berlusconi's vision to transform AC Milan went far beyond just winning trophies. More than just something that could be enjoyed on TV or a stadium on matchdays alone, he wanted AC Milan to represent a lifestyle. With this in mind, he opened an apparel shop in the heart of Milan (near the Royal Palace of Milan and Milan Cathedral), revamped the team's training base with a high-performance center and laboratory, and started publishing *Forza Milan!* magazine. "It sounds old hat now, but it was vibrantly new for Italy at the time," wrote Rome-based journalist Paddy Agnew in his book, *Forza Italia: The Fall and Rise of Italian Football*.

AC Milan stood out from the still largely family-run Italian clubs, which justified losing money each year because of the local prestige and power of ownership and the entertainment and pride of their regional fans, which often included their factory and other employees.

Berlusconi's most important task was to build a team that would not just get Milan's attention, but Europe's, so he and Adriano Galliani (CEO of AC Milan) assembled one of the greatest squads ever. Berlusconi and Galliani appointed rising manager Arrigo Sacchi, a former shoe salesman whose attacking mentality won over Berlusconi, as the manager of the *Rossoneri*. They also signed three world-class Dutch internationals (1987 Ballon d'Or winner Ruud Gullit; 1988, 1989, and 1992 Ballon d'Or winner Marco van Basten; and two-time top three Ballon d'Or finisher Frank Rijkaard) and Roma's Carlo Ancelotti.

Van Basten and Gullit formed an effective partnership up front, while Rijkaard held the midfield beside Ancelotti. Franco Baresi organized the defense with Alessandro "Billy" Costacurta. Roberto Donadoni usually played a right-sided wide midfield role. A young Paolo Maldini also transformed the left side of the backline.

---

* https://thesefootballtimes.co/2019/08/19/the-devils-odyssey-how-silvio-berlusconi-turned-ac
-milan-into-a-superpower/.

The 1982 World Cup*–winning Italy national team and previous Serie A–winning Juventus sides utilized *il gioco all'Italiana* (which means "the game in Italian style," but often referred to as "mixed plan" or "mixed zone") rather than out-and-out *catenaccio*, but caution remained the underlying theme.[†] However, Sacchi wanted a full press with every player looking to win the ball back to attack in a fluid 4-4-2 formation. It was very entertaining for the fans, but more importantly, it was very effective.

Under Sacchi, AC Milan won their first Scudetto (Serie A trophy) in nine years in the 1987–88 season. The following year, the club won their first European Cup in two decades. AC Milan retained their title a year later and was the last team to win back-to-back European Cups until Real Madrid's win in 2016–17 (Real Madrid would win a third in a row in 2017–18). AC Milan went without losing for a remarkable fifty-eight matches, earning the nickname "Gli Invincibili," or "The Invincibles," in the Italian media.

In 1990, Berlusconi bought *Mondadori* and *Einaudi Editore*, two of the historical and most important book and magazine publishers in Italy, and several other small publishers. Now, he controlled broadcasting and publishing (the media) as well as a big club and their sports content.[‡]

---

* In the 1982 World Cup (hosted by Spain), Italy beat Zico's Brazil (often referred to as "the match when football died") and Maradona's Argentina and then West Germany in the final at the Santiago Bernabéu in Madrid. The 1982 semifinal match between West Germany and France is often referred to as "the night in Seville."

† *Catenaccio* is a tactical system in football with a strong emphasis on defense. In Italian, *catenaccio* means "door-bolt," which implies a highly organized and effective backline defense focused on nullifying opponents' attacks and preventing goal-scoring opportunities.

‡ What comes next? Politics. Berlusconi founded his own political party, Forza Italia ("Go Italy")— named after a chant used by AC Milan fans—and was elected prime minister of Italy in 1994. Berlusconi's sudden and spectacular political rise came just as one of the greatest AC Milan sides of all time was marching toward the Serie A title. In the same month that Berlusconi was sworn into power as prime minister of Italy, his AC Milan thrashed a Johan Cruyff–managed Barcelona 4–0 in the Olympic Stadium in Athens in one of the most dominating Champions League final performances ever. AC Milan's success has been inextricably linked to Berlusconi's rise to political power. To the voters, his success with AC Milan proved he is an achiever and innovator—and he brought pride to Italy with European trophies. Berlusconi would frequently use the club to create and re-create a wining political image for himself.

The Real Madrid Match That Led to the Creation of the Champions League

In September 1987, just after purchasing AC Milan and before being elected prime minister, Berlusconi watched a first-round European Cup match that pitted Napoli's Diego Maradona against Real Madrid's *Quinta del Buitre* at the Bernabéu Stadium in Madrid.

Maradona represented the global stars, power, and prestige of Serie A at the time (much more than English football). He also put Napoli football on the map. As for Real Madrid, they represented European football prestige. Real Madrid were led by five local players who came through the Real Madrid youth system—Sanchís, Míchel González, Miguel Pardeza, Rafael Martín Vázquez, and Emilio Butragueño, the "Buitre" or "Vulture." They were often referred to in the Spanish press as *Quinta del Buitre* ("The Vulture Five").

Real Madrid's right-back Miguel Porlán, "Chendo" (another product of Real Madrid's youth system), got the better of Maradona that night. Real Madrid won 2–0 with goals from midfielder Míchel and central defender Miguel Tendillo, but what people always remember was Chendo's cheeky attempt at a nutmeg on the Argentine icon.[*]

Most European football fans don't know that this Real Madrid versus Napoli match is what led to changes in European football competition.[†] Berlusconi was appalled that two big clubs with superstars could meet as early as the first round of the competition and be knocked out. (Since 1987–88, Real Madrid and Napoli have met only one other time in the Champions League, 2016–17, which Real Madrid won.) Meanwhile, clubs like Switzerland's Neuchâtel Xamax, Norway's Lillestrøm, Cyprus's Omonoia, and Poland's Górnik Zabrze all advanced to the second round. In addition, Portugal's Benfica would reach the final that year without beating a single team from any of the Top 5 Leagues.

For Berlusconi, a man that possessed an acute understanding of what the masses craved, it seemed hardly the stage to waste such a highly

---

[*] https://www.theguardian.com/football/blog/2017/feb/14/real-madrid-napoli-champions-league-diego-maradona.

[†] https://www.independent.co.uk/sport/football/european/champions-league-real-madrid-vs-napoli-1987-silvio-berlusconi-a7577996.html.

anticipated clash or to have one of the big clubs with a star like Maradona be
eliminated so early. The European Cup began in 1955–56 with sixteen sides
taking part. The "historical anachronism," according to Berlusconi, followed
a winner-take-all over knockout format right from the start of each season.[*]
Berlusconi naturally feared that a club like AC Milan could lose early on and
miss out on millions in potential revenues.

Armed with a TV network, Berlusconi wanted pay-per-view television to take hold and hoped some of Europe's biggest clubs would play
more matches against each other each season, generating more revenue.

After a two-hour interview with Berlusconi for *World Soccer* in 1991,
Keir Radnedge wrote about Berlusconi's vision, including a European
league:[†]

> To Berlusconi the great clubs, such as Milan, Real Madrid and
> Barcelona represent the future. Television provides the window
> on the game in which the major consumer commercial interests
> will want to be reflected. It's a simple equation: Soccer plus tele-
> vision plus big business represents a circle of success.
>
> In the 1990s Berlusconi looks forward confidently to a Euro-
> pean league which entertains and reflects *"our new commu-
> nications culture."* His vision makes English football's premier
> prospectors look positively minor league.[‡]

In the interview with *World Soccer*, Berlusconi said:

> The concept of the national team will, gradually, become less and
> less important. It is the clubs with which the fans associate. A
> European Championship for clubs is inevitable. The new format
> for the Champions' Cup is a step in the right direction. But it is

---

* https://www.thescore.com/uefa/news/1280677.

† http://inbedwithmaradona.com/retro/2013/7/1/forget-the-world-cup-the-future-according-to-silvio
-berlusconi.

‡ At the time, the big clubs in England were looking to break away and create the English Premier
League.

only a step. The European cups, as they have been organized, have become a historical anachronism. It's economic nonsense that a club such as Milan might be eliminated in the first round. A European cup that lasts the whole season is what Europe wants.

After all, Europe wanted an economic community, with monetary union and a customs union. It's inevitable it should want a football union, too. And the clubs will lead the way—each playing around 80 games a season.

At the time, there were reports that Berlusconi wanted to run two AC Milan teams: one in Europe and one in the league. Berlusconi explained the issues of a congested calendar:

> Next season Milan will play twice every week. On Sundays in the Italian League; on Wednesday in the European Cup, or Italian Cup or television friendlies. This is why we must strengthen our squad. The older players cannot expect to be fit enough to play all the time. In my six years as president, I have never seen our best team play—except in my head. Someone is always injured, or ill, or suspended.

Berlusconi also saw this growth opportunity being driven by fans beyond the local fans in the stadium. He wanted AC Milan to reach all fans. He said:

> Football is currently ignoring part of its support. First are the fans in the stadium; but that means only 50,000 or 60,000. Then there are the fans who watch bits and pieces of soccer on the state channels. But the third audience, which we are not reaching, is to be found on pay-TV. Through cable and satellite, we must be able to reach the committed fan who wants to watch our games . . . They cannot all get into the stadium. But they could watch us through pay-TV.

Impatient for a European League, Berlusconi arranged for AC Milan to play midweek "European Challenge Match" friendlies against Man U and Marseille precisely to feed the high TV ratings big club football matches guaranteed.*

Eventually, Berlusconi, Real Madrid president Ramón Mendoza, and Glasgow Rangers secretary Campbell Ogilvie proposed a new competition with a single round-robin format, called the "Super League," to UEFA. They believed that the competition would be more attractive for international television broadcasters, would allow the contestant teams to earn more guaranteed income, and would give the contestant teams more possibilities to progress through the competition.

That didn't happen, but the idea—and the threat—directly led to the creation of the Champions League in 1992–93—the idea of which started with the 1987 Real Madrid versus Napoli European Cup first-round match. From 1955 to 1991, the European Cup was a knockout format—one club per country (the league champion) plus the defending champion. The Champions League introduced a mini-league group stage system, resembling the FIFA World Cup with an early phase of group play followed by a knockout phase. However, the tournament was still one club per country (the league champion) plus the defending champion.

Over the first two seasons of the new Champions League, the English clubs involved, Leeds and Man U, failed to make it out of the group stage. In the inaugural campaign of 1992–93, Spanish and German sides were absent too. UEFA decided that to maximize revenues, broadcasters from the richest European countries needed more certainty their clubs would play more matches. So, they changed the format in 1994–95. The champions of eight countries, including England, Italy, Germany, and Spain, went straight into a group phase expanded to make four groups of four.

----

* http://jimmysirrelslovechild.co.uk/classic-games/manchester-united-v-ac-milan.

A Regulatory Change That Led to the Top 5 Leagues

In 1995, the Bosman ruling changed employment regulations and salaries for football players.* As a result, UEFA's rule that clubs could only field a maximum of three foreign players (plus two who had played in that country for an uninterrupted period of five years, including three as a junior) had to be scrapped. The European Court ruling unbalanced the entire situation because those clubs who, until then, were able to compete with their own talents on the highest level couldn't do it anymore as they started to lose their talents at a very early age. Players moved to the wealthiest countries that had the wealthiest owners willing to pay and the wealthiest and most populated countries with fan bases willing to pay for tickets and TV subscriptions—and so the Top 5 Leagues with the biggest economies developed.

Postmortem

Berlusconi is the most winning president in the history of AC Milan, having won twenty-nine titles in thirty-one years, including eight Serie A titles and five Champions League titles.

Berlusconi sold AC Milan in 2017. A year later, he bought a little-known club founded in 1912, AC Monza, in Italy's third division, for €2.9 million ($3.4 million) and appointed his brother Paolo club president and long-term collaborator and friend Adriano Galliani as CEO. Galliani had played at Monza as a young boy. Berlusconi's "San Martino" countryside residence near Milan is less than ten kilometers from Monza's stadium.

---

* Players' salaries were increasing due to a 1995 European Court of Justice decision in favor of Belgian soccer player Jean-Marc Bosman. Prior to the Bosman ruling, professional clubs in some parts of Europe (though not in Spain) were able to prevent a player from joining a club in another country, even if the player's contract had expired. The Bosman ruling meant that a player could move to a new club at the end of his contract, without the old club receiving a fee. Players can now agree on a pre-contract with another club for a free transfer if the player's existing contract will expire in six months or less. The Bosman ruling also prohibited domestic football leagues in EU member states, and UEFA, from imposing quotas on foreign players to the extent that they discriminated against nationals of EU states. Salaries were also rising because more billionaires, who could afford personal losses, were investing their private personal fortunes in football clubs.

In 2022, Monza clinched promotion to Serie A—their first time in 110 years. Berlusconi estimated that he has invested over €70 million in the small Lombardy club.* Berlusconi died in June 2023.

1997–2000: RUPERT MURDOCH AND BROADCASTERS WANT TO OWN CONTENT (CLUBS), AND THE CLUBS WANT TO OWN THEIR OWN BROADCASTING

In the 1980s, Berlusconi was a visionary who saw the value of media/ broadcasters owning their own content.† And another media mogul, Rupert Murdoch, had a similar vision. (In full disclosure, I advised Murdoch's News Corp and BSkyB on several investment banking transactions and worked on the sale of Li Ka-shing's Star TV to News Corp while I was at Goldman Sachs.)

In the late 1990s, broadcasters wanted to own part of the content-creation machine. They were panicking at the thought of clubs directly negotiating their own TV deals with the advent of digital TV and the internet, which was just starting to catch on. In 1997, Man U launched MUTV, the first channel dedicated to a single club, with two media partners (BSkyB and ITV) and Man U each owning an equal 33.3 percent of the shares. Man U would bring the brand and content and the broadcasters would bring the technical know-how to drive digital TV subscriptions.

In 1998, BSkyB made a daring attempt to buy Man U amid protests from fans and rival clubs. Although the £625 million bid was accepted by the controlling shareholders, the move was blocked by the Department of Trade and Industry on the grounds that the merger would "adversely

---

* https://www.dw.com/en/italy-silvio-berlusconi-returns-to-serie-a-with-ac-monza/a-61989172.

† In 1970, Ted Turner purchased a low-powered and independent Atlanta TV station, believing he could revive it by adding better content. In 1974, he purchased the broadcasting rights to MLB's Atlanta Braves from the Atlanta-based media giant Cox Enterprises and its prominent network affiliate. Because his proposal tripled both the amount of the payment for the TV rights and the number of games to be telecast, his terms were accepted, even though some people in the Atlanta TV market were unable to receive the relatively weak signal of Turner's station. In 1976, a thirty-seven-year-old Turner purchased the Atlanta Braves for $10 million, putting down $1 million and getting a seller's note for the other $9 million. Eventually, the Atlanta Braves would be marketed in rural areas as "America's Baseball Team" on cable systems that carried his station, which increased viewers and advertising. In 1977, he bought the NBA's Atlanta Hawks. In 1996, Time Warner purchased Turner Broadcasting, and then they sold the sports teams.

affect competition between broadcasters." Competition authorities introduced new rules limiting broadcasters to a stake of less than 10 percent
in a club.*

Over time, Murdoch's companies bought MLB's LA Dodgers, along
with the TV rights for Major League Baseball via his Fox network. He
also owned stakes in the NBA's LA Lakers and New York Knicks basketball teams and NHL's New York Rangers and LA Kings. The New
York teams were actively covered by his own New York tabloid, the
New York Post.

Murdoch believed owning media platforms was good, but if he could
also own the means of (entertainment) production, so much the better.
To him, there was no point owning a satellite or cable station unless you
can show something that people want to watch, and the biggest attraction is live sports (in the U.K. that is football). Therefore, BSkyB tried to
buy Man U, and other broadcasters copied the idea.

Through 1999 and 2000, broadcasters were determined to own a
stake in content, with Sky (Chelsea, Leeds, Man U), NTL (Newcastle
United, Aston Villa, Middlesbrough, Leicester City, Glasgow Rangers,
and Celtic), Carlton (Arsenal) and Granada (Liverpool) all taking up
to 9.9 percent stakes in Premier League clubs.† In 1998, Granada paid
£22 million for its 9.9 percent of Liverpool.

NTL spent hundreds of millions buying minority stakes. The cable
giant believed that buying into football clubs would help break BSkyB's
stranglehold. However, the investments added more debt to the company, which eventually filed for bankruptcy.

In January 2000, ten members of the Premier League and seven members of Division One were publicly traded corporations. Together these
seventeen teams had an equity market capitalization of over $3 billion,
or about $200 million each. The equity market capitalization of Man U

---

* Nasser Al-Khelaifi is chairman of beIN media group, owned by the state of Qatar, which broadcasts UEFA Champions League football. He is president of PSG, which is owned by a state-run
sovereign-wealth fund in Qatar. He also is chairman of the European Club Association (ECA),
representing European clubs, and sits on the UEFA executive committee as ECA's representative.

† https://www.theguardian.com/media/2003/feb/25/broadcasting3. The regulators limited the stakes
to less than 10 percent.

was around $1 billion. As of June 2023, the equity market capitalization of Man U is $3 billion.

Colonel Gaddafi Almost Bought a Stake in Man U, and Did Own a Stake in Juventus

Mehmet Dalman, who brokered the Glazers' takeover of Man U, told the *Sunday Times* that, in 2004, then–Libyan dictator Muammar Gaddafi was "a whisker away" from buying John Magnier and J. P. McManus's 29.9 percent stake in Man U.* Gaddafi was killed in 2011.

In 2002, the Libyan Foreign Investment Company (LAFICO) purchased around 5 percent of Juventus (and subsequently raised its stake to around 7.5 percent over time, spending around a total of €17 million) and Colonel Gaddafi's son, Al-Saadi Gaddafi, joined the board of Juventus (the club he had supported from childhood).† From 2002–2007, the state-owned oil company of Libya, Tamoil, was an official sponsor of Juventus. In 2003, Al-Saadi Gaddafi resigned from the Juventus board and signed a two-year contract to play for Perugia football club in Serie A. While Al-Saadi Gaddafi had played for top clubs in Libya, he had never played in a European football league. Al-Saadi Gaddafi hired Diego Maradona and Ben Johnson as technical consultant and personal trainer, respectively.‡ Luciano Gaucci, Perugia's president, claimed AC Milan owner and then–prime minister Silvio Berlusconi "called me up and encouraged me. He told me that having Gaddafi in the team is helping us build a relationship with Libya. If he plays badly, he plays badly. So be it." (Perugia went bankrupt in 2005.) Presumably, Berlusconi wanted to keep Gaddafi happy because Libyan oil was integral to many Italian businesses, and Berlusconi knew that keeping Gaddafi happy would mean more Libyan investment in Italian companies. Saadi made only one substitute appearance for Perugia (against Juventus) in 2003–04 and played ten minutes for Udinese in an end-of-season match against Cagiliari in 2005–06. He joined Sampdoria during the 2006–07 season but did not

---

* https://www.manchestereveningnews.co.uk/news/greater-manchester-news/colonel-gaddafi-a-whisker-away-14214468.

† In 2002, the Supercoppa Italiana was held in the Libyan capital Tripoli.

‡ https://thesetpieces.com/latest-posts/football-gaddafi-family/.

play a single match. Saadi would later be considered one of the worst players to ever participate in Serie A. It is an example—if one was needed—of the dangers of mixing sport with politics.

For background, Libya and Italy have a long history together—at one time Libya was an Italian colony. In 1977, the carmaker Fiat, controlled by the Agnelli family (which also control Juventus), was in financial trouble and needed cash. Giovanni Agnelli invited LAFICO to buy a 15 percent stake in Fiat for $400 million to help turn things around.[*] LAFICO sold the 15 percent stake in 1986 for $3 billion[†] and bought a new 2 percent stake in 2002.[‡] In 2008, a trading connection between Italy and Libya was formalized when Berlusconi and Gaddafi signed a historic cooperation treaty that committed €4 billion worth of compensation to Libya for the Italian occupation of the previous century in exchange for an increase in Libyan investment in Italian companies.[§]

Libya's oil money also made it a major investor in the U.K. The Libyan Investment Authority (LIA) invested billions of dollars in the U.K., including £155 million for Portman House, a 146,550-square-foot retail complex on Oxford Street in London, and £120 million for an office at 14 Cornhill, opposite the Bank of England in the heart of London.[¶]

Postmortem

In 2003, Rupert Murdoch's News Corp sold its stake in Man U because it was "non-core." At the time, it had already sold its stake in Chelsea to Roman Abramovich and still owned 8.8, 9.9, and 4.8 percent of Leeds United, Man City, and Sunderland, respectively. Eventually, News Corp sold all their stakes in sports teams, including those in the United States.

In 2007 and 2013, ITV and BSkyB sold their MUTV stakes back to Man U, respectively, making MUTV 100 percent owned by Man U.

In the United States, many sports teams started their own regional sports networks (cable channels). The Yankee Entertainment and Sports

---

[*] https://www.latimes.com/archives/la-xpm-1986-09-24-fi-8787-story.html.

[†] https://www.nytimes.com/1986/09/24/business/libya-s-fiat-stake-sold-for-3-billion.html.

[‡] https://www.wsj.com/articles/SB101518824472491640.

[§] https://www.reuters.com/article/uk-libya-italy-idUKLU1618820080830.

[¶] https://www.theguardian.com/world/2011/feb/21/libya-oil-money-major-world-shareholder.

Network (YES) was launched in 2002. Although the Yankees techni-cally don't own YES, they receive a rights fee from YES. In 2012, Rupert Murdoch's News Corp acquired a 49 percent stake in YES. In 2019, the Yankees and other investors, including RedBird Capital[*] (13 percent) and UAE's Mubadala[†] (13 percent), repurchased the News Corp stake.

1997–98: THE G-14, WITH THE HELP OF REAL MADRID, PUSH UEFA TO EXPAND THE CHAMPIONS LEAGUE

In 1997–98, a forty-three-year-old entrepreneur named Rodolfo Hecht, who had previously worked at Fininvest, the holding company of the media empire of Berlusconi, tried to create a European Super League.[‡,§]

Hecht believed there were too many uninteresting games in the Champions League due to its format.[¶] The Champions League was played by the champions of their countries, and the UEFA Cup was played by the teams ranked just below. Therefore, in the Champions League, big clubs from Top 5 Leagues like AC Milan and Real Madrid were pitted against the champions of Poland, the Czech Republic, and Hungary, while the rest of the top clubs in the Top 5 Leagues clashed in the UEFA Cup.[**] There were more matches and more chances of clubs from the big-ger markets meeting in the UEFA Cup. From a commercial standpoint,

---

[*] RedBird owns a stake in Fenway Sports Group, a global sports, marketing, media, entertainment, and real estate company anchored by three iconic clubs, Premier League's Liverpool, MLB's Boston Red Sox, and the NHL's Pittsburgh Penguins. They also own NASCAR's Roush Fenway Racing and 80 percent of New England Sports Network (NESN), an American regional sports cable network that is the primary sports provider throughout New England, including coverage of the Boston Red Sox, Boston Bruins, New England Patriots, and Boston Celtics. RedBird also are owners of both AC Milan and Toulouse.

[†] Man City's parent, City Football Group, is owned by a UAE-based private equity company. City Football Group also owns a stake in New York City FC with the owners of the New York Yankees.

[‡] https://www.independent.co.uk/sport/football-the-man-behind-the-plan-to-change-football-forever -1174196.html; https://ebin.pub/the-european-ritual-football-in-the-new-europe-0754636526-2003045350 -9780754636526.html.

[§] https://showsport.me/football/business-uefa-tv-ucl-114171014.

[¶] https://showsport.me/football/business-uefa-tv-ucl-114171014.

[**] The dissolutions of the Soviet Union and Czechoslovakia as well as the breakup of Yugoslavia drastically affected the sporting level of the countries and significantly increased the number of clubs involved in European competitions. The matches of teams from the Top 5 Leagues against these teams typically generated lesser excitement from overall European fans and media.

ironically, the UEFA Cup became a competition that had more potential than the European Cup.

Hecht's proposed solution was a European Super League, which included two divisions. In the First Division, there would be sixteen big clubs that would be co-founders and safeguarded against relegation. In the second division, there would be sixteen clubs that qualified with high places from the top leagues but could be relegated after each season. Each club would play each other in a fifteen-match round-robin tournament before the competition reached its quarterfinal stage in March. European Super League matches were to be played midweek to not impact domestic leagues. The primary criticism was that the co-founders were protected against relegation.

He tried to seduce big clubs with large amounts of money at the time. Each participant was to be guaranteed a minimum of €30 million per season only from TV rights. For comparison, in the 1996–97 season, Man U reached the semifinals of the Champions League and received only €6 million. The first prize was expected to be $100 million, compared to $14 million for the Champions League winner.* JPMorgan agreed to provide €1.2 billion in financing to the new league, backed by the expected sales of TV rights.

In 1997, UEFA sold the TV rights to European competitions for relatively little money, and matches were often broadcast on state channels. Hecht wanted to package and sell the TV rights, and Hecht's firm would get 5 percent of the value.

Hecht met with the clubs claiming UEFA earned €165 million and kept almost 18 percent for "answering phone calls" and "bureaucracy." Some big clubs feared repercussions from UEFA. Some believed that the European Super League would increase the gap between rich and poor clubs or kill the intrigue inside domestic tournaments.

The *Independent* newspaper wrote that Man U supported a European Super League. A Man U director said, "We are ready to listen and learn more. Its concept is interesting: more transparency, more influence of

* https://www.nytimes.com/1998/08/05/sports/IHT-super-league-would-ruin-competitive-spirit-european-hijackers-have.html.

clubs, more places for English teams in European competitions. But we have an excellent home League and we are not going to let it down." Reportedly, Liverpool were hesitant, and there was a split within Arsenal. The *New York Times* wrote that top clubs held talks directly with JPMorgan to understand their financial guarantee. (JPMorgan would be involved in the European Super League in 2021.)

Generally, the media distrusted Hecht's intentions and some wrote that he really was a "front-man" for Berlusconi. However, many big clubs were at least intrigued by the idea of a European Super League.

In May 1998, Real Madrid beat Juventus 1–0 in Amsterdam and clinched their record-breaking seventh European title, their first title in thirty-two years.* After the final, UEFA held a meeting with clubs in Lisbon in which several big club executives admitted that they were seriously interested in Hecht's proposal. This was a code red for UEFA.

UEFA took a hard stance. They threatened the clubs that supported a European Super League with a ban in all competitions. In June 1998, the general secretary of UEFA said:

> The Super League will divide European football into rich and poor. You'll never get into the Super League and earn that much. Clubs that violate the existing integrity will be subject to certain sanctions. Any team that joins Mr. Hecht's project will be excluded from all FIFA and UEFA competitions, and its players will not be able to play in the World Cup.

The statement had its desired effect—it scared several big clubs. The FA notified English clubs that they would be excluded from the Premier League if they supported the breakaway European Super League (which was ironic considering the Premier League was a breakaway league with FA support). Reportedly, Arsenal and Man U were pressured to write letters guaranteeing that they would not leave.

---

* AC Milan finished first, eleventh, and tenth in Serie A in the 1995–96, 1996–97, and 1997–98 seasons, respectively. Real Madrid finished sixth, first, and fourth in the 1995–96, 1996–97 and 1997–98 seasons, respectively. Since 1997–98, Real Madrid have always been in the Champions League.

In August 1998, rumors persisted about a Super League. Gerd Aigner, then–general secretary of UEFA, said, "We will talk to the clubs, to the leagues and the national associations. No doubt we will be able to make our competitions more attractive, maybe more lucrative. All things are feasible except that we will not allow anyone permanent entry. Sport loses its credibility without two things—national identity and qualification on merit."*

In a 2022 interview with the BBC, Aigner disclosed, "We realized that if UEFA didn't act and take things in our own hands, we would probably lose control of these competitions altogether . . . We wanted to make it [the Champions League] as attractive as possible for the supporters, for TV and for the clubs themselves . . . We managed to have two experts joining us who had just left ISL [Swiss marketing company International Sport and Leisure]. They had marvelous ideas and they developed great ideas about how to present a new product to the public. We also looked across the ocean at the American way of organizing the Super Bowl."†

In early October 1998, UEFA announced proposed reforms to dissuade Europe's big clubs from defecting. The Champions League roster was increased from twenty-four to thirty-two clubs and more Champions League places would go to the continent's strongest leagues. The runners-up in the top leagues were allowed into the Champions League from 1997, but the proposed reforms to start in 1999 had third- and even fourth-placed teams from Europe's top leagues.

The meetings with UEFA led to more interaction and collaboration between big European football clubs. On October 14, 1998, fourteen big European football clubs across seven countries founded the G-14 to provide a unified voice in negotiations with UEFA and FIFA. The founding members were: Real Madrid, Barcelona, Man U, Liverpool, Inter, Juventus, AC Milan, Marseille, PSG, Bayern Munich, Borussia Dortmund, Ajax, PSV Eindhoven, and Porto.‡ (Remember the Bosman ruling was

---

* https://www.nytimes.com/1998/08/05/sports/IHT-super-league-would-ruin-competitive-spirit-european-hijackers-have.html.

† https://www.bbc.com/sport/football/63456291.

‡ In 2002, four more clubs joined the G-14: Arsenal, Bayer Leverkusen, Lyon, and Valencia.

in 1995 and the movement of players and money to the biggest European economies was just starting.)

Later in October, a meeting was held between the general secretary of UEFA and representatives from Real Madrid, AC Milan, Liverpool, Man U, and eight other big clubs. The governing body's general secretary, Gerhard Aigner, said, "UEFA decided to speak directly to the clubs and that's due to the new situation in the world of football."[*]

The parties managed to reach some sort of an agreement. After the meeting, AC Milan's vice president, Adriano Galliani, said: "The 12 clubs present in Geneva have affirmed their wish to work with UEFA. We must make concessions, as must UEFA, but we want to remain within the overall European confederation." Real Madrid's president, Lorenzo Sanz, formerly one of the strongest advocates of the breakaway, said: "UEFA understand perfectly our concerns and have presented a very interesting project of long-term collaboration with the clubs."

Aigner admitted the threat of the breakaway led to action. He confessed, "Plans for an independent Super League forced us to act quickly and improve our co-operation with the clubs."[†]

In May 2000, Real Madrid beat Valencia 3–0 in the final in the Stade de France in Paris. Just after two years of allowing runners-up of the strongest continental leagues to enter the tournament, the tournament expanded to up to four of the strongest teams from Europe's top national leagues. As a result, the tournament was in glaring contrast to 1996–97 (which took place only three years prior), when only top national champions and title holders participated.

The entry of so many "non-champions" into a tournament originally called the European Champion Clubs' Cup (European Cup) and now called the Champions League highlighted that football had significantly changed. In addition, the total payments to participants were increased. Under the reforms, 1999–2000 champions Real Madrid received around €20 million (previously it was about €10 million).[‡] (In 2021–22, champions

---

[*] http://news.bbc.co.uk/2/hi/sport/football/199930.stm.

[†] http://news.bbc.co.uk/2/hi/sport/football/199930.stm.

[‡] https://www.theguardian.com/football/2003/jul/31/sport.comment; http://news.bbc.co.uk/2/hi/business/325977.stm; https://en.wikipedia.org/wiki/1999_UEFA_Champions_League_final#cite_note-111.

Real Madrid collected €83 million in Champions League performance-based prize money, including an additional €4.5 million for winning the UEFA Super Cup in August 2022.)

Lastly, since reforms were implemented in 1999–2000 to include up to four clubs per country, Real Madrid have been in all twenty-four Champions League tournaments and won eight of them (2000, '02, '14, '16, '17, '18, '22, '24)—along with AC Milan (fifteen, won two), Barcelona (twenty-three, won four), Bayern Munich (twenty-three, won three), Juventus (nineteen), Liverpool (fifteen, won two), and Man U (twenty-one, won one).

Postmortem

In the 2006 FIFA World Cup, 22 percent of the participating players were from G-14 clubs. The G-14 demanded and finally received concessions from UEFA and FIFA in 2008 that they be paid compensation for injuries and departures of players to their national teams. Shortly after, in a deal reached with UEFA and FIFA, the G-14 was disbanded and replaced by the European Club Association (ECA), representing over one hundred clubs.*

In May 2022, UEFA announced changes to the Champions League format. In 2024–25, the Champions League will be expanded from thirty-two to thirty-six clubs. The thirty-six clubs will be placed into one giant table, typically referred to as the "Swiss model." A total of 189 matches will be played, up from 125. UEFA expects the broadcast rights for the new-look competition to rise by 40 percent to £3.8 billion a season.

The current format has clubs divided up into eight groups of four, with clubs playing each other home and away over six games. The top two in each group progress to the last sixteen when it becomes a knockout tournament, with ties played home and away over two legs, before the tournament final at a neutral venue over one match.

The new format starting in 2024–25 scraps the group stage. The new format has an initial phase containing one single league table, which

---

* The ECA was the result of the merger of the G-14 with European Club Forum. Today, the ECA represents 232 clubs. At this time, Real Madrid, Barcelona, and Juventus are not members of the ECA.

includes all clubs. Each club will play eight games against different opponents, with four home ties and four away ties over ten match weeks. (Previously, under the old format, sixteen of the thirty-two clubs were eliminated after just six games.) The top eight clubs that accumulate the most points will automatically advance to the Round of 16 knockout stage, while those from ninth to twenty-fourth will compete in a two-legged playoff to progress into the last sixteen as unseeded clubs. The traditional knockout format will then determine the finalists.

Two of the four extra places will be awarded on the performance of a country's clubs in Europe over the previous season. Another place would go to the third-placed league team in the country standing fifth in their rankings. A fourth place would go to one country's domestic champions by increasing from four to five the number of teams who qualify via the "Champions Path."

UEFA rejected a proposal to allow clubs into the competition solely based on historical European performance. Critics argued this would have favored big clubs and provided them with a safety net if they performed poorly in a season.

Some critics believe that UEFA's solution to a group stage that was becoming more boring and predictable was to take that problem of massive inequality and make it worse.[*] They believe there are twelve to sixteen big clubs that the global audience care about and are generally evenly matched, so the bigger you increase the roster, the higher the probability of simply delivering "boring" and "unequal" matches. In addition, some believe that reserving two places for clubs based on UEFA nation coefficients essentially guarantees the Premier League another qualification place—and makes the new format "Super League Lite." Lastly, many players are concerned they will be playing too many matches.

Many clubs are also concerned with even more matches in a congested calendar, including an expansion of the FIFA Club World Cup and FIFA World Cup. More matches usually mean more injuries, which means more depth (more transfer fees and salaries) is required and/or less

---

* https://www.si.com/soccer/2021/03/31/champions-league-future-format-expansion-swiss-system-criticism.

emphasis of domestic competitions. Many clubs and domestic leagues in Europe fear that UEFA club competitions are getting too big and damaging their own domestic competitions. England's FA raised concerns over the impact on the domestic calendar—in particular, the FA Cup and the EFL Cup tournaments.

UEFA generated around €3 billion in TV revenues for the 2021–22 season. Reportedly, experts initially predicted the new Champions League broadcast deal would increase the value in rights by 40 to 60 percent, but that appears to have been too optimistic. The revised forecast is 20 to 25 percent, which is a shortfall of around €500 million annually from the initial predictions. With around 50 percent more matches, 12.5 percent more clubs competing, and around a 40 percent increase in solidarity payments, some are starting to wonder if a 25 percent increase is enough.

According to a September 2023 James Corbett article for Off the Pitch: "Broadcast sources have repeatedly told Off The Pitch that UEFA's projections were fanciful and have said that there has been a difficulty in understanding the benefits of the new Swiss League format. The feedback is that it is too complex. There are a lot of games being played to have nothing resolved . . . Another [source] said that broadcasters globally were having budgets tightened and given a choice between football's premium properties, were choosing the Premier League over the Champions League."

The European leagues collectively also worry that Swiss model competitions are inherently scalable. What is to stop UEFA from asking for even more games in a few years?

For example, from 1933 to 1966, the NFL had a one-game playoff that pitted the league's two division winners against each other. In 1967, the playoffs were expanded to four teams, in 1970 eight teams, in 1978 ten teams, in 1990 twelve teams, and in 2020 fourteen teams.

In 1950, the NCAA college basketball tournament had eight teams, in 1951 sixteen teams, in 1975 thirty-two teams, in 1985 sixty-four teams, and in 2011 sixty-eight teams. There was a recent proposal for as many as ninety teams.

In 1998, two American college football teams were selected to play in the BCS National Championship game. In 2014, the College Football

Playoff National Championship started with four teams to be like the NCAA Final Four. In the 2024–25 season, the playoff will increase to twelve teams.

Lastly, the UEFA president said that a U.S. college basketball sports model of a "final four" format could be on the way: "My opinion is it would be great. It should be more competitive and more interesting for the fans." This would mean that the "final four" could be hosted anywhere in the world, and there would not be semifinal home matches.*

In our next chapter, we'll describe The Real Madrid way of doing things, to provide a baseline about how the club is managed and why the club uses their approach. Much of the information is taken from, or based on, my 2016 book, *The Real Madrid Way*, which covers the subject in more detail.

After that, we'll turn our attention to the systemic changes happening in contemporary football, starting with changes in ownership models. We'll examine what Real Madrid are doing to address the systemic changes—actions that go far beyond the European Super League.

---

* The "final four" is in reference to the final four teams in the annual NCAA basketball tournament: each final four team is the champion from one of four regions of the tournament. These regional champions then travel from the four separate sites of their regional rounds to a common venue for the final four. These four teams are matched against each other on the last weekend of the tournament, usually on Saturday, with the final on Monday night.

Chapter 3

THE REAL MADRID WAY

BACKGROUND

Real Madrid Club de Fútbol are a football club founded in Madrid in 1902. The title *real* is Spanish for "royal" and was bestowed to the club by King Alfonso XIII in 1920, allowing the club to use the royal crown in the emblem. Unlike most European football clubs, Real Madrid's socios (members) have owned and operated the club throughout their history. They elect the president of the club every four years. Real Madrid also have a successful men's basketball team* and women's football team,† in addition to youth teams.

Florentino Pérez (born in 1947) has been the president of the club since 2000 (except for 2006–09). President and board members are unpaid positions. He was born in Madrid and graduated with a degree in civil engineering. Florentino is the chairman of global construction company Grupo ACS and has a net worth estimated over $2 billion. For

---

* The club isn't simply a football club. The club also own a basketball team. The basketball team was added in 1931. Real Madrid basketball play domestically in the Liga ACB, and internationally in the EuroLeague. Similarly to the Real Madrid football club, the basketball team has been the most successful of its peers in both Spain and Europe. Real Madrid are the only European sports club to have become the European champions in both football and basketball in the same season. The Real Madrid squads have won a record thirty-six Spanish League championships, including in seven-in-a-row and ten-in-a-row sequences. They have also won a record twenty-eight Spanish Cup titles, a record eleven EuroLeague Championships, a record four Saporta Cups, and a record five Intercontinental Cups. Real Madrid have also won three Triple Crowns, which constitute a treble of the national league, cup, and continental league won in a single season.

† Real Madrid women's football was founded as the independent Club Deportivo TACÓN in 2014, then underwent a merger and acquisition process with Real Madrid beginning in 2019 and was officially rebranded as Real Madrid's women's football team in 2020.

Florentino, Real Madrid are more than a football club. They are a passion, a club of values, and a way of life. His father took him to matches as a boy and taught him what Real Madrid means.

José Ángel Sánchez (born in 1967) is the CEO and works tirelessly behind the scenes. He was born in Segovia and earned academic degrees in philosophy and law. He has been at the club since 2000, when Florentino recruited him from video-game producer Sega, and he has been promoted many times. When asked about José Ángel Sánchez in June 2022, Florentino said, "[He] is talented enough to run a football club that is very difficult. He has created a good structure, he's the best executive I have seen in my life. I have to boast that we have a good team."[*]

When José Ángel Sánchez accepted Best Executive of the Year 2022 at the Globe Soccer Awards he was asked what Real Madrid's secret was. He replied, "There is no secret, to be honest, and there is not a simple answer to that question either. We just do our best to keep excellence and maintain the good work of our players and employees. Over the last twenty years, the club have suffered many changes in technology and the football industry and the game itself. Maybe the secret is adapting to those changes while staying true to the identity of the club."[†]

SUSTAINABLE ECONOMIC-SPORT MODEL

At the center of The Real Madrid Way for success on and off the pitch are the values of their community and the resulting culture.[‡] Simply put, the shared ethos, expectations, and values of the Real Madrid community dictate the operations, behavior, and mission of every aspect of the entire club—"adapting to those changes while staying true to the identity of the club." The values and expectations of the community drive the decision-making throughout the organization, from on the pitch (in player selection, player behavior expectations, style of play, and priorities)

---

[*] https://twitter.com/themadridzone/status/1537217071360376832.

[†] https://www.youtube.com/watch?v=qrcf2DCA6Bo.

[‡] Much of this chapter is from or based on *The Real Madrid Way* (2016).

to off the pitch (in business and management characteristics, strategy, marketing, investments, financial reporting, human resources, and technology). The Real Madrid management team spend their time reinforcing and solidifying increased personal connections, relationships, and communication directly with their community members. Management also pushes the community's values throughout the organization and to their players. Management's goal is to help the community connect to their intense passion of *living* Real Madrid.

Real Madrid's management team believes that *the community does not exist to serve the business or management; rather, the club exists to serve the Real Madrid community.* While the community has a shared identity as Real Madrid fans, the club recognizes that members and fans are individuals with a wide variety of needs, interests, and responsibilities.

Professor Susan Fournier from Boston University and Lara Lee, former executive at Harley-Davidson, wrote an article titled "Getting Brand Communities Right" in the April 2009 issue of *Harvard Business Review.* According to them, "A community-based brand builds loyalty not by driving sales transactions but by helping people meet their needs."* Essentially, that is what Real Madrid are doing. The club is constantly trying to better understand their community members' values, give them what they want, and improve and inspire their lives. They learned that those needs are not just about gaining status or identity through brand affiliation. Fournier and Lee wrote, "People participate in communities for a wide variety of reasons—to find emotional support and encouragement, to explore ways to contribute to the greater good, and to cultivate interests and skills, to name a few. For members, brand communities are a means to an end, not an end in themselves." To this idea, Real Madrid would most likely add that their members participate in their community to be empowered, inspired, escape, enjoy, celebrate, connect, share, and socialize. Real Madrid seek to help raise the self-esteem, self-confidence, joy, and happiness of hundreds of millions of people around

---

* Susan Fournier and Lara Lee, "Getting Brand Communities Right." *Harvard Business Review.* https://hbr.org/2009/04/getting-brand-communities-right.

the world. The community—the people—is the foundation. The reasons why Real Madrid's community members participate are different, but the jubilation—and sometimes tears—unites them all. For Real Madrid's fans and members, the community is a "means to an end, not the end itself."[*]

Therefore, the management team put at the center of their strategy the members' and fans' values and expectations. For example, if the community wants content to share, Real Madrid seeks to provide the best and most relevant exclusive content in the best and most convenient ways through Realmadrid.com, the Real Madrid app, Real Madrid's social media accounts, Real Madrid TV, or the newly created OTT Real Madrid Play. Technology enables the content for experiences and engagement to be scalable around the world. The access fuels the connection and passion, while the club's traditions and rituals reinforce the identity association. Thus, Real Madrid's community's values, expectations, and desires became the touchstone for developing and aligning strategy, culture, and identity to win on the field and in business.[†]

With this approach, Real Madrid were able to bring together a passionate global community by creating a sense of belonging and shared values felt so deeply by fans around the world that they are synonymous with one's identity and much more. It is impossible to tell where the fan's identity and life as a Madridista and the club's identity and purpose start and stop. There is no question that the identity of a Madridista and of the club is one and the same. The history, feelings, and emotions are intertwined. The closest corporate examples would be Harley-Davidson, Ferrari, and IRON-MAN, where in each case the brand and the identity, life, and lifestyle are absolutely intertwined. Owning a Harley-Davidson motorcycle allows you to be a member of the "HOG" (Harley Owners Group); buying a Ferrari

---

[*] Ibid.

[†] Albert M Muniz Jr. and Thomas C. O'Guinn wrote a paper published by the *Journal of Consumer Research* in 2001 titled "Brand Community." They state that "a brand community is a specialized, non-geographically-bound community, based on a structured set of social relations among admirers of a brand . . . brand communities exhibit three traditional markers of community: shared consciousness, rituals and traditions, and a sense of moral responsibility . . . Brand communities are participants in the brand's larger social construction and play a vital role in the brand's ultimate legacy."

allows you to be called a "Ferrarista"; finishing a 140.6-mile IRONMAN race allows you to call yourself an "Ironman."* The commercial power of the identity, life, and lifestyle is demonstrated by the fact that all three brands have thriving global apparel sales, sold both online and in specialized stores, yet none of them are apparel companies. A HOG, Ferrarista, Ironman, or Madridista benefits from the community with new friendships, a sense of belonging, shared experiences, recognition, and increased self-esteem. In addition, the internet and digital technology have allowed sophisticated, active community engagement.

At the center of everything Real Madrid are and do is their relationship with the community. The Real Madrid management team cares as much about bringing joy to the community and spreading and sharing the community's positive values (far beyond the ninety minutes of a match) as they do about winning championships, in their unique way. In addition, they make efforts to reach well beyond their brick-and-mortar stadium venue via digital technology, television, and social media; international and friendly exhibition matches around the world; and Real Madrid supporters clubs to reinforce and intensify interaction and engagement.

The secret of The Real Madrid Way is creating enterprise value from community values and expectations. Florentino and his Real Madrid leadership team figured out a *sustainable*, circular model to win both on and off the field (this is my interpretation and representation, not Real Madrid's). The word *sustainable* is important because Real Madrid are owned by approximately 94,000 club members, not a billionaire or corporation that can support losses. Many sports teams, including several

---

* Alexander Chernev, Professor of Marketing at Northwestern University's Kellogg School of Management, classifies Real Madrid as a "personality brand," just like Harley-Davidson, Ferrari, and IRONMAN. According to Chernev, "Personality brands express consumers' individual values and preferences. Personality brands are less about asserting an individual's status, wealth, and power; instead, they reflect an individual's idiosyncratic beliefs, preferences, and values. Unlike status brands, which have a price point that makes them unattainable by the majority of the population, personality brands are not differentiated on price, which makes them accessible to a larger segment of the population."

Spanish football teams,* have strong sporting values or expectations on the field; the genius of the executives at Real Madrid are that they have harnessed the values and then developed ways to support them for both on- and off-pitch success.

As demonstrated in Figure 3.1, Real Madrid get the world's best players who match the community's values to play an attacking, beautiful style of soccer with class to win championships and capture the imagination and inspire a current and potential global audience and community. The Real Madrid community expects the management team to sign players to be inspirational to them.

Winning is not enough to the Real Madrid community. This is in direct contrast to the idea of "win at all costs" or "the end justifies the means," or selecting players based on data analytics first, or "taking a calculated risk" in signing a troubled talented player that can "help the team win now." The Real Madrid community has a different standard and demands more. They want the team on the field to reflect the values and expectations of the community, which is winning with a team philosophy, class, style, and elegance. The Real Madrid community wants the club to be "champions and gentlemen."

---

* For example, Athletic Bilbao has a policy of exclusively signing and fielding players meeting the criteria to be deemed as Basque.

Figure 3.1: The Real Madrid Sustainable Economic-Sport Model

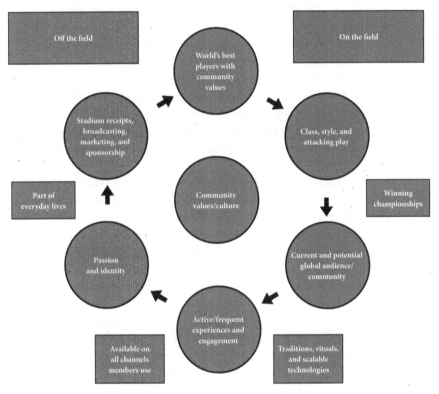

Source: Steven G. Mandis

Señorío and Kindness to Man U

In 2009, Real Sociedad, a football club based in San Sebastián of the Basque region in northern Spain, was celebrating their one-hundred-year anniversary while teetering on the brink of bankruptcy. They were under administration and relegated to the second division, after having been in the First Division for forty consecutive years. They called some other Spanish teams to play them in a friendly exhibition to celebrate the centennial year and raise money. Many turned them down or asked for money. Real Madrid accepted the invitation and agreed to play for free and put its stars in the starting lineup.* This classy behavior is what Real Madrid community members call Señorío.

Señorío is an attitude, an approach for doing things—roughly translated as "gentlemanliness," "chivalry," or, more loosely, "class." It was first introduced into the lexicon of Real Madrid during the first term of Florentino's presidency. Sir Alex Ferguson, the longtime coach of Manchester United, recalls in his autobiography: "I was surprised when, after my last match . . . I received a beautiful gift, a silver replica of Cibeles, the fountain where Real Madrid celebrate title wins, and a lovely letter from president Florentino Pérez."[†]

The community also displayed Señorío when many Madridistas gave a standing ovation for legendary playmaker Francesco Totti of AS Roma when he came onto the field as a substitute in a Champions League game at Bernabéu Stadium in 2016. The thirty-nine-year-old was born in Rome, played three years on the Roma youth team, and then played his entire professional career for Roma. After the game, Totti said his only regret is that he never played for Real Madrid. The Roma captain described his feelings about the standing ovation after the game: "It's a unique emotion . . . I really didn't expect it to be so strong. It means I've given a lot to the game of football, and this is my thanks from an amazing stadium." Real Madrid fans have given similar standing ovations to Italian star players Alessandro Del Piero and Andrea Pirlo.[‡]

However, one of the best examples of Real Madrid Señorío was the warmth and generosity Real Madrid showed Man U after the Munich air disaster in February 1958 claimed the lives of eight Man U players and three staff and the playing careers of two Man U players who never played again.[§]

---

* Oier Fano Dadebat, "LaLiga: Shabby Barcelona Are Miles Away from Real Madrid in Class and Dignity." *International Business Times.* http://www.ibtimes.co.uk/la-liga-shabby-barcelona-are -milesaway-real-madrid-class-dignity-1496194.

† Sir Alex Ferguson, *Alex Ferguson: My Autobiography* (London: Hodder & Stoughton, 2013).

‡ Ben Gladwell, "Roma Striker Francesco Totti Overwhelmed by Bernabeu Ovation." *ESPNFC.* http://www.espnfc.com/as-roma/story/2825492/roma-striker-francesco-totti-overwhelmed-bybernabeu -ovation.

§ The Munich air disaster occurred in February 1958 when British European Airways flight 609 crashed on its third attempt to take off from a slush-covered runway in Munich. The aircraft was carrying the Man U team, nicknamed the "Busby Babes," along with supporters and journalists. There were forty-four people on board, twenty of whom died at the scene. Another three died shortly thereafter in the hospital. The Man U team were returning from a European Cup match in Belgrade,

After Real Madrid won the European Cup in 1958, Bernabéu dédicated the win to the Man U players that died and even offered Man U the trophy. Then, Bernabéu offered to loan Man U the world's best footballer, Alfredo Di Stéfano, for the 1958–59 season. The FA blocked the loan as he would be taking the place of a potential British player.

Real Madrid played Man U in a series of fundraising friendlies to help Man U make money to rebuild their squad. In addition, Real Madrid hosted fundraising banquets and created a memorial pennant with the names of the Munich dead, which was sold in Spain to raise money for the bereaved families.

If the team loses, the community wants at least to see effort until the end, courage, and dignity. This is what makes them happy, and Real Madrid always try to satisfy their needs.

Florentino believes that when Real Madrid represent the ideals of the community members, the community responds with more engagement, passion, and loyalty. Since Real Madrid's community values are inclusive and universal, the community itself grows globally, which leads to world-wide sponsors spending big money for association with and access to the Real Madrid community, as well as television broadcasters paying lots of money to distribute the matches to the large, passionate global audience. The passion leads to an increase in stadium receipts, the value of broadcasting rights, and marketing and sponsorship opportunities, which contribute to higher revenues. Since Florentino and his executives implemented their sustainable economic-sport model, revenues have soared as fans more closely identified with the club and their players and became more passionate and loyal. Coming full circle, the high revenues allow the club to sign the world's best players who share their community values.* Real Madrid want their community to see a player on the team and

---

Yugoslavia (now Serbia), having eliminated Red Star Belgrade to advance to the semifinals against AC Milan.

* On the correlation of revenue and performance, Francisco wrote in his unpublished 2008 thesis: "The point we want to make with this argument is that other things being equal, making money and investing it on players is the best way clubs can make sure they enter in the virtuous circle of winning games, attracting more fans, having more TV audience, selling more merchandising, and making more revenue to reinvest in players."

think, "I want to play like, and be like, that player; I want my son or daughter to play like, and be like, that player; I want to win playing that style and with those values."

The resulting increase in revenues from the community values–centric approach funds not only signing the world's best players but a bigger, more modern venue that makes the stadium experience itself a way to connect with the team. It also provides the best training facilities and a youth academy that develop talented homegrown players who learn, from the age of seven, the history, traditions, values, and expectations of Real Madrid to complement and indoctrinate the imported stars. To the community and to Florentino and his executives, Real Madrid are much more than any one current or past player, coach, or president.

Real Madrid aren't just providing a football match; they are providing a larger experience or entertainment that draws in a community member to actively participate, for a memorable sensation. It is the experience from before and after the match as well as the satisfaction of the work of the club's charitable foundation. Off the pitch, the Real Madrid community wants the club to adhere to accountability, transparency, trust, and good corporate governance. Interestingly, if Real Madrid's community feels the club has not followed their values, the club's unique ownership structure enables those members to express their frustration by—along with not buying tickets or merchandise—voting a president out of office.

Although the team is often referred to as Real Madrid, or simply Real, their official name is Real Madrid Club de Fútbol.* The reason Real Madrid are referred to as a club is that they actually *are* a club. Unlike most professional sports teams that are owned by billionaires or corporations, Real Madrid, since their founding in 1902, have been owned by club members called "socios." As of June 2022, Real Madrid have 93,872 members, of whom 65,883 are between fourteen and sixty-five years old,

---

* While Real Madrid are commonly called "Real," in the city of Madrid the people often refer to the club as "El Madrid." This reflects that although Real Madrid are a global club with a global fan base, the club and the city and their values are synonymous. Both are multicultural, open to the world, welcoming, warm, and global entertainment providers. Many non-Spanish Real Madrid players have declared they love/loved living in Madrid, and many have continued living in the city after they retired.

17,840 are under fourteen years old, and 10,149 are over sixty-five years old or have been a member for more than fifty years. Real Madrid have 72,864 male and 21,008 female members. Adult members pay €149.19 per year as a membership fee. Any person who has been a member for over fifty years is exempt from paying membership fees. Any prospective new members must also be recommended by two existing socios to finalize their application for membership, although membership has been closed to new members since June 2009. A few people have been named "honorary members," including Plácido Domingo (2011), Rafael Nadal (2012), Sergio Garcia (2012), Julio Iglesias (2012),* Fernando Alonso (2017), Luka Dončić (2021),† Carlos Sainz Sr. (2021), and Alejandro Sanz (2021).

A new policy of only admitting descendants of present socios as new socios was established in June 2011 because the demand for season tickets is far greater than the seats in the stadium. Today, if someone is not a descendant of a present socio but wants to be an "official" part of the Real Madrid family, they can join the Official Madridistas Supporters and receive an official supporter card ("Carnet Madridista") and other benefits. Since its launch in 2001 to June 2023, more than 2 million people have been official supporter card holders.‡ They are very much a part of the Real Madrid community but have no season ticket or voting privileges.§ Non-socios can also join a local Official Real Madrid Fan Club and receive other benefits.

---

* Julio Iglesias was a goalkeeper in the Real Madrid Academy until he was seriously injured in a car accident at age twenty. While recovering, he discovered his musical talent.

† In September 2012, at thirteen years of age, Dončić signed a five-year contract with Real Madrid Basketball. In April 2015, Dončić made his professional debut for Real Madrid. In June 2018, Dončić was selected with the third overall pick by the Atlanta Hawks and then traded to the Dallas Mavericks for Trae Young and a protected first round draft pick in 2019.

‡ The number has grown dramatically since June 2022.

§ For more details, see https://madridistas.com/en-US/madridistas/landing. Even though Official Madridistas Supporters may not have "voting privileges," Real Madrid management views them, as well as Real Madrid Fan Club members, as critical active contributors to their global community and values.

A September 2015 General Assembly Meeting of club members representatives. They vote by *a mano alzada* (holding up their hands), a normal practice of Spanish-listed companies. An independent company counts the votes.

On the other hand, socio membership privileges include the right to vote for president and board of directors and to be a candidate for General Assembly (though the socio must have been a member for at least one year and has to be eighteen years or older in these cases). Socios also have easier access to tickets. As noted, Santiago Bernabéu Stadium has a capacity of 81,044. There are 60,127 socio season ticket holders for the 2021–22 season (76 percent of capacity).* All season ticket holders are socios. The remaining seats are for the general public. Socios are subject to disciplinary action for failing to pay any due fees or failing to adhere to a proper code of conduct on Real Madrid property or away matches.

---

* How does a socio become a season ticket holder? There are a limited number of season tickets, and during the last ten years there have been no vacancies. In 2013, the club offered a package of five thousand season tickets for all socios, with a series of priorities such as seniority, number of years as an e-ticket holder (being a socio), number of matches attended during the last seasons, etc. This package was sold out in a few weeks and has not been offered again.

As expected, any operating decisions that require the voting of approximately 94,000 people would be a cumbersome process. Thus, the socios hold an election to form the General Assembly ("Socios Compromisarios"), which comprises around two thousand members elected by the socios for four-year terms. The General Assembly's main responsibilities revolve around the financial aspects of the club, such as approving the club's budget for the season. The General Assembly also has certain other powers such as the ability to discipline the club president, as well as authorizing the club to borrow money.

GROWTH AND BREAKDOWN OF REVENUES

After Florentino and his executives allowed community values to drive decisions, operating revenues have grown on average by 10.3 percent annually—from €118 million in 1999–2000 to €757 million in 2018/19—and then 8.9 percent annually, since COVID impacted results, to €843 million. Today, marketing, which includes sponsorship and partnership deals with global firms, is the largest contributor to revenues (in 2000, the largest contributors to revenues were from membership fees and stadium tickets). Real Madrid's main partnership deals are with Emirates Airlines, Adidas, and HP, and their global sponsors are Mahou, Dubai, BMW, EA Sports, Abbott, Nivea Men, Cantabria Labs, easyMarkets, Adobe, Zegna, Palladium Hotels, Daktronics, Cisco, Softtek, and Canon. There are around forty people on the partnership creation, activation, strategy, and support team headed by Alex Wicks, global head of partnerships, retail, and licensing.

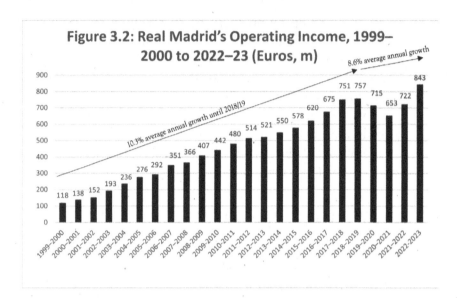

Figure 3.2: Real Madrid's Operating Income, 1999–2000 to 2022–23 (Euros, m)

This growth highlights the effectiveness of the Real Madrid community's values-centric approach in generating extraordinary loyalty and passion—with community members buying merchandise and global sponsors paying to get access to and association with the community members. Real Madrid are driven to personalize as much marketing as possible and make it effective and relevant—which is being driven by technology and data. As an example of how much the passion, loyalty, and community has increased exponentially with personalization, in 2019 Real Madrid reportedly signed an around €120 million per year sponsorship deal with Adidas thought to be the most lucrative kit deal in football history.* It was a significant increase over the reportedly €52 million per year on their previous deal. In 2022, Real Madrid signed a four-year renewal of their partnership with Emirates, which keeps the UAE flag carrier as their main shirt sponsor until 2026. While terms

---

* Financial details are not publicly provided by Real Madrid or Adidas. https://www.goal.com/en/news/real-madrid-sign-reported-11-billion-new-adidas-deal/9y1sooxrnzy714kdrf8spqc39.

of the contract were not publicly disclosed, reportedly the agreement is worth around €70 million annually.*

In October 2023, Real Madrid signed a multiyear tourism partnership deal with Visit Dubai. The announcement of the deal came ahead of the opening of the first Real Madrid–branded theme park at Dubai Parks and Resorts. The park has attractions related to the club, a museum, and football skill games, as well as a wide range of restaurants and commercial spaces selling official merchandise.

Real Madrid also use technology, data, and personalization to grow regional sponsorships around the world by geotargeting sponsorships on various platforms. Real Madrid segment their followers/fans based on several factors including demographics, location, buying habits, incomes, and previous responses to campaigns. The club then targets followers/fans via several digital environments they are signed into (e.g., app/e-commerce/web). Real Madrid also provide digital overlay in the stadium to bring LEDs to different regions.

Environmental Sustainability

Real Madrid ranked in the top three clubs in the Football Environmental Sustainability Index in the 2023 Brand Finance Football Report. Real Madrid promote a range of initiatives to reduce the impact of their activities on natural resources, including material and waste recycling and water usage and planting sustainable forests to offset the carbon footprint. The refurbished Santiago Bernabéu Stadium includes a system for the collection, transport, and subsequent treatment of waste that goes beyond the guidelines set by the European Union. Regarding water usage, the total annual water consumption of the football pitches and ornamental gardening of Real Madrid City Training Grounds comes from the recycled water network of the Madrid City Council, rainwater recovery, and field drainage.

Real Madrid's partners also help support and engage in the club's ESG initiatives. For example, Emirates strive to be leaders in environmental performance within their industry and therefore are looking to share this vision

---

* https://www.sportspromedia.com/news/real-madrid-emirates-shirt-sponsor-2026-laliga-worth/.

with sports brands. This includes a larger sponsorship deal with sustainability leader Real Madrid. In addition, Real Madrid and BMW launched several joint initiatives with a focus on future mobility, sustainability, and diversity. One of the initiatives was the establishment of a collaboration center for sustainability, which serves as a forum for promoting new innovative projects that make a positive impact on the environment. Another collaboration is working with BMW to reduce emissions by electrifying Real Madrid's vehicle fleet and introducing personal mobility solutions (bicycles and scooters) for internal travel at Real Madrid City Training Grounds. Another collaboration with BMW is evaluating the use of special paint capable of absorbing CO_2 to be used in various areas of Real Madrid City Training Grounds.

These initiatives and collaborations highlight how clubs can leverage their sustainability perception in order to draw in stakeholders, in this case sponsors. It is clear that sustainability-related sponsorship has become a key priority for many corporations and is an area of potential growth for sports brands. This includes both attracting sponsorships from large brands looking to associate with sustainability-focused clubs, but also for clubs to partner with sustainable brands.

The community values driving decisions at Real Madrid, as seen through growth in broadcasting revenue, are global. As the community expands, broadcasters are eager to deliver the matches to this loyal, passionate, and very large community. International and friendly match revenues have grown as the community grows around the world and loyally supports the team when Real Madrid physically appears in their area. The awareness of brand and community values increases with the international exposure.

In 2000, when Florentino became president, matchday represented 36 percent and broadcasting represented 35 percent of revenues and were the two largest components of revenues. Commercial revenues (sponsors, licensing, retail, e-commerce, membership programs) represented 29 percent. In 2019 (pre-COVID), matchday only represented 19 percent of revenues and broadcasting was relatively the same percentage, at 34 percent. The biggest growth was commercial revenues, which

represented 47 percent of the total. While Real Madrid revenues grew
542 percent from 2000 to 2019, commercial revenues grew 937 percent.

Matchday revenues grew at the lowest rate because the executives try
to keep ticket prices affordable for socios, which constitutes all of the
season ticket holders. In addition, due to Spanish law, alcohol is not
allowed to be sold to general admissions on matchday. Therefore, it's the
increase in VIP sections and pricing and the commercial exploitation of
the facilities (tour, events, bars and restaurants, shops) that have been the
primary driver of matchday growth.

Table 3.1: Operating Revenue Percentage Breakdown 1999–2000, 2018–19, and 2021–22

	1999–2000 Euros (m)	% total	2019 Euros (m)	% total	% change, 1999–2022	2022 Euros (m)	% total	% change, 2019–2022
Real Madrid								
Matchday	42	36	145	19%	241%	88	12%	-39%
Broadcast	41	35	258	34%	525%	308	43%	19%
Commercial	34	29	355	47%	937%	318	45%	-10%
Total	118		758		542%	714		-6%
Average for top 20 Clubs								
Matchday			75	16%		68	15%	-9%
Broadcast			206	44%		203	44%	-1%
Commercial			184	40%		191	41%	4%
Total			465			462		-1%

For the top twenty clubs in the Deloitte ranking, in 2019 broadcasting
represented the biggest percentage of revenues at 44 percent as compared to
34 percent for Real Madrid. However, if you look at Figure 3.3, which shows
average matchday, broadcast, and commercial revenues split by Deloitte
Football Money League positions, positions #16–20 average 65 percent of
their revenues in broadcasting. Positions #1–5 average 33 percent. After
the top five, there is a big increase to 48 percent. And one can see the
corresponding change in commercial revenues by segment. Positions #1–5

average 49 percent of their revenues in commercial and that drops all the way to 22 percent for #15–20.

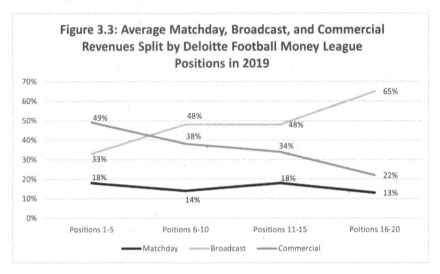

Figure 3.3: Average Matchday, Broadcast, and Commercial Revenues Split by Deloitte Football Money League Positions in 2019

The majority of Real Madrid's revenues, as well as the Top 5 Deloitte Revenue Positions, come from commercial/marketing because they are *both* global brands and media and entertainment companies. Real Madrid and other big clubs are very different than clubs that have most of their revenues from broadcasting and/or matchdays. Even clubs in positions #15–20 are very dependent on domestic league broadcasting deals, which are driven by the big clubs. Real Madrid have the brand and commercial revenues to attract and pay for the very best players—and separate themselves.

The Premier League clubs have an inherent advantage with their larger TV broadcasting deal, but Real Madrid have been able to compete by consistently finishing at the top of LaLiga and getting a larger percentage of LaLiga's TV broadcasting deal and consistently advancing deeper in the Champions League. Real Madrid's real separation comes from more commercial revenues driven by more global sponsors attracted by Real Madrid's values and large global fan base. As previously discussed, Real Madrid having the most social media followers highlights their massive global fan base and reach.

Broadcasting Revenue Ratios
Differences Between Leagues

The broadcasting rights that clubs receive in LaLiga (or any domestic league) are primarily driven by the top clubs or global brands like Real Madrid and Barcelona, which have and attract global audiences and sponsors. An estimated 650 million people watch El Clásico, the most for a regular season football match. El Clásico is a key driver of TV rights for all of LaLiga.

While Atlético Madrid have a global brand, respectfully they are not in the same global brand category as Real Madrid and Barcelona—as demonstrated in commercial revenues. In 2019 (pre-COVID), Real Madrid and Barcelona had €354.6 million and €383.5 million in commercial revenues, respectively—Atlético Madrid had only €99.6 million (and they ranked #13 in the Deloitte ranking overall). In every domestic football league, there is tension between the top clubs with global brands (and global fans) and the remaining others as to the equitable division of revenues.*

In June 2018, Premier League clubs agreed to a new deal over sharing revenue from international broadcast deals for any future international TV right increases divided according to league position. At the time, all the revenue from international TV deals was shared equally among the twenty clubs, but the Big Six had been pushing for a greater share of the money, arguing they are the main attraction for foreign viewers. Under the new agreement, which went into effect in the 2019–20 season, the clubs continue to share current levels of revenue equally, but any increase is distributed based on final league position. Under the new formula, the maximum a club can receive is 1.8 times the amount received by the lowest earning club, and any income above that will be shared to maintain that differential. Keep in mind, that is not total revenues; that is only Premier League broadcasting revenues—sponsorships, stadium revenues, and even broadcasting revenues from the Champions League and other tournaments can create large differences between the Big Six and others.

---

* In 2015, TV rights were centralized for the first time in Spain. Previously, each club marketed its broadcast rights separately. According to LaLiga, the TV revenue gap between the biggest and smallest teams used to be 12:1. Following the 2018–19 season, due to regulatory changes, the ratio dropped to 3.5:1.

While many cite that the Premier League is the most equitable domestic league, the issue for non–Premier League clubs like Real Madrid is that the total Premier League TV rights deals are much greater than the other leagues. And if Real Madrid are going to keep up with the Big Six's Premier League broadcasting revenue to compete at a European level (which helps LaLiga's coefficient with UEFA to get more spots in the Champions League), they need a bigger percentage of the smaller LaLiga pie.

For the 2021–22 season, LaLiga distributed €1,585 million in TV rights revenue. Real Madrid, Barcelona, and Atlético Madrid received €161 million (10 percent), €160 million (10 percent), and €130 million (8 percent), respectively. The lowest club in LaLiga, Rayo, received €45 million. Real Madrid received 3.5 times more.

No team from Serie A, Ligue 1 (PSG: €60 million, three times more than the lowest), or the Bundesliga (Bayern Munich: €90 million, three times higher than lowest) comes close to Real Madrid. However, six Premier League clubs have higher domestic league TV rights than Real Madrid—Man City being the most with €15 million more. The bottom Premier League club earned more in TV rights than the top Italian side, Inter Milan. Inter Milan received €84 million in revenue from television rights in the 2021–22 season (three times more than the lowest in Serie A). The bottom Premier League team (who came twentieth) received almost double the domestic TV money as PSG, who came top of Ligue 1.

The trend shows two very important and fast-growing segments: broadcasting and commercial marketing rights. The growth of these areas illustrates that professional European football is a global entertainment business, in which Real Madrid have been a leader.

WAGES AND TRANSFER FEES

Another key metric explains Real Madrid's financial sustainability: wages-to-turnover ratio—the salaries and wages paid for all employees divided by total business revenues. The lower the ratio (the lower the percentage of revenues going to pay salaries), the more financial flexibility a team has to make other investments. The maximum threshold recommended by the UEFA's European Club Association was 70 percent.[*] New UEFA financial sustainability rules came into effect in June 2022. Among several changes, the new rules also introduce a spending cap (the so-called "*squad cost ratio*") on wages, transfers, and agents' fees to 70 percent of a club's total revenue by 2025–26. In addition, the new rules require all sponsor transactions to be at a fair value. Previously, this requirement only applied to transactions with related parties, which can be debated.

Real Madrid's wages-to-turnover ratio in the financial year 2022–23 was 54 percent, a value close to 50 percent, which is considered the threshold of excellence, and well below the value of 70 percent, which is the maximum level recommended by the European Club Association.

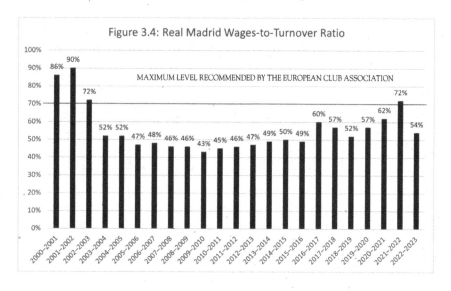

Figure 3.4: Real Madrid Wages-to-Turnover Ratio

In 2019 (pre-COVID), Real Madrid's wages-to-turnover ratio (the club's expenses divided by income) was 52 percent, the lowest among

* The European Club Association (ECA), the only association officially recognized by UEFA, promotes the health of European soccer teams through democratic representation.

the top positions in the Deloitte rankings.* The average for the selected top nineteen clubs was 66 percent, per below. Because of Real Madrid's community values–centric approach in its sustainable economic-sport model, the club generates so much revenue that, despite paying among the highest players' salaries in European football, those salaries are actually among the lowest when expressed as a percentage of revenues. In 2019, Real Madrid ranked number three in total salaries paid, behind Barcelona and Man U. However, Real Madrid, Barcelona, and Man U have lower wage-to-revenue-ratios than the average of the nineteen top clubs because their revenues are high. There were nine clubs that paid over €300 million in wages, with Chelsea and Juventus having higher than the average wages-to-turnover ratio of 66 percent.

Table 3.2: 2019 Revenues, Wages, and Wages-to-Turnover Ratio of Selected Top 2022 Deloitte Football Money League Positions

	2019 Wage/ Revenue Ratio	2019 Revenue Euros (m)	2019 Wages Euros (m)	Revenue Ranking
Real Madrid	52%	757	394	#3
Inter Milan	53%	365	193	
Dortmund	54%	372	201	
Bayern Munich	54%	660	356	#7
Newcastle	55%	200	110	
Man U	56%	712	399	#2
Liverpool	58%	605	351	#8
PSG	58%	636	369	#4
Man City	59%	611	360	#5
Arsenal	60%	445	267	
Barcelona	65%	841	547	#1
Atletico Madrid	66%	368	243	
Chelsea	70%	513	359	#6

* The wages-to-turnover ratio in the North American leagues is around 50 percent, but it varies by team. Collective bargaining agreements with player unions for the various leagues typically address this topic.

	2019 Wage/ Revenue Ratio	2019 Revenue Euros (m)	2019 Wages Euros (m)	Revenue Ranking
Juventus	71%	460	327	#9
West Ham	71%	216	153	
Leicester City	85%	202	172	
Everton	85%	211	179	
AC Milan	90%	206	185	
Leeds United	94%	56	53	
Average	66%		275	

Note: Tottenham was excluded from the 2022 top twenty clubs.
2022 clubs were selected to be able to show their 2019 salary spending pre-COVID
and demonstrate a club that was not in the Premier League.

Everton and Leicester City finished eighth and ninth in the 2018–2019 Premier League table (just outside European qualification dominated by the Big Six)—their wages-to-turnover ratios were 85 percent, which is not sustainable. Their wages were €179 and €172 million, respectively. Arsenal and Man U finished fifth and sixth, and they spent €399 million and €267 million, respectively—more than the total revenues of Everton and Leicester City. This highlights that the Big Six plus Newcastle and growing are their own breakaway league.

The Real Truth About Championship, Promotion, Relegation, and European Qualification in the Premier League

A club that stands out on the table above are Leeds United, which were in the Championship in 2019. Leeds United's wages-to-turnover ratio was 94 percent.

The system of promotion and relegation has produced considerable instability in the bottom one-third of Premier League membership and in the membership of lower leagues.[*] I analyzed the probability of relegation within three seasons of promotion to the Premier League as well as the

---

* https://drive.google.com/file/d/1Tznz8M2qudll6fROOrzHMeMhn0BnHLb_/view.

number of consecutive seasons a newly promoted club to the Premier League stays without suffering relegation. Most of the time (greater than 95 percent probability), newly promoted clubs stay in the Premier League less than five years. Typically, of the three clubs promoted each season, at least one club will suffer relegation the first season after achieving promotion. And most of the time, at least two of the clubs will be relegated within three seasons. There are a few outliers where the club was acquired by or received significant investments from very wealthy owners who subsidized losses to last more than three years. For example, English sports bettor and poker player Tony Bloom made significant investments in Brighton & Hove Albion who gained promotion to the Premier League in 2016–17 after thirty-four years out of the top flight of English football. (In 2018, Bloom completed the takeover of Belgian club Union SG—multi-club ownership model.) Another example is Leicester City. But before you hold them up as a great exception, read the later sidebar, in "Halftime," focused on Leicester City.

In August 2023, Anton Drasbaek Schiønning wrote an article for Off The Pitch titled "If You Don't Spend, You Won't Stay: Transfer Spending Dictates the Fate of Newly Promoted Premier League Teams."[*] Schiønning's analysis uncovered the clear pattern that recently promoted Premier League teams that spend heavily remain in the Premier League, while those with lower transfer spending face immediate relegation. He wrote: "The expectation for promoted teams to spend heavily to compete in the Premier League carries significant financial risks, including potentially burdensome wage costs if they are quickly relegated . . . This analysis underscores a trend that, while potentially longstanding, is now increasingly prominent. Financial strength is crucial for success, a trend likely to intensify, further widening the gap between the haves and the have-nots."

The difference in revenues between each tier of English football provides a significant incentive to try to be promoted. The highest correlations to performance are total salaries and total transfer values of players—better players lead to more wins. Therefore, investment in fan engagement or infrastructure or youth academies come second behind player salaries and transfer fees. Without Financial Fair Play in the EFL Championship (LaLiga has FFP

---

[*] https://offthepitch.com/a/if-you-dont-spend-you-wont-stay-transfer-spending-dictates-fate-newly -promoted-premier-league?wv_email=sgmandis%40me.com&wv_id=0b33e863-2b87-44e3-82bb-a46d d11bfd0d&wv_name=.

in the top two tiers), clubs in the second tier are gambling beyond their means in the hope of reaching the promised land and money of the Premier League.

A 2018–19 (pre-COVID) review of football finance by Deloitte calculates that Championship clubs spend 107 percent of their entire revenue on wages, which obviously is unsustainable. Keep in mind, 107 percent wage-turnover ratio is only the Championship's average—Reading's were 226 percent. Aston Villa and Sheffield United gained promotion with ratios of 181 and 190 percent, respectively.[*] Spending in the English Football League (EFL), particularly the Championship, is by and large recklessly unsustainable and is just getting worse. Why? Clubs are risking it all for the windfall moment of reaching the Premier League.

The Championship playoff final to get promoted to the Premier League is often referred to as "the world's richest game." In 2020, Deloitte calculated that promotion would mean an increase in revenue of at least £135 million over the next three seasons for the victorious club and that could rise to £265 million over a five-year period if the club avoids relegation in their first season in the Premier League.

While the world's richest game is certainly exciting with so much on the line, one has to wonder if this is sustainable or even good for English football.

Lastly, most of the money going to players in the Championship isn't going to homegrown British players; the majority of the players are foreign (and they typically get more money).[†] Six out of the top ten and twelve out of the top twenty earning football players in the Championship were foreign.[‡] And the Premier League has the highest percentage of foreign players (69 percent) of any European League. Seven out of the top ten and fifteen out of the top twenty earning football players in the Premier League were foreign.[§] For context, foreign players represent less than half of the Bundesliga, LaLiga, and Ligue 1. Ironically, one reason for the breakaway Premier League was for more money to go to the development of players to help England win a World Cup.

---

[*] https://inews.co.uk/sport/football/championship-finances-football-premier-league-gamble-444133.

[†] https://www.skysports.com/football/news/11661/10725849/premier-league-has-highest-percentage-of-foreign-players-uefa-report.

[‡] https://salarysport.com/football/sky-bet-championship/highest-paid/.

[§] https://www.spotrac.com/epl/rankings/.

The Merengues have a strict salary structure, which also helps keep harmony in the locker room. This was a reason why Ronaldo had to be sold after making demands to match Messi's pay at Barcelona. If Ronaldo was paid more, then other players would also ask for more. This is precisely what happened at Barcelona—and contributed to their difficult financial situation. Real Madrid also has a strict policy of not extending player contracts for more than one year after the contract expires and the player is in his thirties. This led to Sergio Ramos leaving. While Real Madrid's prudent approach and sustainable economic-sport model may upset fans who don't want to lose exceptional players like Ramos and Ronaldo, Real Madrid's approach and model have played a key role in helping Real Madrid have strong financial performance and avoid violating any Financial Fair Play regulations. The on- and off-the-pitch are interrelated and codependent.

As transfer fees have skyrocketed, Real Madrid have generally focused paying transfer fees for younger players with potential, rather than more established players with higher transfer fees. For example, in 2017, Real Madrid agreed to pay a reported transfer fee of €46 million for Vinícius Júnior (according to transfermarkt.com, his market value in March 2023 was €180 million), which was, at the time, the second most expensive sale of a player in the history of Brazilian football (behind only Neymar), and the highest amount ever paid by a club for a footballer under the age of nineteen. In 2018, Real Madrid agreed to pay a reported transfer fee of €45 million for Rodrygo, who was then under the age of nineteen (according to transfermarkt.com, his market value was €110 million in March 2023). Real Madrid's focus has risks as the players are younger and less proven. In 2022, the CIES Football Observatory released a report listing the average age of transfers for every club across Europe's Top 5 Leagues from 2013 to 2022—and it shows just how heavily Real Madrid have invested and focused on youth. Real Madrid had the lowest average age: (22.87 years old), followed by Borussia Mönchengladbach (23.36), Borussia Dortmund (23.57), OGC Nice (23.73), LOSC Lille (23.88), and Real Sociedad (23.90).* Signings like Vinícius Júnior, Rodrygo Goes,

---

* https://www.managingmadrid.com/2022/10/19/23412976/real-madrid-rank-first-in-youngest-average-age-of-player-recruitment-over-last-decade.

Eduardo Camavinga, and Brahim contributed to Real Madrid having such a remarkably low average age.* In June 2023, Real Madrid acquired nineteen-year old England midfielder Jude Bellingham from Borussia Dortmund for a reported €103 million.†

Four teams stood out in the CIES Report when it comes to the percentage of players recruited aged thirty and over: Man U (23.5 percent), AC Milan (23.4 percent), Inter (23.0 percent), and Chelsea (20.3 percent).‡ *Real Madrid did not recruit any player over the age of twenty-nine during this period—the only club among the fifty analyzed.* However, all transfers have risks. Real Madrid essentially took the reported approximately €100 million they received from Juventus for Ronaldo in July 2018 and spent €140 million in July 2019 signing twenty-eight-year-old Eden Hazard—who, for a variety of reasons, didn't meet expectations.

FINANCIAL RESULTS

Lastly, the financial results demonstrate a sustainable economic model. *Sustainable* means that the model funds itself and doesn't constantly need equity injections or excessive borrowings to continue. In fiscal year 2022–23, which ended in June 2023, Real Madrid's revenues were €843 million (excluding player transfers), up 17 percent on the previous year and surpassing pre-pandemic revenues for the first time (€757 million in 2018–19). Their EBITDA (Earnings Before Interest, Taxes, Depreciation, and Amortization), a simple proxy for cash flow, was €158 million.

A profit after tax of €12 million was obtained in 2022–23 compared to €13 million in 2021–22. Thus, in an economic context characterized by widespread and very significant losses in the vast majority of the most relevant European clubs in the period 2019–20 to 2021–22, losses that also persist in the results of relevant clubs announced so far relating to the financial year 2022–23, the club closed in profit all the financial years

---

* In December 2022, Real Madrid agreed to sign sixteen-year-old Brazilian forward Endrick from Palmeiras, with Endrick to Real in July 2024 when he turned eighteen, staying with Palmeiras in the meantime.

† https://aktie.bvb.de/IR-News/Ad-Hoc-News/Jude-Bellingham-vor-Wechsel-zu-Real-Madrid.

‡ https://football-observatory.com/IMG/sites/mr/mr78/en/.

of the four-year period covering the financial years 2018–19 to 2022–23, which have been affected by COVID-19 and, in the specific case of the club, by the completion of the remodeling works of the stadium. This has been achieved through cost containment and business improvement measures in all areas.

As a result of the profits made, Real Madrid increased the value of their net assets on the 2022–23 fiscal year to reach a value of €558 million. Cash and cash equivalents were €128 million. Net debt (total debt minus total cash) remained negative at €47 million (excluding stadium renovation project), meaning they have more cash than debt, and a net debt to EBITDA ratio of 0.0x.

Table 3.3: 2021–22 and 2022–23 Real Madrid Economic and Financial Summary (Excluding Stadium Renovation)

	2021–22 Euros (m)	2022–23 Euros (m)
Revenues (before results from disposal of fixed assets)	721.5	843
EBITDA*	203	157.6
Profit after tax	12.9	11.8
Equity at June 30	546.4	558.3
Cash and cash equivalents at June 30	401.5	128.2
Net borrowings at June 30	-263.1	46.7
Debt/EBITDA Ratio	0.0x	0.0x
Debt/Equity Ratio	0.0x	0.0x
STADIUM REMODELING PROJECT		
	2021–22	2022–23
Accumulated Investment	537.8	892.7
Loan Drawn	800	800

* Earnings Before Interest, Taxes, Depreciation, and Amortization

It is estimated that an increase in revenue from the full commercial availability of the stadium would start in early 2024 and would develop progressively. All this leads to estimate that the revenues of the stadium in 2023–24 will increase significantly compared to the financial year 2022–23, although they would still be significantly lower than the expected level to be achieved from 2024–25 when the different business lines are fully operational.

Real Madrid's sustainable economic-sport model pursues self-sustainable growth where, through a combined effort of growth/diversification of income and cost control, profitability is obtained, along with a financial structure whose solvency allows the club to meet the investments necessary for the development of its activity.

Real Madrid's "Debts"

I regularly read or hear materially inaccurate and misleading statements about Real Madrid's financial condition—including suggestions that Real Madrid needed the European Super League because they were in a disastrous financial situation or have a comparable financial situation with Barcelona or Juventus. And the statements are usually from people who have not done any research or have any education or background in business or accounting, or who are acting in bad faith. Real Madrid have one of the strongest balance sheets (and earnings power) in football (and sports)—which is truly remarkable considering they can't raise/sell equity as a member's club.

Real Madrid's gross debt on June 30, 2022 (excluding the stadium remodeling project), was €253 million (which includes €53 million owed to clubs for player transfers and €47 million of advances on income accruing in the future). But the key metric is net debt (gross debt minus cash and cash equivalents). It does not make sense to discuss what one owes without factoring in what cash one has. Real Madrid had €425 million of cash and cash equivalents plus €91 million in player transfer receivables on June 30, 2022, for gross cash and cash equivalents of €516 million (excluding the stadium remodeling project). So Real Madrid has *net cash* (not net debt) of €263 million (excluding the stadium remodeling project). It also does not make sense to discuss what one owes without factoring in what cash one produces, and Real Madrid produces cash flow.

One popular British newspaper article in 2017 referred to Real Madrid's "debts" and provided gross debt. When I wrote to the editor in 2017 to explain how simply using gross debt was misleading, this was their response: "We referred to 'debts' . . . Our purpose was not to report Real Madrid's absolute cash position but to illustrate the scale of the potential liability . . . While Real Madrid has considerable assets, many are held in Southern European banks and capital markets that carry significant risk . . . it was fair and accurate to report the absolute debt."* The newspaper's response makes no business or economic sense. It's materially inaccurate and misleading to not state both debt and cash (and assets and liabilities). In addition, the prejudice from the British press on Spain's financial system is impertinent, especially considering the U.K. government had to support their banking sector.

To be fair, including the stadium remodeling project adds €800 million of long-term financing, but it also adds more cash (not spent yet) and assets (the value of the remodeling to the stadium at cost) to the balance sheet— which gets to the concept of "net worth" or "equity" (assets minus liabilities).

Another newspaper article just mentioned Real Madrid's total liabilities of €1,723 million, *including* €800 million of long-term financing related to the stadium remodeling project, which had not been spent yet—that sounds like a very big and scary number! It does not make sense to discuss liabilities without factoring in what one owns—assets. The article neglected to mention that there were €2,269 million of total assets, for a positive net €546 million of equity.† (This is the same including or excluding the stadium remodeling project as the debt is offset by the cash/assets.) This is accounting's way of saying if Real Madrid sold/liquidated all their assets and then paid off all of their liabilities, they would have €546 million left over. Of course, if Real Madrid could be sold, it would be for far more than €2.269

---

* In 2008, the U.K. government had to support the banking sector, including Royal Bank of Scotland and Lloyds TSB, and Barclays took capital from Middle East investors. The letter was from 2017. In 2010, Spanish bank Santander's U.K. business PLC reached an agreement to acquire the parts of the banking businesses of the Royal Bank of Scotland Group, which are carried out through its RBS branches in England and Wales and its NatWest branches in Scotland. In 2015, TSB confirmed a takeover bid by the Spanish banking group Sabadell for £1.7 billion, less than a year after it rejoined the stock market through Lloyds Banking Group's sale of 50 percent of its holding.

† Remember, Real Madrid are a nonprofit club and do not make distributions; the profits stay in the club.

billion of total assets. In 2024, *Forbes* valued Real Madrid at $6.6 billion—the world's most valuable football club.[*]

Any reasonable person would think it would be materially inaccurate and misleading to state their "net worth" or financial condition by just stating either their "absolute" assets (or cash) or liabilities (or debt)—of course they would "net" them.

The €800 million of debt for the stadium matures in 2049 (twenty-six years from 2023) and has an average fixed interest rate of 2.23 percent (a very low fixed rate, considering the twenty-year and thirty-year U.S. Treasury rates were both around 3.8 percent in February 2023).[†] Some try to add the €800 million of debt from *net cash* of €263 million and get to €537 million of net debt—fast-forwarding the cash from the loan being spent. However, Real Madrid are operationally cash flow positive and are generating cash, so it would be misleading to not take that cash into account. It also does not make sense to discuss what one owes without factoring in what cash one produces—Real Madrid's EBITDA, a simple proxy for cash flow, was €203 million in 2021–22, which was impacted by COVID and the stadium renovations.

Lastly, the new stadium, which will be a multipurpose facility for concerts, commercial events, and restaurant spaces, is reportedly expected to generate over €150 million per year more in revenues than what the stadium made pre-pandemic.

In addition, if Real Madrid's members wanted to, they could sell the naming rights of the stadium for hundreds of millions of Euros over ten years. In 2010, JPMorgan Chase signed a $300 million, ten-year marque marketing partner deal for Madison Square Garden for assets inside MSG that do not include rights to the arena itself (it's not the "Chase Madison Square Garden" but "Madison Square Garden presented by Chase"). In May 2022, Barcelona sold the Camp Nou's stadium naming rights to audio streaming platform Spotify and will now be referred to as "Spotify Camp Nou" for four years.

---

[*] https://www.forbes.com/sites/mikeozanian/2024/05/23/the-worlds-most-valuable-soccer-teams-2024/#.

[†] The stadium financing was structured to be as easy to service as possible and as easy to explain as possible to the socios and Real Madrid community. It was structured as a mortgage style financing with a fixed amortization, after a grace period on principal during construction work years, not leaving future potential risk for the club in the form of bullet maturity structures or refinancing risk.

To provide some more context for Real Madrid's financial strength:

Barcelona's net debt (gross debt minus cash), as of June 30, 2022, was €608 million. Barcelona had negative equity of €353 million (the liabilities were more than the assets). In 2023, *Forbes* valued Barcelona at $5.5 billion, the third most valuable football club.

Man U's net debt, as of June 30, 2022, was £514.9 million. Man U had positive equity of £154 million (the assets were more than the liabilities). The Glazer family received £33.6 million in dividends throughout the financial year. In 2023, *Forbes* valued Man U at $6.0 billion, the second most valuable football club.

VALUES AND CULTURE

Management consulting firm McKinsey & Company has highlighted the importance and value of culture.[*] The firm, through a survey of hundreds of companies in North America, Europe, and Asia, found 66.7 percent of business leaders felt culture provided their greatest source of competitive advantage. In addition, McKinsey & Company found that companies with effective organizational culture outperformed peers significantly. In fact, those companies with high-performing cultures delivered significant performance improvement, 300 percent higher annual returns to shareholders than companies with undefined cultures.

Real Madrid suggesting culture as the most important ingredient to winning on and off the field poses some challenges. Culture is hard to define, let alone analyze, measure, and compare, and it is difficult for the media to report on culture. It is much easier to reference and compare performance data and statistics for insights. It is more straightforward to try to hire data analysts to assemble a theoretically competitive team by selecting undervalued players based on analytics. Maybe our fascination with fantasy league sports has made us lose sight of the fact that, at the end of the day, a real team has to be able to afford these theoretically winning players, which requires loyal and supportive fans and sponsors. It's also easy to forget that even the most talented superstars are real

---

[*] In full disclosure, I have worked with McKinsey & Company as a senior adviser and as a client.

people from different backgrounds, at different stages in their lives and careers, who have to rely on one another and perform as expected, even when tired and injured after a long season, in actual high-pressure games, to win championships. What is the glue for this? Real Madrid believe it is culture.

Every winning culture has its own authentic personality and soul that can't be invented or imposed. In organizations, culture is an invisible but powerful force that influences the behavior of the members of that group. Most often the values of the founder or owner or a legendary top executive are instilled in the organization and shape its culture.

Real Madrid Mission and Values

When Florentino took over the presidency of Real Madrid, there was no documented mission statement and no written values. Although having such a statement or set of governing principles is relatively common practice for the best-performing businesses, in sports it was highly unusual. Conventional thinking in sports was that the single mission and value of every team was simply to win—nothing complicated about that.* What Florentino was tapping into was why the club exists and how community members wanted to win on and off the field.

Conventional wisdom is that the mission of a sports team is simple and obvious: "Win a championship." However, there is a difference between a "goal" and a "mission with values." A mission statement is a statement that is used as a way of communicating the purpose of the organization. The purpose of a values statement is to describe the desired culture and provide a behavioral compass or set of behavioral expectations for the organization.

Real Madrid's employees and community members seemed to know implicitly what the answers were, but they had never formally written them down. Florentino wanted to spell them out explicitly so that everyone in the community could read them and the club could be held accountable to them, especially as the organization grew.

---

* At least this is how most fans think about it. Some owners have the mission of breaking even or making money.

In many corporations, senior management, sometimes with the input of employees or consultants, typically writes the mission statement. In this case, Florentino wrote the mission and values statements based entirely on what the community members had said in surveys, which was a highly unorthodox approach. He believed that since the club members owned the team, they should be the ones to guide management's thinking on strategic issues, provide focus and common goals, help define performance standards, guide employees' decision-making, and help establish a framework for behavior. He believed that if the club closely followed the mission and values, the club members would be even more passionate and loyal because the club would be a reflection of what was important to them.

After board approval, he included them in the first annual report Real Madrid published during his presidency.

Mission

To be a multicultural club that is both appreciated and respected throughout the world both for its sporting successes and for the values it disseminates, which, based on the search for excellence both on and off the field of play, contribute toward fulfilling the expectations of its members and followers.

Values

WILL TO WIN. Real Madrid's main objective is to strive, to the best of its abilities, to win all of the competitions it enters while showing its commitment, its belief in hard work, and its loyalty to its supporters at all times.

SPORTSMANSHIP. Real Madrid is a worthy and fair opponent on the field of play, upon which it competes with goodwill and respect toward all rival clubs and their respective supporters. Away from the field of play it is Real Madrid's overriding desire to maintain relations with all other clubs based on fraternity and solidarity and to collaborate with them and with the Spanish and international sports authorities on a permanently ongoing basis.

EXCELLENCE AND QUALITY. Real Madrid aspires to have the best Spanish and foreign players within its ranks, to imbue them with the values to which the Club aspires, and to repay the support of its fans with a sporting project based on quality, discipline, and sacrifice for the common cause. With respect to the management of its activities, the Club adheres to the principles of good governance and strives for excellence at all times.

TEAM PHILOSOPHY. All those who form part of Real Madrid, be they sportspeople or other professionals, make a commitment to working as part of a team and to give the best they have to offer for the good of the whole without putting their personal or professional aspirations first.

TRAINING. Real Madrid constantly devotes a great deal of effort to the discovery and instilling of new sporting values. This involves channeling the necessary attention and resources into the youth teams of all its sporting disciplines and nurturing not only the sporting development of its youth players but also their social, ethical, and civic education.

SOCIAL RESPONSIBILITY. Real Madrid is aware of the high social repercussion of its activities and it is for this reason that it dedicates all the resources within its power to complying with the very highest standards of good corporate governance and the promotion of the best sporting values, to strengthening its relations with its members, former players, fan clubs, and supporters, and to the development and implementation of solidarity projects in favor of the needy both within Spain and beyond its borders.

ECONOMIC RESPONSIBILITY. Real Madrid is aware that it manages tangible and intangible assets of exceptional value and importance, and it is for this reason that it pledges to administer them responsibly, efficiently, and honestly in benefit of its members.

Each employee and player is to adhere to the mission and values, which sponsors are to implicitly support. The mission and values pervade every corner of the organization, from the marketing department to the player development staff, to the coach and to the players on the field. For the club members, fans, and community, winning wasn't everything: they want to win with values.

SELLING FUTURE MARKETING, LICENSING, AND
SPONSORSHIP RIGHTS TO PRIVATE EQUITY

Sorting out Real Madrid's financial mess after Florentino won the club's presidential election in 2000 was something of a challenge. Florentino hired Deloitte & Touche, the accounting and consulting firm, to review the club's financial statements and get to the bottom of what was going on. The independent auditor's results showed the situation to be as bleak as Florentino had feared. An August 2000 letter from a group of Deloitte & Touche auditors expressed concerns about Real Madrid's ongoing existence: "The budget that has been provided to us for the year 2000–01 has an excess of expenses over revenues . . . [which raises] important doubts about the ability of Real Madrid to continue its operations so that it can . . . meet its obligations . . . in the normal course of its business."

Florentino had to give a personal pledge of €18 million ($19 million), 15 percent of the budget by Spanish law, to run for president. The club had no money and huge debt. However, it had immediate working capital needs. To get the banks to agree to lend Real Madrid an additional €78 million, Florentino had to personally guarantee the amount. The club signed seven new players, including Figo, Conceição, Makélélé, and Solari, at a total cost of €151 million. To borrow to pay for two of those signings, Makélélé and Conceição, Florentino personally guaranteed another €39 million to the banks. (Real Madrid sold some players, including Redondo and Anelka, and received €67 million; otherwise the club would have had to borrow more.) Finally, when the budget for the 2000–01 season was approved, the expenditures were higher than the previous year's budget, and, by law, Florentino had to personally guarantee an additional €12 million. So, in 2000, after becoming president of the club, Florentino personally guaranteed €147 million ($155 million) in total [18+78+39+12]. Only €30 million [18+12] of the €147 million was required by law. Without Florentino's additional €117 million personal guarantees, the club wouldn't have been able to afford the necessary investments required to start their turnaround. The personal financial risk was so large that it would be fair to say that Florentino's passion really was both an obsession to save the club and a conviction of the strategy he was to apply.

Real Madrid didn't have the money or time to invest up front in an untested theory and wait to see if it produced the anticipated results. The team was heavily in debt and losing money. The outcome of Florentino's personal financial gamble for the club was at stake. The players would need to be paid up front, and the projected theoretical marketing dollars from aligning Real Madrid's passionate global community's values, expectations, and desires with the club's strategy, culture, and identity would come later. And Real Madrid couldn't sell or raise equity since it was owned by socios. Florentino and his team would have to innovate.

Florentino and some of his executives, including Carlos Martínez de Albornoz, had experience in the infrastructure construction business and had helped raise equity for the infrastructure projects they were involved with as construction and engineering executives by projecting highway and bridge toll cash flows. They applied the same ideas of selling projected cash flows to Real Madrid, except in this case, the future income would be tied to marketing, licensing, and sponsorship revenues.

No precedent existed for estimating what Real Madrid's new strategy would yield over the next ten to fifteen years from marketing, licensing, and sponsorship revenues. Real Madrid developed a stand-alone legal entity (named "Sociedad Mixta") to own and manage the future marketing, licensing, and sponsorship, player-image rights, and online business revenues of Real Madrid, and developed a credible financial model with projections for the next eleven years. The Sociedad Mixta, managed by the club's marketing division, handled all such interactions with current and potential customers and partners.

Florentino and his team went to meeting after meeting with various companies to explain the concept and the financial model and its underlying assumptions. The idea was for the companies to pay up front for a percentage of Real Madrid's future revenues based on the potential financial return they would get. The challenge was that with no historical track record, this strategy required investors to take a big leap of faith.

Once projections and assumptions were agreed upon, the parties had to negotiate the discount rates to present value projected future cash flows

that would reflect the risks to come up with a valuation—but there were
no good comparable precedents. Finally, in October 2000, Caja Madrid
(a Spanish savings and loan institution that would later become part of
Bankia, and now CaixaBank) paid €78 million for a 20 percent share. In
February 2001, Sogecable (the leading pay TV group in Spain) signed a
€39 million deal for a 10 percent share. There were risks on both sides—
Real Madrid didn't want to sell too low and the investors didn't want
to overpay—which were mitigated by establishing put-and-call arrangements at various prices and times for protection. By October 2000, Real
Madrid had sold a total of 30 percent of the rights for eleven years for
a total of €117 million, which gave the club some financial liquidity for
operations. In the end, the venture was a financial success for both sides.
Real Madrid got the immediate financial stability they needed, and the
investing companies saw an 11 percent annualized return by 2014. "Sociedad Mixta" is an example of Real Madrid being creative and innovating
to adjust to their organizational structure and needs to compete.

In 2018, Real Madrid were looking ahead and wanted to build a "digital stadium" of the future. They would need to raise cash, and they had
a very valuable asset—a global brand with values that attracted sponsorships from global companies. Florentino and his management team
wanted to utilize their experience from the Sociedad Mixta deal to raise
capital. However, this time Florentino didn't need to try to explain and
sell the model to banks or companies. Private equity firms who were
starting to focus on the value of sports clubs were aggressively looking
for opportunities to invest. Real Madrid closed a €200 million, four-year
sponsorship (with a two-year extension to the partnership depending
on certain targets) rights deal with U.S. private equity firm Providence
Equity Partners.* Providence Equity assumed influence on some of the
club's future sponsorship direction, with exception to stadium naming
rights, training ground naming rights, and shirt sponsorship deals. The
deal was significant because the traditional and conservative management

---

* https://www.sportspromedia.com/news/real-madrid-sell-sponsorship-income-providence-dave
-hopkinson-mlse-la-liga/.

team at Real Madrid figured out how a member's club could utilize private equity capital without selling control or equity.

The partnership with Providence Equity coincided with Real Madrid's appointment of former Maple Leaf Sports & Entertainment (MLSE) chief commercial officer Dave Hopkinson as global head of partnerships for Real Madrid.* While the original four-year deal was signed in 2018, there was also the option for a two-year extension. With the pandemic and other factors, the parties renegotiated the deal before the contract expired.

STADIUM

Located in the center of Madrid, Santiago Bernabéu Stadium is a football history monument and a key asset of the club. Initially called the Nuevo Estadio Chamartín (it received the name of the club president eight years later), it was inaugurated as the first big football stadium in continental Europe. Initially, it consisted of two uncovered tiers that could hold just over 75,000 spectators. Capacity was further increased to 124,000 in 1954, when one of the long sides got expanded with a third tier.

The stadium represented a revolution for the football industry as it was a key piece of Santiago Bernabéu's sustainable economic-sport model. Bernabéu wanted to get the best players for Real Madrid. To pay for them, he did something innovative at the time. He took a huge financial risk and built the biggest football stadium to increase ticket revenues, predicting that the best-playing stars with an attacking style would not only win there but would also draw large crowds to the stadium to see them do it. To finance the stadium, he sold bonds to the club members and fans. (Keep in mind, by 1921, eighty-four out of the eighty-six English football clubs had converted to private corporations and sold equity to pay for stadiums and infrastructure and fund losses due to player wages.)

At the time, many thought 75,000 capacity, and then 124,000 capacity, was "too much stadium for so little a club." Bernabéu's gamble paid off, and with the larger ticket receipts, Real Madrid were able

---

* Hopkinson left to become president and chief operating officer of Madison Square Garden.

to afford the best world-class players from abroad, the most famous being Argentine forward Alfredo Di Stéfano. Real Madrid won LaLiga in 1953–54 over defending champion Barcelona. It took Bernabéu ten years to win his first LaLiga championship as president (the club's third Spanish title).

Just five kilometers, or three miles, down the Paseo de la Castellana ("Castellana Street") from the Museo Nacional del Prado ("Prado Museum"), which housed some of the works from the greatest artists, Bernabéu showcased the greatest football players in the world playing in a mesmeric style never seen before in Europe.

Together with his gifted teammates, Di Stéfano invented modern professional club football and embodied all that is magical about it. Fans could see that eleven highly skilled players, when given paint (the ball), could go onto a canvas (the field) and paint a ninety-minute picture of imagination and beauty that expressed them. Anything less than ninety minutes of full effort and beautiful, exciting, and attacking soccer with elegance, style, and class—whether the players were winning by several goals or losing—was considered an "unfinished painting" or disrespectful to the art and viewers. Their artistry fit perfectly because Madrid has a community rich in history and culture that could appreciate the beauty and talent.

By the 1990s, the stadium was old and run-down. When Florentino Pérez became the president of the club, he launched a "master plan" with one goal: to improve the comfort of the Santiago Bernabéu and the quality of its facilities, and maximize revenue for the stadium.

Florentino invested €127 million in five years (2001–2006) by adding an expansion to the east side of the stadium, as well as adding a new facade on Padre Damian Street, new boxes and VIP areas, new dressing rooms, a new Presidential Box on the east side, a new press area (also located on the east side), a new audio system, new bars, integration of heating in the stands, panoramic lifts, new restaurants, escalators in the tower access, and implementation of the multipurpose building in Padre Damian Street. Following the enlargement of the lateral east side and the creation of new galleries, the capacity of the Santiago Bernabéu was expanded to around eighty thousand.

Florentino had an even bolder vision than Bernabéu. Similar to Bernabéu, Florentino wanted to have a large stadium that marked the future of the club and would help pay for the world's greatest players, but he saw beyond the around twenty-five home matchdays at the stadium to generate revenues.

So the Santiago Bernabéu is undergoing a massive restoration that will ensure the arena continues to be a global benchmark within the worlds of sport and architecture. According to Florentino Pérez, "The new stadium will continue to be the setting that generates the emotions which will leave their mark on Real Madrid's future. It'll be the best stadium in the world in which to see us once again recognized at the end of the century as the best club of the twenty-first century. It'll offer a new stadium, heritage, and be a new source of pride for our members and fans."

The project is being led by GMP Arquitectos, L35, and Ribas & Ribas. The renovation work will see the Bernabéu become a state-of-the-art arena that satisfies the demands of club members, while also increasing the club's revenue streams. One standout feature will be the stadium wraparound facade, which consists of strips of steel and stripes that can be lit up and upon which images can be projected. The renovation will make the Santiago Bernabéu a more modern, comfortable, and safe venue and see it enhanced with the addition of leisure, restaurants, and organized entertainment areas.

The new arena will also offer the option for the pitch to be covered by both permanent and retractable roofs, a feature that will ensure that all of the seating areas are covered, and that the stadium can be used all year round, regardless of weather. In addition, the grass will be retractable to allow the stadium to be used not only on matchdays or for playing football. This is a unique piece of engineering, the largest vertical greenhouse now in operation worldwide. The pitch is divided in trays, each self-sufficient to maintain the grass in the greenhouse anytime. Conceptually speaking, the system (patented by the engineering company SENER in collaboration with Real Madrid) works differently from any other similar concept: the grass will only be deployed to play football, and then kept again in the greenhouse, so full maintenance is secured. This will enable Real Madrid to host various events, from football matches and concerts to trade shows and basketball games, throughout the year, independent of weather—all in the downtown convenience of a capital city. In February 2024, the NFL announced that it would play a regular season game in 2025 at the Santiago Bernabéu Stadium.

Florentino wants the stadium to be in use 365 days per year and develop a business for corporate, entertainment, and tourism events—beyond matchdays.

The redevelopment will see the Santiago Bernabéu become a digital arena, in which technological advances and the use of audiovisual tools will be available across many areas of the stadium. For example, fans will be able to enjoy club-generated content that enhances their matchday experience on their mobile phones and tablets, in what is known as the use of a second screen. The arena will be fitted out with an impressive 360° scoreboard. Bernabéu Stadium will be a data-driven facility, from building management to content supply. By logging in on the stadium app, visitors will have access to a full array of exclusive content while the system will be able, according to the data provided and always within the boundaries of the European data regulations, to provide a personalized experience. When completed, the stadium will be one of the world's largest and most technologically advanced venues.

Many call the new stadium the "infinite stadium," as there'll be a seamless transition between the physical experience and the online one. Single sign-on technology will allow the multiple touch points of the stadium to recognize the visitor and push personalized content/offers/experiences to his/her app / handheld device / display.

The Bernabéu Stadium will have more than 2,500 screens, considering each unit with a unique IP address, and so able to display different content. In addition, digital signage software (Adobe) will help Real Madrid manage a unique experience for fans through the screens in different modes.

The club's museum (which is the third most visited museum in Madrid after Reina Sofía and the Prado) is undergoing massive improvements. The museum is being extended in size and will benefit from a new interactive section, featuring the latest augmented-reality technology. The route included within the Tour Bernabéu will also be extended with the launch of a panoramic tour that will take visitors around the stadium's outer rim.

The shopping provision will be improved with a Real Madrid store that will be the largest sports store in the city (three thousand square meters). The new stadium will also include the launch of a new shopping experience with digital points of sale offering goods sold by the world's most prestigious electronic and consumer goods brands, turning the public areas into a window for the planet's latest products.

Florentino sees the stadium as an important part of boosting revenue streams to compete with new ownership models. Florentino said, "Real Madrid must do things like this because we are the number-one club, and the only way we will remain there is by always being the first big innovator."[*] In addition, LaLiga and UEFA, not Real Madrid, are in control of TV rights, so Real Madrid are focused on revenue opportunities they can control, like the stadium.

The €800 million renovation project began in 2019. In November 2023, the Extraordinary General Assembly approved an additional €370 million for the stadium renovation project. The renovation team is utilizing Roman techniques to raise the top so as not to affect the operation of the stadium during the football season. The project is very complex because Real Madrid did not stop playing football in the stadium during redevelopment, since they see the stadium's atmosphere and history as a competitive advantage. But that complicates working on the redesign, which includes a roof that encloses the whole stadium.

Over the long run, Real Madrid can make significantly more revenue because the stadium will be available 365 days a year, and the stadium, which is turned into an entertainment district, will further diversify the club's revenue streams.

---

[*] https://futballnews.com/florentino-perezs-plans-of-moving-santiago-bernabeu-stadium-to-real madridland-crumbled/.

The renovated Santiago Bernabéu will be a crown jewel of the socios during Florentino's tenure.

Selling Future Stadium Revenue Rights to Private Equity

In 2022, Real Madrid received approximately €360 million from U.S. private equity firm Sixth Street Partners to be invested across any of the club's activities. Through this alliance and long-term partnership, Sixth Street acquired the right to participate in the operation of certain new businesses of the Santiago Bernabéu stadium for twenty years. In addition, Legends will contribute its experience and knowledge in the operation of large stadiums and leisure centers, allowing for the optimization of the management of the Santiago Bernabéu Stadium. U.S.-based investment firm Sixth Street has $60 billion in assets under management.* The arrangement with Sixth Street, which also owns a portion of the NBA's San Antonio Spurs, is limited to sharing in profits, not revenues, from the venture. The deal includes Legends, an American sports and live events management company that's majority owned by Sixth Street, which has overseen Real Madrid's retail business since 2020.

The deal reduces the financial risks for the socios. However, one of the key elements of the Sixth Street transaction is the alignment of interests among the three parties to achieve success: Real Madrid investing heavily to create the best venue in Europe; Legends coming to Europe with one of the biggest clubs; and Sixth Street making a large investment dependent on alignment and success. Alan Waxman, a founding partner and the chief executive of Sixth Street, said, "Real Madrid's Santiago Bernabéu is hallowed ground in the world of football, and we are honored to be joining this partnership to invest in the innovative, long-term strategic vision that has guided the club's consistent success over its storied history." (In full disclosure, Alan and I worked in the same proprietary trading and investing area at Goldman Sachs.)

---

* In 2022, Sixth Street also announced a deal with Barcelona to purchase 25 percent of the club's LaLiga TV rights for the next twenty-five years.

Socios are primarily responsible for what Real Madrid are today—not one president or a league. Real Madrid had won LaLiga only twice from LaLiga's founding in 1929 to 1953–54 when Real Madrid won their third. Athletic Bilbao (five), Atlético Madrid (four), Barcelona (six), and Valencia (three) had won more Spanish titles before Real Madrid won their third. Santiago Bernabéu's economic-sport model and his push for the European Cup certainly helped make Real Madrid the global brand with the most fans. However, it's the socios who elect and support the presidents, and who are primarily responsible for what Real Madrid are today. Real Madrid's socios took the economic risk to build one of the largest stadiums at the time to help recruit and pay the best players in the world. It was (and is) the socios who filled the stadium, provided the inspiration, atmosphere, and spirit, and created the traditions. And it's the socios who take the risk for the renovated Santiago Bernabéu Stadium.

Florentino Pérez put the values of the community at the center of the entire sustainable economic-sport business model and strategy.

Understanding how and why Real Madrid executives manage the club and the club's financial performance provides a baseline to put other clubs' strategies and information into context. Next, let's focus on the changes in football and sports and entertainment and content, starting with different ownership models, and how Real Madrid are addressing those changes.

One of the biggest systemic changes in football relates to ownership. Closely government-related entities (or people) have relatively recently increased their investments in football. In addition to investment returns, among many things, involvement in football can be a way for owners to build relationships and deliver positive messaging and legitimacy. The most prominent example is the Abu Dhabi United Group, which bought control of Man City in 2008. The money from the Middle East has changed the financial landscape of football. It increased the financial stakes by sending transfer fees and salaries soaring. This environment caused many owners to sell out or seek the investments of capital that can usually come from large institutions, like private equity (or people of such vast wealth, their family investment offices are essentially institutions). In 2022, U.S. private equity firms Clearlake and RedBird acquired control of Chelsea and AC Milan, respectively. More than one-third of the top clubs in Europe have some connection to a U.S. private equity firm or their principals. In addition, both closely government-related entities and private equity firms have acquired multiple clubs for synergies to improve returns. The next chapter goes deeper into these new players (and their interconnected relationships) and their strategic rationale, as well as the potential consequences.

The new Santiago Bernabéu stadium.

Real Madrid president Florentino Pérez with Jude Bellingham, upon signing Bellingham in June 2023.

Chapter 4

CLOSELY GOVERNMENT-RELATED, PRIVATE EQUITY, AND MULTI-CLUB OWNERSHIP MODELS

THE OWNERSHIP AND control of football clubs has changed dramatically in the last few decades, especially for football clubs. Closely government-related entities, including sovereign wealth investment funds from Arab states of the Persian Gulf, own stakes in clubs such as Man City, Newcastle, and PSG. With their backing, the clubs' spending has skyrocketed.

In 2022, private equity firms, which typically raise pools of capital from high-net-worth individuals and institutional investors to invest in private companies, invested €4.9 billion (about $5.3 billion) in Europe's five largest football leagues, up from just €66.7 million in 2018. More than one-third of European football clubs in the Big Five Leagues, including Chelsea and Milan, have financial backing from private equity or private debt firms. The clubs have spent a lot of money since these investments took place.

Sometimes, private equity firms are also co-investors in clubs with closely government-related entities, including Man City and PSG, or sovereign wealth funds are investors in private equity firms that own clubs, including Chelsea.

The rise of closely government-related and private equity firm back-ers has coincided with a sharp uptick in multi-club owners. These MCOs control over 40 percent of the Big Five clubs. The most active MCOs tend to be U.S. private equity investors.

This chapter will give some background on how and why ownership models are changing, and the potential implications to football.

MAN CITY'S CLOSELY GOVERNMENT-RELATED + MULTI-CLUB + PE MODEL

In 2008, Sheikh Mansour was interested in purchasing one of the top English Premier League football clubs.*

Sheikh Mansour, born in 1970, is the fifth of former Emir of Abu Dhabi Sheik Zayed's eighteen sons through seven marriages. His mother is Sheikha Fatima and he has five full brothers (known as sons of Fatima), including Sheikh Mohamed (known as MBZ), current president of the United Arab Emirates (UAE) and the ruler of Abu Dhabi.† Sheikh Man-sour's second wife is the daughter of the ruler of neighboring Dubai. Man-sour is the Deputy Prime Minister and Minister of Presidential Affairs of the UAE and reportedly has a personal net worth estimated at $30–40 billion and family net worth of over $1 trillion.

Sheikh Mansour has significant business interests and helps manage over $1 trillion in UAE and its capital, Abu Dhabi, including stakes in many important global companies. He is the vice chairman of the UAE

---

* Around 2007, reportedly, Dubai International Capital investment group had considered a pur-chase of Liverpool. In 2007, Americans George Gillett and Tom Hicks Sr. purchased Liverpool. They were two of the American pioneers of multi-club ownership extending to European football. (In full disclosure, I worked with Tom Hicks Sr.'s son Mack Hicks, and we are friends.) Malcolm Glazer purchased his first shares in Man U around 2003, and gained control of the club in 2005.

† The United Arab Emirates, or simply the Emirates or UAE, is located at the eastern end of the Arabian Peninsula and shares land borders with Oman and Saudi Arabia and maritime borders with Qatar and Iran. During the nineteenth and early twentieth centuries, the pearling industry thrived in the area. The decline of the pearling industry after World War II and the rise of the modern cultured pearl industry resulted in extreme economic hardship. In 1953, subsidiaries of British and French oil companies obtained concessions from the ruler of Abu Dhabi to drill for oil, and in 1958 they struck oil in Abu Dhabi waters. In 1971, the UAE received independence from treaty relation-ships with the United Kingdom and was admitted to the UN. Abu Dhabi is the nation's capital while Dubai, the most populous city, is an international hub. Today, UAE has the sixth largest oil reserve in the world.

state-owned Mubadala Investment Company (MIC), which owns stakes in numerous companies, including semiconductor firm AMD, regional sports network Yankee Entertainment and Sports Network (YES Network), investment firm Carlyle Group, and private equity group Silver Lake. In 2019, Silver Lake would buy a 10 percent, $500 million stake in City Football Group, and increase the stake to 18 percent over time. In 2020, MIC bought a 5 percent stake in Silver Lake. In 2021, Silver Lake acquired a 33 percent stake in the Australian A-League.

MIC has an estimated $284 billion in assets under management. Mansour is a board member of the UEA state-owned Abu Dhabi Investment Authority (ADIA), which is estimated to manage $790 billion. He is chairman of UAE state-owned Emirates Investment Authority (EIA), focusing on investing in asset classes considered to help strengthen and diversify the UAE economy. EIA manages over $87 billion, including stakes in important companies in the Middle East and North Africa (including Etisalat, an Emirati-based multinational telecom services provider). The reason for the investments is to help solidify UAE and Abu Dhabi's wealth, because one day the natural resources can run out.[*]

While Sheikh Mansour was looking to buy a top English football club, Man City's owner, Thaksin Shinawatra (the former prime minster of Thailand), needed to sell. Shinawatra had his over $2 billion in assets frozen by a Thai court, and Man City were losing tens of millions of dollars a year. Unable to keep funding the losses, Shinawatra decided to sell the club. But the club was not a member of the Big Five, had terrible player contracts, leased the stadium from the city, and was considered #2 in Manchester after Man U. Shinawatra had bought Man City in June 2007 for £81.6 million.

While Man City weren't a Big Five club, Sheikh Mansour saw a bigger picture. As a business investment, he would be buying membership into the most-watched sports league in the world, with growing international TV rights and investment value. In addition, owning a Premier League

---

[*] In December 2022, former CNN and NBCUniversal head Jeff Zucker, private equity firm RedBird Capital Partners, and Abu Dhabi–based International Media Investments formalized plans for a joint venture called RedBird IMI with $1 billion in committed funds aimed at "large-scale" media and sports investment opportunities.

7

club would give him even more legitimacy and a platform to build relationships and deliver positive messaging. For example, no one had ever
heard of Roman Abramovich or had a view about him until he bought
Chelsea. However, the bigger picture that Sheikh Mansour saw was that
owning a Premier League club would provide an opportunity to present
the UAE as a globally relevant, dynamic, relatable, and welcoming Gulf
nation. He hoped that over time his ownership could improve relations
and understanding between his country and the West.* This was important because of the West's criticism of the Emirates human rights record,
and common misconceptions and stereotypes about the Middle East.
Michael Rosenberg of *Sports Illustrated* explained: "Sports seem like they
aren't political, which is precisely why they are so often used for political
purposes. The drama seduces us, and our passion distracts us, and so
we swallow whatever government officials feed us without even realizing
it."† Football can also be a positive tool for change. The UAE women's
national football team was formed in 2009—and ever since has been
breaking barriers and changing perceptions.

Traditionally, the UAE's Abu Dhabi Tourism Authority and Etihad
Airways used sports sponsorships to build brand awareness, engagement, and sentiment as well as to grow business and leisure traffic to

---

* It can be challenging and complicated to evaluate or judge (or reconcile) the complex cultures of
other countries based on the standard of one's own cultural norms, values, or beliefs for lots of reasons (e.g., lack of historical perspective or understanding; one's own cultural biases, misconceptions,
or stereotypes; or the impact of time). One also may need to consider the time period, rates of trans-
formations over time, and the constraints of the cultural norms, values, or beliefs of countries (both
of one's own culture as well as other countries). This is not to indiscriminately justify or defend any
actions or policies or cultural norms, values or beliefs, but rather be a reminder that one may need
to carefully think about context before objectively evaluating or judging the complex cultures (or
even ethics) of other countries (and possibly one's own). In addition, tourism, cultural exchange, and
interaction can be an overwhelming force for mutual good. Many people do not know much about
and/or have never visited countries in the Middle East, which encourage visitors to explore. Sports
and entertainment are reasons for more people to visit and see what the countries are all about, meet
the people, and learn what the countries are doing for the future of their citizens. Sports can be a
positive tool to help transformation over time.

† https://www.si.com/olympics/2022/12/29/sportswashing-olympics-world-cup-daily-cover. Rosenberg
also wrote: "After Russia invaded Ukraine, the International Olympic Committee and FIFA moved
to ban both Russia and its ally Belarus from competition. That might not seem like much of a penalty for Russia's atrocities in Ukraine, but don't think of it as a punishment. Think of it as taking
away a weapon."

the emirate.* But buying a club was a bold and visionary tactic. Technically, the acquisition was not undertaken by a state-owned entity, but was funded with Sheikh Mansour's own money via Abu Dhabi United Group (ADUG). Officials in UAE have consistently insisted that ADUG is completely unconnected to the government of UAE or the Emirate of Abu Dhabi, and Sheikh Mansour's involvement with Man City is a completely private investment.

Sheikh Mansour bought the club within weeks of being presented the opportunity but had one condition: Man City had to sign a superstar player. The problem was that there was limited time left before the transfer deadline. So, reportedly, Man City started a rumor with Sky that it was bidding for several star players. And that got the attention of agents and clubs. In the end, they bought twenty-four-year-old Brazilian winger Robinho from Real Madrid for £32.5 million, outbidding Chelsea. On the same day, Sheikh Mansour bought Man City for £150 to £210 million.

There were no protests from fans or politicians, as when Man U initially agreed to be sold to Rupert Murdoch's BSkyB in 1998, or to the Glazers in 2005. No one seemed particularly worried about the Premier League's "Owners' and Directors' Test."† For decades, Man City had finan-

---

* Emirates, sponsor of Real Madrid, is one of two flag carriers of the UAE (the other being Etihad Airways). Emirates is based in Dubai and owned by the government of Dubai's Investment Corporation of Dubai. Etihad Airways is based in Abu Dhabi and owned by ADQ, an Abu Dhabi state-controlled sovereign wealth fund.

† The Premier League defines its process of identifying whether or not an interested party is deserving of owning a club in England. The Owners' and Directors' Test outlines requirements that would prohibit an individual from becoming an owner or director of a club. These include criminal convictions for a wide range of offenses, a ban by a sporting or professional body, or breaches of certain key football regulations, such as match-fixing. The test is applied to prospective owners and directors, who are then subject to a review on a seasonal basis. After the U.K. government review in 2022–23, the Premier League is examining if more tests and transparency is needed, and whether those decisions should be approved by an independent body. In addition, the Premier League has had conversations with Amnesty International about human rights. The FA and the EFL have to agree on what the test should be, how it should be implemented, and how it should be communicated to fans. One condition proposed by the U.K. government review would assess a candidate's integrity, or whether "the proposed owner is of good character such that they should be allowed to be the custodian of an important community asset." Sacha Deshmukh, Amnesty International U.K.'s CEO, said: "In an era of global sportswashing and with the horror of what is currently unfolding in Ukraine, the Premier League has a clear moral responsibility to change its ownership rules to put a stop to top-flight English football being used as a PR vehicle for those complicit in serious human rights violations." https://www.theguardian.com/football/2022/mar/03/premier-league-considers-adding-human-rights-to-new-owners-test.

cial challenges, and on the pitch they paled in comparison to cross-town rival Man U.* For many fans, Sheikh Mansour was seen as essentially bringing unlimited money to enable their club to compete. He stood in stark contrast to Man U's American owners, who to many fans seemed to be too focused on dividends and returns on investment.

After the takeover was complete, Sheikh Mansour wrote in an open letter to Man City fans: "In cold business terms, Premiership football is one of the best entertainment products in the world and we see this as a sound business investment."† Around that time, according to Robinson and Clegg's *The Club*, one of the club's executives internally said, "We're not a football club, we're actually a sports entertainment company. So, we must create content. We must create events, we must create shows, we must create drama. And we must be part of the news, front page and back page, in every way. Am I competing with the other football club down the road, Manchester United, or am I competing with Walt Disney, with Amazon?"

Khaldoon Al Mubarak was appointed Man City's new chairman. He is thoughtful, professional, and sensitive to Man City's heritage. He also runs UAE state-owned Mubadala Investment Company (MIC) and runs the Executive Affairs Authority, a key branch of the Abu Dhabi government. Under Khaldoon Al Mubarak, Man City was quickly and completely revamped with significant capital investments. One year after the acquisition, an unofficial group of Man City fans bought a stadium banner that read: "MANCHESTER CITY THANKS YOU SHEIKH MANSOUR."

Man City executives greatly admired Barcelona's success. In 2012, they failed to sign Barcelona's manager Pep Guardiola (he would later sign in 2016) but hired Barcelona's former finance vice president Ferran Soriano. During Soriano's 2003 to 2008 tenure, Barcelona's revenues had

---

* "City had managed to tumble into that hapless predicament despite a gift of outrageous fortune: a new, 48,000-seat stadium, built for the 2002 Commonwealth Games with public money—£78m from the national lottery, £49m from Man City council—and converted at the public's expense." https://www.theguardian.com/football/2012/may/18/fall-and-rise-manchester-city.

† Two years later, Sheikh Mansour attended his first and only Man City match in person at Etihad Stadium. A club representative said, "He loves the club in his own way," and has not missed watching one match.

increased from €123 million to €308 million, and a €73 million loss was turned into an €88 million profit. In 2008, Soriano and seven other Barcelona board members resigned amid disagreements with then-president Joan Laporta.

Man City needed someone experienced to be CEO and help balance the books. At the time, since buying Man City, Sheikh Mansour had spent close to $785 million on thirty transfers in four years and reported a then football world record loss of £197 million ($310 million) for the 2010–11 season.

In his book *Goal: The Ball Doesn't Go In by Chance* (2011), Soriano mentioned how Man City was changing football: "They [Man City] were threatening to buy up the best players at whatever price, creating another wave of inflation."

In 2011–12, Man City won their first Premier League title, beating Man U, who finished tied with them on 89 points, on goal difference. While Man City lost close to £100 million during the 2011–12 season, they crashed the seemingly closed Arsenal (three Premier League titles), Chelsea (three), and Man U (twelve) trophy party, being the fifth club (Blackburn Rovers won in 1993–94) to win the Premier League in its twenty-year history.* Man City won the Premier League before Liverpool (who won their first and only Premier League title in 2019).

Soccernomics: High Correlation Between Salaries and Wins; Most Clubs Lose Money

Before Ferran Soriano's book *Goal: The Ball Doesn't Go In by Chance* (Palgrave Macmillan, 2011) was published, he had read *Soccernomics* (New York: Nation Books, 2009). Simon Kuper, writer for the *Financial Times*, and Stefan Szymanski, former professor of economics and current professor of sports management at the University of Michigan, made the argument that there was a high correlation between total spending in salaries and total league

---

* At the time, Arsenal, Chelsea, and Man U had won all the titles.

points.* The authors also pointed out that most football clubs lose money. According to them, the buyers of football clubs are wrong if they assume that if they can get their teams to win trophies, profits will inevitably follow.

The authors analyzed the Premier League and discovered that even the best clubs seldom generate profits. They also detailed how unprofitable the overall industry is. In addition, they showed that there was little correlation between success on the pitch and making money. However, Kuper and Szymanski found that most clubs didn't care about profits. Instead, they kept spending what they believed it took to win matches. The majority of clubs even paid players more money than they had or could produce, so the teams would borrow money, and most had a precarious amount of debt. The club owners were often (not always) bailed out by the rising broadcasting rights correspondingly increasing the value of the clubs above the debt and losses.

UEFA would try to address clubs losing money, saving owners from themselves. In 2009, UEFA set regulations to prevent football clubs from spending more than they earn in pursuit of success, called Financial Fair Play (FFP). The regulations provide for sanctions, fines, or player transfer bans to be taken against clubs who exceed spending, over several seasons, within a set budgetary framework. Implementation took place at the beginning of the 2011–12 season. Initially, clubs could spend up to €5 million more than they earn per assessment period, although under this monitoring period, total losses of €45 million were permitted over three seasons as long as clubs had owners who could cover such amounts. Starting in 2015–16, the monitoring period again covered the previous three seasons, but the limit dropped to €30 million. In the following years, the limit would be lower.

A frequent criticism of FFP is that it entrenches existing high revenue clubs at the top of a hierarchy by making it more difficult for new disruptors to spend on an equal plane until revenues match. And that this quirk in FFP would make football more predictable and less exciting. Another criticism at the time was that FFP would be extremely difficult to police. According to *The Guardian*, UEFA warned PSG and Man City that they would be unable to "cheat" the FFP rules.† At the time, there were media reports that the clubs were already engaging in questionable sponsorship practices designed

---

* In 1997, Szymanski co-authored an academic paper that I believe was the first to demonstrate statistically the link between pay and performance. Szymanski, S., & Smith, R. (1997). "The English Football Industry: Profit, Performance and Industrial Structure." *International Review of Applied Economics*, 11(1), 135–153.

† https://www.theguardian.com/football/2013/feb/04/manchester-city-financial-fair-play.

to keep them in line when the regulations went into effect. The last criticism was that it would be fans who would have to pay more for tickets, subscriptions, shirts, etc., to help clubs increase revenues to pay increasing player wages and be compliant with FFP as owners could no longer fund the losses.*

In 2011, Man City signed on to a £400 million, ten-year new sponsorship arrangement with Etihad Airways, which was initially owned by members of Abu Dhabi's royal family and later switched to ADQ, an Abu Dhabi state-controlled sovereign wealth fund. Man City described it as "one of the most important arrangements in the history of world football." It was the largest deal of its kind in sport. The ten-year agreement, in which Man City's stadium was renamed the Etihad Stadium, was worth more than twice the previous record, JPMorgan Chase's $300 million (£187 million), ten-year partner marketing deal for Madison Square Garden in 2010 ("MSG presented by Chase"). The deal was seen as especially remarkable because Man City don't even own the stadium.

To put the Man City deal into English football context, the deal Arsenal struck with Emirates in 2004 was valued at £90 million over fifteen years. Around £48 million of that came via shirt sponsorship, with the naming rights worth only £2.8 million a year. At the time, Chelsea and Tottenham had both scoured the market for a deal in the region of £10–15 million a year but found no serious interest. An Arsenal's Supporters' Trust spokesman said: "The deal at Manchester City stretches credulity to the limit. The numbers just don't stack up."

Following an investigation process for circumventing FFP, in 2014 UEFA fined Man City €60 million and placed restrictions on their European squad and incoming transfers for FFP breaches, including the value of certain sponsorship revenues being overstated to reduce financial losses. Shortly thereafter, Man City reluctantly accepted a reduced

---

* Many believe FFP—now FSR—works better today in one crucial respect: there are sporting sanctions, not just financial. Clubs are banned from playing in competitions, and that has affected each club's approach. At most clubs, FFP and not being banned from the UCL are the overwhelming factors driving every significant financial decision.

€20 million fine for breaking the rules, even if they disagreed with the process and conclusion.

In 2018, German magazine *Der Spiegel* published documents posted on the whistleblower platform Football Leaks which alleged that Man City's owners, ADUG, had deliberately misled UEFA by inflating its sponsorship revenues to circumvent FFP in the investigation that concluded in 2014. The sponsorship agreements called into question were those that concerned Man City's shirt and stadium sponsor, Etihad Airways, and also Abu Dhabi–based telecoms company Etisalat. One document appeared to show that Etihad Airways was paying only £8 million of a £67.5 million sponsorship agreement, with the shortfall coming directly from ADUG.* Man City and ADUG absolutely and categorically deny this.

The series of *Der Spiegel* articles also described how allegedly Man City's owners were apparently circumventing rules by disguising direct funding to the club as sponsorship payments. They allege the money in question was apparently sent to the companies based in Abu Dhabi, which would then wire the money onward to the club. The system supposedly allowed the club to claim a low volume of direct investment by the owner and a higher total of marketing revenues—in direct violation of FFP. The FFP rules were designed to prevent clubs from spending more than they earn and thus going into financial difficulties or distorting competition on the pitch. Once again, Man City and ADUG absolutely and categorically deny this.

As a result, in 2019, UEFA launched another formal investigation process, and in February 2020 announced that it had found that the club had deliberately overstated its sponsorship revenue, in its accounts and in the break-even information submitted to UEFA between 2012 and 2016. In addition to this, UEFA stated that Man City had failed to cooperate with the investigation—which was also against FFP rules. Again, Man City and ADUG absolutely and categorically deny this.

The punishment was that Man City were banned from participation in the UEFA club competitions in the next two seasons (the 2020–21 and

* https://www.brabners.com/blogs/manchester-city-football-club-v-uefa-closer-look.

2021–22 seasons) and had to pay a €30 million fine. The lead investigator was the former Belgian prime minister Yves Leterme (PM from March 2008 to December 2008).*

Man City appealed the punishment to the Court of Arbitration for Sport (CAS). In July 2020, the CAS said Man City did not disguise equity funding as sponsorship contributions, but did fail to cooperate with the UEFA investigation. The CAS lifted the ban from participation in UEFA club competitions and reduced the fine to €10 million.

The CAS explained that the burden of proof in establishing that Man City committed the breaches was on UEFA, and UEFA had to establish that not only did the leaked documents portray the picture they seemed to paint, but that the arrangements that the documents described *actually occurred*. The CAS concluded that there was insufficient evidence that payments made by Etihad to Man City actually came from ADUG. In addition, FFP regulations provide that prosecution for any breaches is time-barred after five years (a statute of limitations). The CAS determined that any alleged breaches that related to Man City's financial statements for the years ending in May 2012 and May 2013 are time-barred, together with the break-even information submitted for the 2013–2014 monitoring process. The CAS determined that Man City's lack of cooperation throughout the investigation process was a severe breach of FFP and should be fined.

It was hardly an exoneration for Man City, as some of UEFA's allegation were simply dismissed on the basis that they were more than five years old. Some critics commented that the ruling undermined the credibility and effectiveness of UEFA and FFP and that the size of the fine (when considering the wealth of the owner) was insufficient and would not be a future deterrent, especially since the burden of proof was determined to be on UEFA—going forward, a club could simply not cooperate

---

* Man City believed that UEFA were behind the leaks and that should have halted the investigation. Man City also cited an interview Leterme gave to the magazine *Sport & Strategy* in 2018, shortly after the hacked emails had been published by German magazine *Der Spiegel*. "If it is true what has been written, there might be a serious problem," said Leterme. "This can lead to the heaviest punishment: exclusion from the UEFA competitions." https://m.allfootballapp.com/news/EPL/UEFA-chief-slams-Manchester-Citys-unacceptable-claims-of-a-leak/2234059.

and only receive a relatively small fine.* Others also pointed out that the original formal investigation failing to discover the leaked documents, and the fact that clubs could easily hide or fabricate information or not fully cooperate, demonstrated the ineffectiveness of FPP.

The investigation also highlighted the actual or perceived (or potential) conflicts of interests. The dividing lines between a government and a private football club can seem (or become) almost indistinguishable. When the FFP rules were designed, authorities hardly anticipated a situation where the owners of football clubs and their largest potential sponsors were at such scale and so tightly intertwined, to possibly include closely government-related, private equity, and multi-club ownership models.

Under new ownership, the perception of Man City relative to their historical crosstown rival, Man U, had changed. Man City had so much more success than Man U. Liverpool legend Jamie Carragher said, "Liverpool vs. Man City has become the greatest, most intense and highest quality rivalry in English Football History [over Liverpool vs. Man U]."† In many ways, Man City's rivalries transitioned to the established big continental clubs like Real Madrid and Bayern Munich and Premier League clubs like Liverpool and Chelsea, who were regularly contenting for Champions League titles. Man U haven't won the Champions League since 2007–08, and haven't really been a threat to win a Champions League trophy in over a decade.

The identity of the club also changed. Before Sheikh Mansour, Man City's identity was *the* working-class club of Manchester. They struggled and had bad luck, in contrast to their neighbor Man U with their global brand and squad full of international superstars. Today, Man City are a global brand with international superstars and a perennial favorite to win trophies, but with an interesting twist. In April 2021, *The Athletic* wrote: "Manchester City fans have come to think of themselves as outsiders. That is something the club have embraced too. Over the past couple of years, as City's war against UEFA and its financial fair play (FFP)

---

* https://www.spiegel.de/international/europe/sponsorship-money-paid-for-by-the-state-a-2ad5b586
-1d82-4a21-8065-f3c081cd91a4.

† https://www.eurosport.com/football/premier-league/2021-2022/liverpool-v-manchester-city-greatest
-rivalry-in-english-football-history-jamie-carragher_sto8876406/story.shtml.

regulations came to a head, the arguments were spelt out. Namely, that FFP was cooked up by a cabal of elite clubs desperately trying to protect their status at the top of world football, to the exclusion of the likes of City, Paris Saint-Germain and, those clubs argued, others who may now have the backing and wherewithal to break up the game's old hegemony."* While a global power, Man City represent "outsiders"—in contrast to established, traditional clubs with long histories of winning.

In his book, Soriano wrote: "We [Barcelona] reached the conclusion that in the football industry there was a startling gap between the clubs that had become entertainment providers with global brands and the other clubs who were limited to their local markets." The commercial sponsorship opportunities and revenues for Man City becoming a global brand would do precisely what he said in his book—create a wave of player transfer fees and salary inflation. However, he and other Man City executives had a brilliant strategy to deal with the inflation Man City was helping create—the multi-club ownership (MCO) model. An MCO model would provide financial and commercial synergies, including helping clubs to save on transfer fees.

MULTI-CLUB OWNERSHIP (MCO) MODEL

In 1998, UEFA implemented regulations related to the integrity of UEFA club competitions. A key clause of the regulations was that no two clubs can be directly or indirectly controlled by the same entity or person to the point where they have "decisive influence."† The regulation's aim was to prevent and prohibit a conflict of interest between clubs in the same competition.

In 2000, ENIC (an investment company with stakes in six European football clubs) lodged a complaint with the European Commission

---

* https://theathletic.com/2528722/2021/04/19/european-super-league-manchester-city-have -swapped-sides-they-are-betraying-their-fans/.

† Interest in another club is defined by three main points: having majority voting rights in two or more clubs, having the right to appoint or remove board members and authoritative figures in two or more clubs (such as a manager or sporting director), and, finally, owning shares in two or more clubs competing in the same competition.

against the rule, claiming that it distorts competition by preventing and restricting investment in European clubs. The Commission, however, rejected ENIC's claim, stating that the rule can be justified by the need to guarantee the integrity of the competitions.

Following the initial implementation of the UEFA rules, the Court of Arbitration for Sport (CAS) ruled that any shareholding of 50.1 percent or more in a second club would potentially breach the UEFA rules. However, there is considerable disparity in the regulations around club ownership in different national associations. For example, the Premier League rules define control as having a shareholding of 30 percent or more (therefore, anyone with a stake of 30 percent or higher in a Premier League club can't own another English club), whereas under the UEFA rules, it would be possible for someone to have 100 percent ownership in one club and a 49.9 percent stake in another club competing in the same competition.

At the end of the 2016–2017 season, both Red Bull Leipzig (German Bundesliga) and FC Red Bull Salzburg (Austrian Football Bundesliga) qualified on merit from their respective leagues for the UEFA Champions League 2017–18 season. Since both clubs are ultimately funded and affiliated in some manner by Red Bull, questions had arisen as to whether UEFA's rule against common ownership would mean that both clubs would be prevented from competing in the UEFA Champions League at the same time. After an investigation, UEFA made a statement in June 2017:

> Following a thorough investigation, and further to several important governance and structural changes made by the clubs (regarding corporate matters, financing, personnel, sponsorship arrangement, etc.) . . . [UEFA] deemed that no individual or legal entity had anymore a decisive influence over more than one club participating in a UEFA club competition . . . [therefore UEFA] has decided to accept the admission of both FC Salzburg and RB Leipzig to the UEFA Champions League 2017/2018, having found that Article 5 (Integrity of the competition) of the competition regulations is not breached.

The key decision gave the multiple-club ownership (MCO) model a huge boost.

Multi-club ownership has grown significantly in football since the decision, and the trend isn't slowing down. According to research by international professional services firm Deloitte, over seventy MCOs were thought to be in existence in 2022, more than double the amount only five years ago (twenty-eight MCOs).

The practice is becoming noticeably common in the Premier League, as nine clubs in the league (Arsenal, Brentford, Brighton, Crystal Palace, Leicester City, Man City, Nottingham Forest, Southampton, West Ham) have an MCO model. One division down in the Championship, there are six MCO model clubs (Cardiff, Queens Park Rangers, Sheffield United, Sunderland, Swansea, Watford). A combined twenty clubs from LaLiga, Serie A, and Ligue 1 are MCO model clubs.

Closely government-related entities, private equity funds, Red Bull, and others are utilizing the MCO model in multiple sports, or just football, for several reasons.

Intellectual Property (IP) / Know-How. Knowledge of how to operate a sports business on the field (health, performance, data analytics) and off the field (sponsorship, pricing, stadium experience, entertainment) is a key asset because of the scarcity of teams. Gaining exposure across regulatory and league contexts enhances an organization's global insights, adding to group knowledge and best practice sharing.

Scale. The ability to use or shift fixed cost resources (marketing, scouting, technology) over more clubs and larger revenues base. Also, the ability to cross-brand or cross-sell more clubs to sponsors as a package to reach more fans. This enables an entity to collect more data on their fans, which is very commercially valuable, and to place more salespeople in more markets to build and service more global sponsor relationships, which increases total addressable market. It also allows the costs of specialist expertise to be spread across a large portfolio, and supports more experimentation, with more clubs available to introduce new technologies or experiments.

Risk Diversification. Access to revenues from different sources reduces the impact of idiosyncratic league shocks and financial volatility from on-pitch performance. Also, it can increase organizational and operational stability. In football specifically, diversification could also mean dampening the negative financial impact of relegation, as resources (including players) could be moved.

In Football, Better Scouting. Having a global network of scouts enables clubs to capture more players playing at their academies. It also makes more player data available and brings access to more local knowledge. Finding players at younger ages and saving on transfer fees has become increasingly important in football.

In Football, Better Player Pathway. Clubs save on transfer fees as players can be developed and moved from different academies and clubs under the same ownership. Players at the affiliated clubs learn a particular style and understand the culture, and are more likely to stay (even if for slightly lower salaries). Clubs can be patient with young stars and keep them within their system, and get them playing time (instead of loaning out players and losing control of their development). Longer talent retention can maximize value creation. And in concert with scouting, the finding, developing, and selling of elite players has become increasingly important to generating profits and cash for football clubs.

In Football, More Power. It's a simple equation: owning more clubs can mean more power and influence.

There can be significant synergies in multi-club ownership—and various MCOs are at various stages of execution and realizing those synergies. In most of the cases of the MCO model, there is a "star" club, with one club that's the pinnacle in terms of brand and philosophy, and a number of other clubs that are associated with or feed into that organization. The star club has the institutional knowledge of how to operate a sports business on the field (health, performance, data analytics) and off the field (sponsorship, pricing, stadium experience, entertainment). This IP is very valuable because there are few sports teams, and even fewer that are professionally run. For example, when the Glazers bought Man U, they brought new professional American sport management ideas, especially regarding marketing, sponsorship, and stadium experience, from their experience with the NFL and Tampa Bay Buccaneers. All of which increased Man U's revenues.

In 2022, Man City's holding group owns majority or minority stakes in thirteen football clubs worldwide, including Man City (UK), NYCFC (USA), Melbourne (Australia), Yokohama F. Marinos (Japan), Montevideo City Torque (Uruguay), Sichuan Jiuniu (China), Mumbai City FC (India), Lommel SK (Belgium), Esperance Sportive Troyes Aube Champagne (France), Club Bolivia Club (Bolivia), Palermo (Italy), Girona FC (Spain), and Bahia (Brazil). They have created a network of clubs that gives them an ability to develop and extend a commercial presence and fan engagement as well as football scouting and development. They control the contracts and data of more football players, and the data of more fans, than any other entity worldwide. The value is in the system that puts it all together and makes it useful to everybody. Other investors and investment groups have multiple football clubs, but none operates at a similar scale.

Having many clubs grants the ability to use or shift fixed cost resources (marketing, scouting, technology) over more clubs. The MCO model enables a larger revenue base, and the capability to cross-brand or cross-sell to sponsors to reach more fans.

The MCO model also interacts with player development. City Football Group (CFG), which is the holding company of Man City and their other clubs, has established a consistent way of playing, one that has come to be associated with Guardiola's Man City: possession, constant pressure on the ball, short passes, building from the back. This consistency allows players to move between CFG's clubs more easily. That in turn both enhances player pathways, establishing particular player development goals, and supports a style-of-play brand. If a fan is attracted to that style, then CFG has other clubs for you. The scale of the ownership group enables them to spread the costs of a global marketing department or global scouting network. An MCO club has lots of data on their players, beyond their performances in matches, that it can share with its affiliates. Most importantly, the MCO model helps clubs track player development and save on transfer fees, one of the biggest expenses for a big football club.

Let's consider an MCO case study. Founded in 1987, Red Bull is an Austrian energy drink brand, probably the most famous energy drink in the world. However, the company's co-creators—Dietrich Mateschitz, an Austrian entrepreneur, and Chaleo Yoovidhya, a Thai businessman— were always keen to expand beyond an energy drink.

In 2005, Red Bull purchased SV Austria Salzburg, a football club in Mateschitz's native country. They changed the club's name to FC Red Bull Salzburg. In the subsequent years, they bought up other clubs in other countries, creating a global network united by a shared owner- ship and a consistent set of principles and business practices. In total, the brand has now invested in six football clubs (FC Red Bull Salzburg, RB Leipzig, NY Red Bulls, Red Bull Bragantino, FC Liefering, Red Bull Ghana*), and a total of over fifteen sports teams across eleven sports (including Formula 1, Rallycross, Ice Hockey, Skateboarding, Surfing).†

The Red Bull franchise allows each team within the multi-club own- ership model to compete in their domestic leagues, while maintaining close links with the other Red Bull clubs, who can act as feeder clubs. RB Leipzig are at the center of this network (parent club), essentially the final destination for talent that has been nurtured by the other clubs. Once feeder clubs such as the MLS's New York Red Bulls and Brazil's Red Bull Bragantino (who are highly competitive domestic sides in their own right) have developed and nurtured talent, they'll generally be trans- ferred to Europe, where they can then be sold for profits.

The success of their model hinges on clever strategic planning and close synergy between clubs. Many duties in HR, finance, marketing, and information are centralized.

Red Bull's MCO model is arguably the most visible multi-club own- ership model at the elite level in Europe, with both Leipzig and Austria's

---

* Red Bull Ghana was founded in 2008 and abolished in 2014.
† https://jobsinfootball.com/blog/red-bull-soccer-teams/.

RB Salzburg.* Unlike Red Bull, which has put versions of its energy drink logo on football clubs, City Football Group is a holding company, not a consumer brand. It does not exist from a consumer perspective. CFG's link between its clubs is subtle. At clubs that had little or no history when they were acquired, such as New York, Melbourne, and Mumbai, they adopt Man City's light-blue color scheme. When CFG adds a club that already has a strong identity, it retains the acquired club's branding.

The recruitment, development, and selling of players is just one aspect of the game that looks set to change profoundly as a result of the MCO model. By owning a club in Brazil, for example, Red Bull will gain better insight into the most promising players. It has also bought itself access to domestic infrastructure in Brazil, and a better understanding of the marketplace. On top of that, Red Bull has an easy proposition for players it might want to acquire: a place at a club in the player's home country where they can develop, before a riskier move to Europe.

Red Bull is essentially creating a supply chain for talent. For example, Brazilian player Igor joined Red Bull's youth academy in Brazil. After impressing with the U-20 side, in 2016 he was transferred to Austrian second-tier club FC Liefering, which are owned by Red Bull and function as a feeder club for RB Salzburg. He was promoted to RB Salzburg, and then later sold to Italy's SPAL for €3 million in 2019.

The development of Igor, resulting in €3 million over just a few years, was profitable for Red Bull. To use a baseball analogy, Igor's transfer was a single that helped cover the costs for the potential home run. The transfer of Guinean player Naby Keïta from RB Leipzig to Liverpool for €60 million in 2018 also highlights the potential "home run" power of the MCO model. In 2016, RB Salzburg sold Keïta to RB Leipzig for €29.75 million. RB Salzburg did even better than Leipzig. They brought Keïta to Austria from the French third division side Istres two years before for €1.5 million.

---

* While Man City and Red Bull may be among the most recognizable multi-club owners, Italian businessman Giampaolo Pozzo was one of the pioneers. He currently owns Udinese in Italy's top-flight Serie A and English club Watford. Girona, of the Spanish top-tier LaLiga, were also under his stewardship between 2009 and 2016. He believes MCO allowed him to expand Udinese's know-how and align elements of the clubs' developments, both on and off the pitch, as is still the case between Udinese and Watford.

The MCO model has some critics. Antonia Hagemann, chief executive officer of Supporters Direct Europe, says: "It creates different tiers of clubs: the parent and a feeder club. If you are a fan of a parent club then you are lucky, but not if you are a fan of a feeder club. It could also be the end of transfers as we know it, as there could only be transfers between clubs. As a player you can start off with a feeder club and move up to a parent club, but this promotes inequality and poisons the competitiveness of the market. If you have this group of clubs that trade between themselves and shift players back and forth, it is cheaper and puts them at a competitive advantage." [*][†]

At some MCOs, there is a clear attempt to establish a group philosophy in terms of pooling resources and imposing a common playing style, which can allow players to move more easily from smaller to larger clubs within the network. Although international players union FIFPRO has said any clauses in contracts that force players to move to another club in an MCO against their will would be "abusive," this type of intra-group trading has benefits for the owners.[‡]

Shifting players between clubs within the same MCO means the transfer fees stay in-house. However, some critics believe that fees agreed between affiliated clubs can be manipulated, such as shifting costs onto one club to potentially reduce taxes or circumvent FFP. In addition, if eventually there are a handful of MCOs with a lot of clubs, that gives

---

[*] https://www.playthegame.org/news/multi-club-ownership-in-football-challenges-governance-at-many-levels/.

[†] John Textor's multi-club ownership model is a little different. While Man City's approach has been to buy relatively smaller clubs than Man City as a part of a pyramid to feed talented players to itself, the American businessman has been trying to buy stakes in relatively similar clubs. He controls Olympique Lyonnais (France), Botafogo (Brazil), and RWD Molenbeek (Belgium) and owns a 40 percent stake in Premier League's Crystal Palace (U.K.). Textor argues that the goal of his MCO model is to create synergies and aims to become more efficient, save money, and get joint sponsor deals. He sees close collaboration between relatively similar clubs as a part of their competitive advantage.

[‡] The Fédération Internationale des Associations de Footballeurs Professionnels, generally referred to as FIFPRO, is the worldwide representative organization for around 65,000 professional football players. FIFPRO, with its global headquarters in Hoofddorp, Netherlands, is made up of sixty-six national players' associations.

them more power and influence within the football ecosystem than single-owned clubs.

Regulators are studying and considering the purposes and implications of MCOs.

Man City: "Existential Threat"

From Robinson and Clegg's *The Club*:

> There was, however, one topic nearly all of the [Premier] League seems to agree on . . . Manchester City was turning into an existential threat to English football . . . It wasn't the astronomical sums of money that they were spending either . . . there had been individuals prepared to buy success on the football pitch . . . The Premier League had welcomed them in, emptied their wallets, and continued along its merry way. But there was something about the way Manchester City combined these two things that made this time feel different and more dangerous . . . they weren't just merely outspending the rest of the league, they were spending them into oblivion . . . the most expensive squad ever assembled . . . the world's most brilliant coach . . . And a youth academy stacked with top-class teenage talent. When would it all end?
>
> Those inside English football had a different question on their minds: When does it start to undermine the whole point of showing up? . . .
>
> It wasn't the team on the field or the money in the bank. It was the vision. Unlimited ambition, laser like focus, and all the money in the world to execute it. No team had ever offered such a complete threat . . .
>
> Now its [Premier League] supremacy was threatening to fall apart. Because when it comes to outsize global ambition, it turned out that the best empire builders were from places like Abu Dhabi. And they weren't interested in the picayune details of competitive balance or health of the league or the way things had been done.
>
> They were interested in building monuments.
>
> In November 2022, Man City released its annual report for the 2021–22 season, announcing the highest-ever revenues in the club's history. In

June 2023, Man City won the UEFA Champions League for the first time thanks to a 1–0 win over Inter in Istanbul.

From my perspective, many new wealthy owners blindly spend money thinking that money and talent leads to trophies. Or perhaps they overly rely on data analytics. However, Man City are unique—they have all three (money, talent, and data analytics), *plus* they have quickly established a culture and style of play that take precedence over any individual star player. Their style of play, like Barcelona's, gives players defined roles in a system so that when substitutions or rotations are required, there is less disruption. And with a congested calendar, rotations for rest and recovery are very important. This gives Man City (and Barcelona) an advantage over a thirty-eight-match domestic league season. The culture and style of play are distributed to their other clubs. And with the largest MCO model, they also have the most data about the most players and fans. They also can test various strategies, techniques, and technologies at different clubs.

The real questions are: What will happen to the culture and style of play when Pep Guardiola leaves? Have they codified them and put in place lasting supporting pillars? Only time will tell. Man U and Arsenal struggled after the departure of their legendary managers, who created and embodied their cultures.

Will Man City ever break even? The group lost £138 million in 2021–22 and their total losses over the last decade top £1.3 billion.* Is this sustainable, and good for football?

MCO MODEL + PRIVATE EQUITY

City Football Group's MCO model became a blueprint for groups with money, including other closely related government entities and U.S. private equity investors. In particular, private equity and institutional investors started looking for opportunities to buy a scarce "platform" asset (parent club) benefiting from growing revenues (growing TV rights), and combine it with financial engineering (acquisitions of "feeder clubs") to create synergies (parent club with global network with feeder clubs) to generate returns.

* https://theathletic.com/4432985/2023/04/20/newcastle-united-kv-oostende/.

In 2019, U.S. private equity firm Silver Lake purchased a 10 percent stake, which has grown with additional investments to an 18 percent stake, in Man City (UAE state-owned Mubadala Investment Company [MIC] also owns a stake in Silver Lake). Silver Lake focuses on investments in technology and technology-enabled and related industries and invested in Dell and Skype.* In addition, they own a 33 percent stake in the Australian A-League. They see sports as digital media outlets that can create new ways via technology to connect with more fans globally and make money from them. A Man City spokesman said:

> We and Silver Lake share the strong belief in the opportunities being presented by the convergence of entertainment, sports, and technology and the resulting ability for CFG [City Football Group] to generate long-term growth and new revenue streams globally . . . CFG's teams play 2,500 games each year and employ more than 2,000 people in 12 locations around the world . . . a large network of scouts and consultants and commercial and marketing team members based all over the world serving these different clubs . . . So the usage of technology helps us to stay connected to our staff, to our partners, to our fans, and we really have made an effort to find the right partners that can help us develop those tools to be able to do everything.

Silver Lake also saw the value in customer data. Sports fans are unique and devoted consumers. A sports fan is the optimal customer, frequently promoting and communicating about their favorite brand. Imagine how many CFG fans entered their stadiums using a smartphone that held their ticket on an application, or purchased a jersey, and could be tracked. Some believe that a sports team's database of fans (including their contact information and ticket and retail purchase history) is one of their most valuable assets.

---

* In 2016, Silver Lake invested in mixed martial arts organization UFC. In 2021, Silver Lake purchased a 33.3 percent stake in Australian national association football leagues. In 2022, Silver Lake bought a 5.7 percent stake in New Zealand's All Blacks rugby team.

The owners of the data can send customized messages or promotions to targeted groups of fans. They can tell sponsors the demographics, behavior, and preferences of fans and demonstrate how they match with a sponsor's brand, image, and messaging. Brands are investing more resources into becoming consumer- and fan-centric because they see the continuously changing landscape driven by tightening data privacy regulations and heightened consumer expectations. Today, brands want to build longer-term relationships with their consumers that are more tailored, personalized, and rewarding. By maximizing the value of their customer data, sports teams can differentiate themselves by creating revenue-generating ideas for boosting attendance, driving engagement and brand affinity with unique fan and consumer experiences, and growing sponsorship opportunities.

Lastly, the benefit of having a portfolio of clubs is that owners have more clubs to introduce new technologies or other experiments. In 2019, Man City's owners were the anchor investor in Sapphire Sport, a new $115 million venture capital fund focused on technology and digital sports, including gaming, digital health, digital commerce, and next-generation media. CFG can introduce the venture capital portfolio companies to its portfolio of clubs and help create value for both parties. Some CFG clubs may be early adopters, and interested based on their local conditions, and others may want to see the results of their affiliates before trying new technology.

The biggest splash for private equity so far was in May 2022. A consortium led by Los Angeles Dodgers 20 percent owner Todd Boehly and Clearlake Capital completed its takeover of Chelsea in a deal with a commitment of up to £4.25 billion ($7.4 billion)—£2.5 billion for the club itself, plus £1.75 billion toward investment on and off the pitch over the next decade.* The deal was the most expensive for a sports team in

---

* Boehly is the face of the consortium, but the bulk of the financing comes from Clearlake Capital, a private equity firm based in Santa Monica, California, and owned by Behdad Eghbali and Jose E. Feliciano. Clearlake will be the majority shareholder, but other prominent figures involved include Swiss billionaire Hansjörg Wyss; chief executive of Guggenheim Partners Mark Walter, who also owns a stake in the Dodgers and the L.A. Lakers; London-based property developer Jonathan Goldstein; and Danny Finkelstein, former adviser to ex–U.K. prime minister David Cameron.

history at the time, and includes a commitment not to sell a controlling stake in Chelsea for at least ten years.

Boehly revealed that his hope is for Chelsea to follow the examples of CFG and Red Bull by adopting a global MCO model in order to aid the development of players. At a conference in September 2022, he revealed: "We've talked about having a multi-club model . . . I would love to continue to build out the footprint. There are different countries where there's advantages to having a club. Red Bull does a really good job at Leipzig and they've got Salzburg, both of which are playing in the Champions League so they've figured out how to make that work. You have Man City which has a very big network of clubs . . . The challenge Chelsea has, when you have 18, 19, 20-year-old stars, you can loan them out to clubs but you hand their development to someone else. Our goal is to ensure we show pathways for our young stars to get on to the Chelsea pitch while getting them real game time. The way to do that is through another club in a really competitive league in Europe."[*]

There are other U.S.-based private equity groups pursing an MCO model. RedBird Capital Partners followed up their acquisition of French Ligue 1 club Toulouse in 2020 by purchasing AC Milan for around €1.2 billion ($1.2 billion) in 2022. The firm also holds a stake in Premier League giants Liverpool after acquiring an 11 percent stake in the club's owners, Fenway Sports Group (FSG), in 2021. RedBird's managing director, Gerry Cardinale (in full disclosure, Gerry and I were in the same analyst and associate classes at Goldman Sachs), is a big proponent of MCO. Speaking at the Leaders Business Summit in London in 2022, he explained:

> We've been pioneering the multi-team concept for two reasons. Firstly, diversification is risk-prudent, but more importantly with the things we do, we're so integrated operationally and investment-wise that to put that kind of effort and infrastructure in place, you really want to be able to federalize that out to all the

* https://www.espn.com/soccer/english-premier-league/story/4745442/chelseas-todd-boehly-eyes-us -style-all-star-game-for-premier-league; https://www.dailymail.co.uk/sport/football/article-11210789 /Todd-Boehly-held-talks-purchasing-Portuguese-club-summer.html.

pieces of intellectual property that you touch . . . The team that we put together, whether it's in the U.S. with FSG, Toulouse, or now with Milan, they're doing the same thing, it's all the same construct. There is a synergy there and best practices that you can do across all these assets. I believe the sum of the parts is greater than the whole if you can put these together and what is coming to sports is different types of capital.

In July 2023, UEFA cleared RedBird's AC Milan and Toulouse to compete in European tournaments. UEFA said, "Following the implementation of significant changes by the clubs and their related investors, [UEFA] accepted admission of the aforementioned clubs to the UEFA club competitions for the 2023/24 season . . . More specifically, the significant changes that were implemented relate to ownership, governance, and financing structure of the concerned clubs . . . The clubs will not be allowed to transfer players to each other—permanently or on loan—until September 2024 and cannot share scouting databases."*

In addition to RedBird, another private equity group, 777 Partners, has been extremely active in football with several acquisitions. The firm has invested hundreds of millions of dollars to take controlling stakes in several clubs: Italy's Genoa, Belgium's Standard de Liege, France's Red Star FC, Brazil's Vasco da Gama, and Germany's Hertha BSC.† 777 Partners has minority stakes in Australian A-League's Melbourne Victory and LaLiga's Seville.

PSG: CLOSELY GOVERNMENT-RELATED + MCO + PE MODEL

On November 23, 2010, French football icon Michel Platini (and head of UEFA and vice president of FIFA at the time) walked into the Élysée Palace, the official residence of the president of the French Republic, near

---

* https://www.reuters.com/sports/soccer/uefa-relax-multi-club-ownership-rules-allow-milan-villa -compete-europe-2023-07-07/.

† A planned acquisition of Everton by 777 Partners encountered a long and drawn-out process with several challenges.

the Champs-Élysées, to have lunch with French president Nicolas Sarkozy and his chief of staff, Claude Guéant. Platini discovered he wasn't
the only one—other guests included officials from Qatar, including then-
crown prince Sheikh Tamim bin Hamad Al Thani of Qatar (who has
since succeeded his father, Hamad, as the country's emir) and the then-
prime minister, Sheikh Hamad bin Jassim.*

Nine days later, on December 2, 2010, Qatar was awarded the rights
to host the 2022 FIFA World Cup.† Qatar has repeatedly denied any alle-
gations of acting improperly in securing its World Cup bid. Qatar main-
tains that it strictly adhered to all rules and regulations for the FIFA
World Cup bidding, and any claim to the contrary is baseless. A two-year
inquiry by FIFA's ethics committee found no significant concerns.

Qatar explained that their aim was to build bridges between East and
West and better the world's understanding of the Middle East—offering
fans around the world a chance to see the region's natural beauty, the
richness of Arab culture, the positivity and warmth of its people, their
passion for football, and their aspirations for the future. Like Sheikh
Mansour and the UAE, this was important because of the West's criticism of Qatar's human rights record and common misconceptions and
stereotypes about the Middle East.‡

One week after Qatar won the right to host the World Cup, on
December 10, 2010, Barcelona signed a deal to have a commercial sponsor

---

* Qatar is on the northeastern coast of the Arabian Peninsula and shares its sole land border with
Saudi Arabia to the south, with the rest of its territory surrounded by the Persian Gulf. The capital
is Doha. Following Ottoman rule, Qatar became a British protectorate in 1916, and gained independence and joined the UN in 1971. Oil reserves were first discovered in 1939, but development was
delayed by World War II and oil exports began in 1949. In the 1990s the exploitation of natural gas
grew, and concurrently the nation's economy grew quickly. Before discovering oil and gas within its
borders, Qatar's population was one of the poorest in the world. Pearling, fishing, and trade were the
main ways to make a living.

† Reportedly, Platini cast the deciding vote in Qatar's favor (allegedly he had been leaning toward a
bid from the USA). In 2015, Platini said: "Sarkozy never asked me to vote for Qatar, but I knew what
would be good." He claims that he had made his decision to vote for Qatar before the lunch, and
he had requested the lunch with Sarkozy to inform him of his decision. https://www.ft.com/content
/d45b1e6e-91df-11e9-b7ea-60e35ef678d2. Sarkozy has denied influencing Platini to vote for Qatar.

‡ Again, it can be challenging and complicated to evaluate or judge the complex cultures of other
countries. See note on page 148.

on their shirt—for the first time in their 111-year history.* The sponsor was the Qatar Foundation, a not-for-profit organization founded in 1995, dependent on the Qatari state, and dedicated to education, science, and community development.† The Qatar Foundation was to pay the Catalan club €30 million (£25 million) a year for five years, with further bonuses payable according to success on the field. The €150 million deal was the biggest shirt sponsorship deal in football history at the time, and was worth double the €15 million a season earned by Real Madrid from the bookmakers Bwin.‡ A Barcelona vice president described the deal as the "biggest in the history of football—and at a time of economic crisis, too . . . [and] would not have been signed if it were not for the debt which, as we have said before, is between €420m and €430m." Qatar would get its name not only on the shirts but on the Camp Nou facade, on the iconic stadium's seats (next to the Nike logo), and the museum.

In February 2011, before the lunch, the royal family of Qatar reportedly prepared a new £1.5 billion bid for Man U after the Glazers allegedly rejected an earlier offer of just over £1 billion. The bid was turned down by the Americans, who were supposedly holding out for closer to £1.8 billion. Reportedly, the Al Thanis were partly motivated by the rivalry with the Abu Dhabi royal family, whose wealth had transformed Man U's archrivals Man City into title contenders.§ At the time, Man U was third in the Deloitte Football Money League, behind Real Madrid and Barcelona (neither of which could be bought since they are owned by members).

Around six months after the lunch in Paris, in May 2011, Qatar Sports Investments (QSI) purchased control of French football club Paris

---

* UNICEF was the first name ever to appear on Barcelona's blue-and-red shirts when a deal was signed in 2004. Unlike traditional sponsorship deals, Barcelona pay UNICEF €1.5 million a year toward AIDS projects to carry its name on the shirt.

† Barcelona's then-manager, Pep Guardiola, was an ambassador for Qatar's 2022 World Cup bid. Guardiola has past ties to Qatar, having played for Al-Ahli SC (Doha) toward the end of his career. Guardiola declined an invitation to go to the 2022 World Cup in person in Qatar and took Man City players not playing in the World Cup to Abu Dhabi for a week for warm training.

‡ The deal included a clause allowing a switch in sponsor after the first two seasons, so Qatar Airways took over as the main sponsor in 2013.

§ https://www.dailymail.co.uk/sport/football/article-1360043/Qatari-royal-family-1-5bn-bid-buy-Manchester-United-Glazers.html.

Saint-Germain (PSG) from U.S. private equity group Colony Capital, for a reported €70 million.* (It is important to note that QSI was in discussions to buy PSG two years before the acquisition and before the lunch with Sarkozy and Platini.)

PSG had been in financial difficulties. Sarkozy is a die-hard fan of PSG. While president of France, Sarkozy wanted Qatar to buy PSG and played an active role in brokering the purchase.

PSG immediately went on a spending spree to construct a team to challenge for the Champions League trophy. And the Qatar media conglomerate beIN (at the time a part of Al Jazeera) brought competition into domestic TV rights by buying the rights to broadcast Ligue 1 matches—which increased the broadcasting and sponsorship money into French football.

In August 2012, PSG signed a huge "nation branding" deal with the Qatar Tourism Authority (QTA) to promote Qatar. The Qatari government branch agreed to pay PSG €1 billion over five seasons, including €100 million for the first season. The partnership was made official in October 2013, but the contract stipulated two retroactive payments of €100 million and €200 million for the 2011–12 and 2012–13 seasons, respectively, thus effectively eliminating PSG's losses for that period— which was important as it relates to FFP.†

Fast-forward to August 2017. PSG activated the €222 million release clause of Barcelona for Brazilian player Neymar, making him the most expensive transfer in football history. Later that month, PSG signed a loan and option to buy a deal for €180 million (divided into three installments) with Monaco for French national player Kylian Mbappé.‡

---

* Qatar registered its bid for the 2022 World Cup in 2009.

† In 2014, UEFA halved the value of the deal from €200 million to €100 million. UEFA's revised valuation saw PSG's deficit for the 2013–14 season reach €107 million, more than double the amount allowed under FFP rules, which at the time limited losses to €45 million over the last two years. Inevitably, UEFA fined PSG for violating FFP rules in May 2014. In August 2016, PSG and the QTA renewed their partnership until June 2019, after their initial four-year contract expired in June 2016.

‡ In the January 2023, transfer market Chelsea have spent more than €600 million on new signings ($650 million), including €120 million for World Cup winner Enzo from Benfica. When asked about the spending of Chelsea at a news conference, Guardiola said: "It's none of my business. *It's a surprise because it's not a club state* . . . There are regulations, I don't forget the eight or nine teams that sent a

To outsiders, it seemed that the signings couldn't be compliant with FFP—how could PSG pay the two highest transfer fees in history in the same month, and then pay their enormous salaries and stay within the rules? UEFA subsequently started an investigation, and eventually the lead investigator (former Belgian prime minister Yves Leterme, who also worked on the Man City case) cleared PSG.* According to documents obtained by the *New York Times*, PSG's defense lay in its accounting, and its argument that rich sponsorship deals with Qatari entities like the telecom company Ooredoo, the Qatar National Bank, and, most crucially, the Qatar Tourism Authority had helped make possible the purchases of Neymar and Mbappé and other world-class players.

The agreement with the Qatar Tourism Authority for "nation branding" was PSG's highest sponsorship deal, more than €100 million ($111 million) per season. According to the *New York Times*, sports marketing company Octagon Worldwide valued the deal at less than €5 million, but UEFA used an amount closer to the amount (reportedly €60 million) that was provided by media measurement and data company Nielsen. In 2014, UEFA halved the value of the deal from €200 million to €100 million.†

With the help of their sponsorships (and player sales), PSG incurred a loss of €24 million over the three-year period—less than the FFP limit. Javier Tebas, the head of LaLiga, said, "There are clubs who could not care less what their real incomes are when they want to sign a player because they receive incomes from a state. It forces other clubs into an economic situation which is really living on the edge. It skews the

letter to the Premier League to get us banned." https://www.espn.com/soccer/liverpool-engliverpool/story/4867959/kloppguardiola-question-chelseas-transfer-spending.

* Diplomatic relations between the State of Qatar and Belgium were established in the 1970s. Since 2004, bilateral relations witnessed noticeable improvements in different aspects of development and cooperation between them. Bilateral economic ties were enhanced in 2007; a contract regarding supplying the Kingdom of Belgium with the Qatari liquefied natural was signed in March 2007. https://brussels.embassy.qa/en/belgium/qatar-belgium-relations. On December 21, 2007, Yves Leterme became vice prime minister of Belgium and minister of Budget, Transport, Institutional Reform and the North Sea.

† UEFA also warned PSG that the QTA contract would not be taken into account beyond June 2019. PSG also brought in the €50 million and €60 million in player sales before the end of June 2018 and 2019, respectively, that UEFA demanded to comply to FFP. https://www.nytimes.com/2019/07/24/sports/psg-uefa-ffp.html.

balance of the entire European football structure."* The case raised questions about UEFA's commitment to enforcing its FFP rules. A July 2019 article by Tariq Panja for the *New York Times* was titled: "In P.S.G. Case, Documents Show UEFA Surrendered Without a Fight: Disputed Facts and an Investigator's Calculations Raise Questions About European Soccer's Commitment to Enforcing Its Financial Fair-Play Rules."†

LaLiga's FFP

LaLiga implemented their own Financial Fair Play regulations for Spain's top two divisions in 2013. Many believe the rules are far stricter and more effective than those imposed by UEFA and most domestic leagues. In Spain, LaLiga sets each team a different squad-cost limit, limiting the money spent both on transfers and staff wages, including non-playing staff. This is set before the summer transfer window to prevent any unsustainable or anti-competitive spending before it can even take place, unlike in the rest of Europe. This limit is calculated looking at a range of factors, from clubs' prospective earnings to past profits and losses to savings. The league employs several accountants to do the calculations, and when a club signs a player and attempts to register them with the league's "LaLiga Manager" software, the signing must be first deemed within FFP by LaLiga before they can be registered.

In November 2023, LaLiga introduced a series of measures designed to relax its economic controls as a part of efforts to allow Spanish clubs to be more competitive in the transfer market. In the summer of 2023, LaLiga teams spent the lowest amount on new signings among Europe's Top 5 Leagues, with a total spend of €453 million—compared with €3.018 billion and €767 million for Premier League and Bundesliga teams, respectively.

LaLiga received criticism when Barcelona were unable to register several players in the summer of 2021, which led to Lionel Messi leaving for PSG. However, LaLiga FFP rules saved Barcelona from incurring even more losses

---

* Tebas is president of the European Leagues, which represents Ligue 1 and other leagues. The financial sustainability rules he repeatedly complains about are the very same rules that he helped create and approved as recently as the UEFA ExCo on May 10, 2022.

† https://www.nytimes.com/2019/07/24/sports/psg-uefa-ffp.html.

and facing far bigger challenges. It was Barcelona's unsustainable wages and transfer fees and lack of foresight that led to Messi leaving, not LaLiga.

Real Madrid have a strict salary structure, which also helps keep harmony in the locker room. This was a reason why Ronaldo had to be sold to Juventus in 2018 after making demands to match Messi's pay at Barcelona. In 2018, *Diario AS* journalist Manu Sainz wrote, "The market last summer [2017] went crazy . . . Messi is earning €40 million net with his new contract. Neymar is on €30–35 million, and Cristiano, who has just won the Ballon d'Or, is far behind them on around €24 million net."* If Ronaldo was paid more, then other players may also ask for more. This is precisely what happened at Barcelona—other players' salaries increased commensurately with Messi's, and all of the increases (not just Messi's contract) contributed to Barcelona's difficult financial situation.

UEFA wanted to reopen the case due to concerns over the lead investigator's work, but PSG appealed to the Court of Arbitration of Sport (CAS) that the lead investigator's decision should stand. The CAS ruled in PSG's favor. PSG issued a short statement: "The club reiterates that we have always respected the [FFP] rules and that we have endeavored to respond calmly and transparently to repeated requests from UEFA."

The outcome of the case also highlighted the close relationship between the club's Qatari ownership and UEFA. PSG's president, Nasser Al-Khelaifi, sits on UEFA's executive committee, is the chairman of the powerful European Club Association (ECA), and is also the chairman of beIN Media Group, the Qatar-based broadcaster that has committed billions to secure television rights from UEFA and other sports partners.† The U.K. had put restrictions in place for Rupert Murdoch and

---

* https://bleacherreport.com/articles/2752348-why-cristiano-ronaldos-contract-is-again-becoming-an-issue-for-real-madrid.

† The roles of PSG president, ECA chairman, and UEFA ExCo member are the exact same Lineage—each role is, in turn, and by definition, only possible by having the former. Just like Andrea Agnelli of Juventus and Karl-Heinz Rummenigge of Bayern Munich before, Nasser's role on the UEFA ExCo is as an ECA representative—he is there representing the ECA, which is different from being a UEFA representative. The ECA is to hold UEFA accountable. Nasser is chairman, not operational executive CEO, of beIN. Each company Nasser is connected to has their own legal conflicts process. If there is even a risk or perception of conflict—not even an actual conflict—he is recused from meetings. Ironically, when selected stakeholders request Nasser's help (e.g., French domestic

other broadcasters from controlling football clubs, limiting them to a less than 10 percent stake. Fans protested Sky owning Man U. Imagine if Murdoch sat on the Premier League board, controlled Man U, and controlled Sky (which bought the Premier League rights). In interviews, Nasser Al-Khelaifi insists that he is helping the football ecosystem and that his lawyers advise him when conflicts exist and when he should recuse himself.

Fears That Rules Don't Apply to All

In August 2022, *New York Times* reporter Tariq Panja wrote an article titled: "At Top of European Soccer, Fears That Rules Don't Apply to All." In March 2022, Real Madrid came from behind in remarkable fashion to eliminate PSG in the Round of 16 in the Champions League. After the match, Nasser Al-Khelaifi and his sporting director, Leonardo, allegedly went to the referee changing rooms to express their frustration about the refereeing. The *New York Times* reviewed a report by the referee that described "aggressive behavior" and even blocking the door when asked to leave. Panja wrote: "The events created a crisis for European soccer's governing body, UEFA. Al-Khelaifi is one of the most powerful men in the European game, an executive whose multiple roles—including a place on UEFA's top board and a post as chairman of a media company that funnels hundreds of millions of dollars into European soccer through broadcast deals—have long aroused conflict-of-interest concerns." (In interviews, Nasser Al-Khelaifi insists that he is helping the football ecosystem and that his lawyers advise him when conflicts exist and when he should recuse himself. UEFA president Aleksander Čeferin says he understands the potential conflicts of interest for Al-Khelaifi "but I don't agree that these are the right concerns."*)

TV broadcaster collapses or Super League is launched and ECA needs a new head), the selected stakeholders seem to overlook any notion of conflicts, which, in fairness, can put Nasser in a difficult situation. Nasser Al-Khelaifi (born in 1973) was a professional tennis player ranked as high as 995 in the world in December 2002. He met Sheihk Tamim bin Hamad Al Thani (who became the eighth Emir of Qatar in June 2013) through playing tennis when they were younger.

* https://eu.usatoday.com/story/sports/soccer/2019/02/07/the-latest-uefa-president-ceferin-wont-be-a-yes-man/39020441/.

UEFA announced that it was going to investigate. However, no results were publicized. (UEFA said that it was prioritizing issues involving clubs that were still in the tournament.) Panja wrote:

> Weeks passed. Then months. Other incidents that had taken place at UEFA matches held after the game between Real Madrid and P.S.G. were investigated and adjudicated. But UEFA's investigation into Al-Khelaifi—who in addition to his role at P.S.G., one of Europe's richest clubs, is also the chairman of beIN Media Group, the Qatar-based company that is one of UEFA's biggest partners—dragged on. Only in June, after the European soccer season had finished, after much of the attention on the incident had faded, did UEFA quietly publish a short paragraph. It appeared on Page 5 of a six-page document listing outcomes of recent disciplinary cases: UEFA said it would ban Leonardo—who had since left P.S.G.—for one game for violating "the basic rules of decent conduct."

Curiously, there was no mention of Al-Khelaifi, who according to the referee's report had engaged in behavior that was worse. (UEFA declined to explain to the *New York Times* why Al-Khelaifi was not disciplined. PSG declined to comment to the *New York Times*.)

Panja spoke to Alex Phillips, who, according to his LinkedIn profile, had worked at Deloitte for four years before working at UEFA from 2005 to 2020, with his last position at UEFA as Head of Governance and Compliance from 2018 to 2020. Punja wrote: "He [Alex Phillips] told *The Times* that the timing of the resolution alone felt intentional." Panja quotes Phillips saying, "They would have waited to find a quiet time to bury it and hope people would have forgotten and it would blow over." UEFA categorically denies this, and Phillips does not currently work at UEFA.

Phillips suggested that UEFA's disciplinary mechanism has been undermined in recent years. "The so-called independent judicial bodies are in reality far from independent, instead now being used as a power tool to ensure specific outcomes . . . We would tell the public that they are independent decisions when they really are not." Once again, UEFA categorically denies this.

In October 2022, *L'Equipe* reported that PSG would report losses of €370 million for the 2021–22 season.[*] And then in March 2023, *L'Equipe*

---

[*] https://offthepitch.com/a/psg-have-lost-more-eu600-million-2019-and-made-no-penalty-deal-uefa-how-can-happen.

published another article explaining that PSG are not expected to face any sanctions (such as being rejected from playing in the Champions League) from UEFA's Financial Fair Play (FFP) rules for the 2022–23 season due to a "settlement agreement." Reportedly, PSG were avoiding any punishment despite their heavy losses and debts but had to stay within FFP regulations to avoid future penalties.*

If PSG indeed lost €370 million for the 2021–22 financial year, the club would have lost more than €600 million in the last three seasons. Some speculate that the main reason UEFA may enter these settlements is to avoid lengthy and costly legal battles because of the ambiguity in the changes in the FFP rules. Others point to Al-Khelaifi being a close ally of Čeferin as a member of UEFA's executive committee, as the chairman of the European Club Association that helped stop the breakaway Super League project in 2021, and as the head of one of UEFA's most important commercial clients—Qatari broadcaster beIN SPORTS. Any settlement agreement would need to be approved by the executive committee, of which Al-Khelaifi is a member (he would most likely recuse himself from the vote).

UEFA is making the rules, enforcing them, and at the same time organizing the competitions with a clear business interest (which could be a reason to try to have PSG in the Champions League). Maybe some separation of these roles or more independence between the roles would give football better governance and fewer potential or perceived conflicts.

After the *L'Equipe* article, in March 2023, Kasper Kronenberg, editor in chief of Off The Pitch, wrote: "Ultimately, UEFA risks seriously sabotaging its own new financial regulation of European football if the governing body fails to show everyone that the new rules must be taken seriously."† Kronenberg interviewed Henning Zülch, professor at HHL Leipzig Graduate School of Management, about the latest report about the PSG settlement. Zülch

---

* Following UEFA's announcement of nearly thirty clubs being affected by FFP regulations (eight-plus clubs being sanctioned and nearly twenty clubs being on the red flag list and being monitored), it is important to note, along with seven other clubs, for the three seasons affected by COVID, PSG have entered into a settlement agreement with CFCB, which will chart PSG into conformity with the new financial sustainability rules; over thirty clubs are included in the announcement and at least two clubs received sporting sanctions, but not PSG; PSG made significant reported profits for the two seasons prior to COVID—both 2017–2018 and 2018–2019; and for the three COVID seasons, French clubs faced singularly unique financial circumstances not faced by any other clubs in any other league, including the league being canceled and the domestic broadcaster collapsing.

† https://offthepitch.com/a/interview-uefa-has-opened-pandoras-box-and-other-non-compliant-clubs-will-invoke-case-if-they-do?wv_email=sgmandis%40me.com&wv_id=0b33e863-2b87-44e3-82bb-a46dd11bfd0d&wv_name=.

said, "For the sake of its [the new financial regulation's] credibility and in order to preserve the legitimacy of the new rules, UEFA is recommended to keep the clubs on a tight leash, report any misconduct and monitor the clubs that don't comply with the framework closely. Consequently, clubs that have not progressed in the right direction and don't fulfill the criteria after the transition phase must be sanctioned."

Zülch is concerned with the football industry in terms of transparency and its inability to adapt to the professional corporate governance structures that are the backbone of financially sustainable sectors. He said, "The lack of transparency of comprehensive financial data in Europe's football industry remains inherent. In this sense, UEFA could make a valuable contribution and lead by example by closing the transparency gap in today's football industry . . . Full transparency in its [UEFA's] decision-making processes strengthens legitimacy and acceptance of UEFA's regulation. UEFA would be well-advised to avoid any backroom deals and to show each club the limits."

Kronenberg explained one reason why it matters: "The new institutional investors in football won't accept continued losses at their clubs. In the long-term, they would leave the industry if UEFA doesn't punish clubs breaching financial regulations."

In 2022, after analysis of the financial years from 2018 to 2022, UEFA found that PSG, along with seven other clubs, had failed to comply with the FFP rules. PSG were given the biggest immediate fine of €10 million. However, UEFA said that clubs were only being asked to pay 15 percent of the total agreed, and that PSG's fine could rise to €65 million if they fail to comply with the settlement reached with UEFA for the next three years. LaLiga's president said, "€10 million for them is a cup of coffee . . . sanctions have to be dissuasive and also affect the sporting side of things . . . over the last six or seven seasons, PSG have lost €1 billion. They are breaking the European football ecosystem. How can other clubs compete?"

Earlier in 2022, UEFA announced that it was phasing out the existing FFP rules that allowed clubs to report losses of no more than €30 million over a three-year period. FFP is being replaced by new licensing and "sustainability" regulations that will allow clubs to report losses of €60 million over three years, and the permitted figure can even reach €90 million for a club "in good financial health." The new regulations also limit spending on wages, transfers, and agent fees to 70 percent of club revenue—before, the 70 percent was a recommendation and not a strict requirement. Obviously, the higher the value of sponsorships deals (which can be difficult to value if not truly independent, third-party transactions), the higher the amount on wages that could be spent.

Summer of 2022: The Mbappé Saga + Haaland

In May 2022, Real Madrid were reportedly very close to finalizing a deal with Mbappé (born December 1998) on a free transfer, ending a long-running transfer saga. Playing for Real Madrid was Mbappé's childhood dream. Real Madrid had beaten Mbappé and fellow PSG's stars Messi and Neymar just two months before, en route to a Champions League final against Liverpool. However, in an abrupt U-turn, Mbappé reportedly texted Florentino via WhatsApp:

> I inform you that I have decided to stay at PSG. I want to thank
> you for giving me the opportunity to play for Real Madrid, the club
> I have been a fan of since I was a kid. I hope you understand my
> decision, good luck in the UCL Final.*

At a press conference, Mbappé said he personally called Florentino to inform him about his decision to remain at Paris Saint-Germain.

> I have a lot of respect for Real Madrid and Florentino Pérez. They
> did everything for me and tried to make me very happy—that's
> why I had to call him personally. We've got a close relationship.

---

* https://twitter.com/elchiringuitotv/status/1528050162739949569; https://www.dailymail.co.uk/sport /football/article-10842211/Kylian-Mbappes-devastating-text-message-Real-Madrid-president-Florentino -Perez.html.

Reportedly, Real Madrid were willing to pay a total amount of around €300 million, including a signing bonus. According to *Le Parisien*, PSG more than doubled the amount—a total of €630 million if he stayed in Paris for the next three seasons. It was the most valuable sports contract in history—higher than Messi's 2017 four-year contract renewal of €555 million (which allegedly instigated Ronaldo to ask Real Madrid for a higher salary, and after Real Madrid said no, Ronaldo was sold to Juventus).

According to *Le Parisien*, Mbappé's total package includes a €70 million gross salary per season (total €210 million), a €180 million signing bonus, and additional bonuses of €70 million, €80 million, and €90 million, respectively, for staying each of the following three years (total €240 million). In an interview with *Sport Illustrated*, Mbappé revealed that Emmanuel Macron, president of France, actively participated in the renewal deal. When asked earlier about Liverpool's chances in signing Mbappé, Klopp said, "But it is about the money of course. No chance. Absolutely No Chance."*

In June 2022, Borussia Dortmund striker Erling Haaland (born July 2000) had signed with Man City. Man City activated the Norway striker's release clause and paid a total of £85.5 million including agents fees and other add-ons. According to GOAL, the total cost of buying Haaland in the five-year deal was around €300 million, including his transfer fee, salary, agent fees, and competition-linked bonuses over several seasons.† Liverpool manager Jürgen Klopp said the Haaland deal "set new levels" in the transfer market.‡

After the Haaland and Mbappé deals were announced, LaLiga filed complaints with UEFA against Man City and PSG, alleging both "are in continuous breach of the current Financial Fair Play rules . . . LaLiga understands that the irregular financing of these clubs is carried out either through direct injections of money or through sponsorship and other contracts that do not correspond to market conditions and do not make economic sense. LaLiga considers that these practices alter the ecosystem and the sustainability of football, harm all European clubs and leagues, and only serve to artificially inflate the market, with money not generated in football itself."

* https://bleacherreport.com/articles/2861901-jurgen-klopp-says-liverpool-have-absolutely-no-chance-of-signing-kylian-mbappe.

† https://www.goal.com/en-us/news/live/live-erling-haaland-transfer-news-and-rumours/bltcc2eac74 1dc861e1.

‡ https://www.eurosport.com/football/transfers-1/2021-2022/erling-haaland-passes-manchester-city-medical-as-liverpool-boss-jurgen-klopp-says-massive-deal-will-_sto8918227/story.shtml.

UEFA president Aleksander Čeferin said in an interview that he rejected LaLiga's criticism of Mbappé's new deal:

> I absolutely don't agree. There are too many insults anyway in football, and I think that every league should worry about their own situation. I don't think it is right that one league criticizes the other league. As much as I know, the offer from Real for Mbappé was similar to PSG's offer.[*]

Even if Real Madrid's offer was the same (which reportedly is not true), that's actually not the point. The question is which club could afford signing Mbappé within FFP—to answer that question, one needs to examine the financials of each club.

In June 2022, the annual report from French football's financial authority stated PSG suffered a €224.3 million loss in 2020–21, up from a €124.2 million loss in 2019–20. In 2021–22, Off The Pitch reported PSG lost €370 million.[†]

In contrast, Real Madrid managed to remain in profit over the financial years affected by the pandemic, making a profit in both 2019–20 (€313,000 after tax) and 2020–21 (€874,000 after tax), being one of the few major clubs in Europe that did not incur losses over those two financial years. In June 2024, Real Madrid announced the signing of 25-year-old French captain Mbappé to a five-year contract on a free transfer.

In January 2023, Qatar Sports Investments (owner of PSG) said it was looking to acquire a minority stake in a Premier League club to "turbocharge" the fund. Reportedly, PSG president and QSI chairman Nasser Al-Khelaifi met with Tottenham chairman Daniel Levy.[‡] Many believe that the Premier League will continue to separate itself even further from the other four big European leagues, including Ligue 1 (where PSG play).

---

[*] https://www.france24.com/en/live-news/20220615-la-liga-confirms-complaints-to-uefa-against-city-and-psg. Tebas is president of the European Leagues, which represents Ligue 1 and other leagues. The financial sustainability rules he repeatedly complains about are the very same rules that he helped create and approved as recently as the UEFA ExCo on May 10, 2022.

[†] https://offthepitch.com/a/psg-have-lost-more-eu600-million-2019-and-made-no-penalty-deal-uefa-how-can-happen.

[‡] Tottenham denied talks took place; QSI sources said there were two "exploratory" meetings with Levy and said speculation that talks had been held with Liverpool and Man U was untrue.

QSI also have a minority stake (22 percent) in Portuguese side Braga and control of Belgian club KAS Eupen.

Why Do Many MCOs Own Football Clubs in Belgium?

QSI controls a Belgian club. MCG and John Textor too. Reportedly, Newcastle are looking to buy a Belgian club. Why?

Belgium has a relatively small population of only eleven million. The country is loaded with talented sons of first-generation migrants from Congo, Morocco, Burundi, Mali, and beyond. Many of these sons play lots of football in the constrained spaces of poor, working-class neighborhoods—quickly developing unique skills because they touch the ball so often and also in imperfect conditions. In addition, Belgium has very good grassroots youth development focused on technical skills.

In 2021, Man City had six Belgian players on their squad. Big clubs habitually scout players in Belgium. In addition, there are very few restrictions on players. Only eight players on each squad of twenty-five have to be homegrown, meaning teams can import large numbers of foreigners. Even more alluringly, for players from outside the European Union, Belgium offers a fast track to European citizenship, making it ideal for African players in particular. Lastly, the costs are low. The clubs are relatively inexpensive. In addition, the players make less money. For example, in the Netherlands, any team planning on registering a non-EU player must pay the player at least €300,000 a year. In Belgium, it is less than €100,000, including bonuses. There are tax breaks too. When a club is sold, the profit is not taxed under Belgian law.

In December 2023, US private equity firm Arctos Partners and QSI reached an agreement for Arctos to buy up to 12.5 percent of PSG, valuing the club at around $4.6 billion, according to people familiar with the matter.[*]

Arctos has stakes in more than 20 sports teams, including the NBA's Golden State Warriors, Utah Jazz, Sacramento Kings, Philadelphia 76ers;

---

* https://www.sportico.com/business/finance/2023/arctos-buys-into-paris-saint-germain-1234754448/.

MLB's Los Angeles Dodgers, Boston Red Sox, Chicago Cubs, San Francisco Giants, Houston Astros, San Diego Padres; NHL's Tampa Bay Lightning, New Jersey Devils; and MLS's Utah Royals. In addition, the firm bought a minority stake in Formula 1's Aston Martin.

Lastly, PSG have a similar strategic issue as Man City (as well as Newcastle and Chelsea)—they don't own their own stadium, which impacts their ability to grow stadium revenues.*

PRIVATE EQUITY STAKES IN LEAGUES' MEDIA RIGHTS

In aggregate, it is estimated that top European clubs lost $8.5 billion in revenues in the 2020–21 season. When KPMG looked at the financial performance of the winners of the six major European leagues, it saw average losses of ~15 percent of previous years' revenues.

In February 2021, amid opposition from seven clubs, including Inter Milan, Juventus, Lazio, and Napoli, Serie A announced that it had ended exclusive talks to sell 10 percent interest in a newly formed company managing the league's media, sponsorship, and media rights business to a CVC-led consortium. In 2023, the topic was raised again. Aurelio De Laurentiis, the owner of Napoli, said he is still against external investment into the league's media business. He told Reuters: "We should produce the content and then place it with the various platforms—Amazon, Netflix, Apple, DAZN and Sky."†

In December 2021, amid a lack of consensus opinion among its thirty-six member clubs, the Bundesliga decided to end talks over private

---

* Most of PSG's peers in the UEFA Champions League own their own stadiums and have modernized them to increase revenue opportunities. In addition, they have much larger capacities. The Parc des Princes, which is owned by the City of Paris, holds just 48,000 spectators. Real Madrid's stadium has around 80,000 seating capacity, Barcelona's over 99,000, and Bayern Munich and Man U are around 75,000. Reportedly, Paris won't sell or is asking for too much money, so PSG is considering buying the national stadium, the 80,000-capacity Stade de France, from the government, or moving to a couple of unidentified greenfield sites. Clubs that don't own their own stadiums include: Man City, Chelsea, Newcastle, Nottingham Forest, Hertha Berlin, West Ham, PSG, Club Brugge, AS Roma, Lazio, AC Milan, and Inter Milan.

† https://www.reuters.com/lifestyle/sports/napoli-owner-says-serie-should-keep-hold-media-business-2023-03-06/.

equity investment into a new league entity that would hold a license to commercialize their international media and sponsorship rights for twenty-five years. In May 2023, a €2 billion ($2.15 billion) investment from a private equity firm for the Bundesliga's TV rights was voted down. Reportedly, the three potential candidates (Advent, Blackstone, and CVC) offered to purchase 12.5 percent of the Bundesliga's television broadcasting rights over a twenty-year period. German fans (in particular Dortmund fans) campaigned vigorously against the idea.[*] They were concerned about outside investor influence for such a long time, their clubs losing some of their freedom to make decisions, the further fracturing of the weekly schedule for the benefit of television, antisocial kickoff times to suit foreign audiences, and the prospect of competitive games abroad.[†] The fresh capital was to be invested in digitalization and a new online content platform (40 percent), stadiums, youth academies and other club infrastructure (45 percent), and the rest free to invest in players (15 percent). Advocates of the proposed deal had argued that German football is in need of significant investment in order to avoid being left behind by the English Premier League.[‡] In 2021–22, Dortmund ranked thirteenth in the Deloitte Football Money League with €357 million in revenues, compared to €731 million for Man City. In December 2023, German clubs approved a plan to sell a share of broadcast revenues to an outside investor, even though the plan was opposed by many fans.

In December 2021, LaLiga ratified a deal with private equity firm CVC Capital Partners (CVC) taking a stake in the league's commercial ventures and media rights. However, four of the forty-two Spanish clubs (Real Madrid, Barcelona, Athletic Bilbao, and UD Ibiza) opted out of the deal, and three of them (Real Madrid, Barcelona, and Athletic Bilbao) took legal action against the deal (as well as the Spanish Football Federation). Real Madrid, Barcelona, and Athletic Bilbao are all owned by socios.

---

[*] In a survey of over 56,000 fans conducted by Kicker magazine at the start of May, 67.65 percent of respondents said they were against an investor in the league, with only 24.47 percent in favor. Only at Red Bull–backed RB Leipzig were a majority of fans (53.42 percent) in favor.

[†] https://www.dw.com/en/bundesliga-investor-plan-rejected-after-intense-fan-protests/a-65725420.

[‡] In November 2023, it was reported that the Bundesliga had held positive talks with German clubs about a new plan to attract external investment because it will provide greater focus on the digitalization and internationalization of the league.

Established in 1981, CVC is a world leader in private equity and credit with €133 billion of assets under management. One of their specialties is the sports industry. CVC's former and current sports investments include Formula 1, Moto GP, Six Nations Rugby, Women's Tennis Association (WTA), and IPL Cricket. (In full disclosure, I am friends with CVC's co-founder Donald Mackenzie, who led the firm's purchase of Formula 1.)

The private equity firm will spend €2 billion in exchange for an 8.2 percent stake in a new company (LaLiga Group International with the project investment company called Boost LaLiga) that will hold the league's commercial ventures, including TV rights and all the other businesses and incomes it's currently generating through different methods, like its own OTT called LaLiga SportsTV. The most significant revenue stream for LaLiga is, of course, the TV/media rights that it's selling to third parties. However, the creation of LaLiga SportsTV is a significant step toward LaLiga streaming all their matches through their own OTT and not selling the TV rights to third parties anymore. Or, most likely, it will be a hybrid solution, with fans able to buy a season pass through LaLiga's own OTT or watch the games through traditional channels.

The money will then be shared with the LaLiga teams over the next three years. Most of the cash is to be given to clubs to spend on new infrastructure and modernization projects, as well as to increase how much they can spend on players. There are specific rules on how the money can be used. Seventy percent of the money should be used to improve the club's infrastructure, which means improving the stadiums and training grounds and implementing new technology. Fifteen percent of the money can be used to clear previous debt and to cover losses caused by the pandemic, whereas the remaining 15 percent can be used to sign new players, renew contracts, etc.

CVC's arrangement lasts fifty years, but the firm said it is likely to sell the rights within ten years. The deal was due to be worth €2.7 billion, but those clubs who did not want to participate were given the chance to opt out. It seems that, among other things, at least Real Madrid and Barcelona feel that fifty years is too long, and the value of their rights is much higher than what was agreed with CVC.*

---

* Subsequently, in 2022, Barcelona did their own TV rights deal for twenty-five years with Sixth Street.

An article in the *Financial Times* reported that under certain assumptions "CVC could treble or even quadruple its money in the next decade. Since the league is not on the hook for clubs' costs, the vast majority of CVC's revenue is profit." A rival football dealmaker quoted in the article said, "It's the best deal in the history of private equity. They are not going to lose money here."*

A key driver behind the deal was opportune timing—the pandemic had a significant negative financial impact to every club. Most had to postpone projects, cut expenses, and had difficulty getting access to capital. With this financial boost, many clubs can move forward with their projects that were put on hold because of the pandemic. The explanation of Miguel Ángel Gil Marín, the principal owner of Atlético Madrid, of why he supported the deal helps clarify this point:

> As of today, the audiovisual rights managed by LaLiga represent 30 percent of Atlético's ordinary income, excluding the players' market and transfer fees. That is to say, the loss that the club would have in the future if revenues were as they are today would be 3 percent. I sincerely believe that Atlético will recover that 3 percent in two ways: the first, via LaLiga, as a result of the increase in the value of the rights thanks to the synergy with CVC, and the second, through the profitability of the investment that Atlético will make with that money in a new infrastructure, which will allow the club to offer its fans an actual city of sport and entertainment.

In the last sentence, Gil Marín is referring to a new training grounds and smaller stadium that are already designed right next to the Atlético Stadium, Civitas Metropolitano (was Wanda). The pandemic put the plan on hold, but with the CVC money, it's moving forward.

CVC's investment approach in trying to capture what they believe will be growing TV rights value is very interesting. Most private equity firms seem to be investing in clubs, which would benefit from the cash flows of increasing TV rights values. In contrast, CVC's investment is a "pure play" on TV rights. CVC doesn't appear to want to take the

* https://www.ft.com/content/86ce59dc-8625-4000-a52f-603046354d19.

financial risk of a club, including the risk of relegation or inflation of transfer fees or salaries or FFP compliance. In 2022, U.S.-based private equity firm Carlyle tried to buy a stake in Serie A and said it had no plans to take a minority stake in the football club itself. In 2023, a Carlyle executive stated: "Football and sports in general have proven to be a very valuable property that has further potential to exploit."[*]

Real Madrid's socios want more (not less) control and full ownership of their TV rights. Private equity firms typically seek returns over 20 percent per annum, and Real Madrid can get much cheaper cost of capital because of their profitability, strong balance sheet, key assets, and global brand and fan base. Most, if not all, of the other clubs that supported the deal could not get the same financing (at either the interest rate or amounts or terms) as Real Madrid. By pooling all together in the league, the LaLiga clubs got better capital markets access, but a deal for fifty years is a long time.

In April 2022, the French soccer league announced a €1.5 billion investment deal for 13 percent with CVC as part of a new commercial subsidiary in charge of marketing media rights. Following the collapse of its record-breaking TV rights contract with Spanish-based broadcaster Mediapro, the French soccer league was forced in 2021 to ask the government to set up a financial rescue plan amid huge revenue losses exacerbated by the pandemic. The deal with Mediapro should have been worth more than €4 billion over four years for the top two leagues but collapsed after only four months.[†]

---

[*] https://news.bloomberglaw.com/private-equity/carlyle-sees-more-chances-to-exploit-footballs-growth-potential.

[†] French football has yet to recover from the bankruptcy of Mediapro, which had raised the rights for the 2020–21 to 2023–24 cycle to €1.153 billion per year, which was never paid. The renegotiated deal totaled €624 million per year. For the domestic rights, Canal+ currently pays €332 million for two matches per round, with Amazon Prime spending €250 million for the other eight matches, while the telecoms firm Free pays €42 million for the deferred broadcasting rights of the ten weekly Ligue 1 matches. For the overseas rights, beIN pays a reported €70 million per year to market Ligue 1 rights overseas. Any income earned over the guaranteed figure is then split between the LFP and beIN.

HALFTIME

REVIEW OF CHANGES

The changes in the leaders in the Deloitte Football Money Rankings and ownership models (not to mention the announcement of the European Super League and subsequent reactions and opinions) led me to believe some things really have systemically changed in European football and deserved further investigation.

In the previous chapter, I explained the serious systemic changes in ownership: closely government-related, private equity, and multi-club ownership models have proliferated.

Money from a club owner can be disguised as sponsorship income, and commercial contracts with closely affiliated sponsors can be artificially inflated to circumvent Financial Fair Play. In addition, some people or entities have many roles that can at the very least be perceived as potential conflicts of interest. This ranges from controlling both a broadcaster and club and having a board seat on the regulating body, to owners funding two clubs (i.e., the multi-club ownership model) within one competition, or transferring players between two related entities. As a members-owned club, Real Madrid are focused on keeping the integrity of competition for themselves and football.

Last chapter, our ownership discussion highlighted that football's regulation system has been exposed as a patchwork of rules that often differ by jurisdiction, are inconsistently enforced, and challenged in court.

FIFA and UEFA control the multibillion-dollar transnational activity of football (including the regulatory function over clubs, the money-making hosting of tournaments function utilizing clubs, and the judiciary and discipline function over clubs) but are subject to limited regulation or oversight (including potential conflicts).

Football is structured in a pyramid with FIFA at the summit, then the continental confederations like UEFA and CONCACAF beneath, and then national associations and leagues. The paradox of this governance structure is that all of its actors cooperate, but also compete with each other to organize competitions within the limited number of days that players can play at peak performance. For example, UEFA's expansion of the European Champions League can be competitive with domestic leagues and tournaments or the FIFA Club World Cup (and vice versa). Meanwhile, the football economy is highly dependent on the biggest clubs in Europe, with global brands who have the economic risk of buying and paying the best players from clubs around the world, because together the biggest clubs attract the most global fans, sponsors, and viewers.

FIFA's and UEFA's Missions May Not Be in Harmony

FIFA's mission: "Ultimately, FIFA's key mission is to truly globalize, popularize and democratize football for the benefit of the entire world . . . to further modernize the football world, make it increasingly inclusive and pave the way to a landscape in which, one day, we will have at least 50 national teams and 50 clubs from all continents at a top competitive level."*

I recognize that FIFA has its issues and controversies and faces criticisms. However, on a personal level, I really enjoy helping FIFA precisely because of its mission and impact. I get to teach and share best sports management business practices, research, and data with club and league executives from all over the world who want to learn and improve but often have limited resources and access.

UEFA Mission: "UEFA's core mission is to promote, protect and develop European football at every level of the game, to promote principles of unity and solidarity, and to deal with all questions relating to European football."†

---

* https://publications.fifa.com/en/annual-report-2020/the-global-game/the-vision-2020-2023/.
† https://www.uefa.com/newsfiles/374875.pdf.

Both missions make complete sense and are admirable. However, they may not always be in harmony. FIFA is trying to improve national teams and clubs from *all continents*, not just Europe. UEFA is trying to improve national teams and clubs *in Europe*.

This gets back to my question in the beginning of this book to football fans: "So, when pundits in Europe, for example, say 'football belongs to the fans,' who exactly do they mean?"

UEFA currently runs the world's most popular club competition—the UEFA European Champions League. While the competing clubs are based in Europe, the clubs essentially transcend Europe and are global brands. UEFA wants to make the tournament more global and leverage the global appeal of the clubs to reach and attract global fans and grow—and possibly even play the European Champions League final in the United States. In 2023, UEFA president Aleksander Čeferin said, "It is possible [a Champions League final in the U.S.]. We started to discuss about that, but then one year it is World Cup, 2024 is Euro, this year is Istanbul, '24 in London, '25 in Munich. And after that let's see. It's possible, it's possible."[*] UEFA redistributes around 97 percent of the money to the clubs and the nations. However, the revenues from this event are primarily directly distributed to football *in Europe*.[†]

Meanwhile, FIFA runs the FIFA Club World Cup, which in its current format contains seven teams from six different continental confederations. In 2023, Real Madrid won the Club World Cup for a record-extending fifth time after beating Saudi Arabia's Al Hilal 5–3 in the final in Rabat, Morocco. The revenues from this event are directly distributed to football *globally*, like the World Cup.

In December 2022, FIFA president Gianni Infantino first unveiled proposals for a new thirty-two-team event to be played every four years from 2025. The idea is to give fans more of a global product they already desire, and give more clubs, players, and fans from around the world an opportunity to dream of playing the big clubs (which are global brands). Initially, the European Club Association (ECA) and the international football players' union FIFPRO raised several concerns, including calendar congestion and

---

[*] https://www.espn.com/soccer/story/_/id/37638269/champions-league-matches-us-possible-uefa -president-ceferin.

[†] European clubs redistribute the money globally when they sign players outside Europe. However, there are restrictions in various leagues as to how many foreign players can be on a squad.

impact to the players and European Champions League. After discussions, in March 2023, UEFA and the ECA came to an agreement with FIFA.

The new FIFA Club World Cup will attract a much larger global audience because it will include twelve European clubs (UEFA): the eight finalists of the last four versions of the Champions League and the other four with the best coefficient; as well as five South American clubs (CONMEBOL), and two clubs each from Africa (CAF), Asia (AFC), and North America (CONCACAF), and a final team from Oceania (OFC). (Details subject to change.) Fans from around the world can root for their favorite clubs or clubs representing their favorite leagues.

Global fans will now have the UEFA European Champions League every year and a FIFA Club World Cup every four years.

Reportedly, the founders of the proposed European Super League were going to participate in an expanded FIFA Club World Cup.[*]

Sports account for 3.5 percent of the EU's GDP. To put it in perspective, this is more than twice the GDP from agriculture. Yet despite their enormous public (social and economic) relevance, European sports are, for the most part, regulated by private systems of governance. This is why most sports organizations are headquartered in Switzerland, which offers them almost total regulatory autonomy and exemption from oversight.

One does have to ask if the current football regulatory system makes sense or is working effectively.

In November 2021, Alex Phillips, who worked at UEFA for twenty years including Head of Professional Football and Head of Governance and Compliance, did an exclusive and wide-ranging interview with Off The Pitch.[†] He said:

> For as long as the competition organizers are doing both the commercializing and regulating, then there will always be this conflict of interest. If UEFA the regulator excludes those big clubs, then UEFA the competition organizer sees a massive decrease

---

[*] https://www.nytimes.com/2021/05/20/sports/soccer/super-league-fifa-infantino.html.

[†] https://offthepitch.com/a/uefa-cant-be-both-regulator-and-competition-organizer-its-actually-massive-problem.

in interest and value in its own competitions. The solution, that I have been advocating for some time now, is to separate their three main functions—competitions, regulation, development—into autonomous bodies so they can do their jobs properly without fear or favor . . . in terms of its [UEFA's] regulatory role it is a pale shadow of what it once was.

The Verdict

A22, the company behind the European Super League (ESLC), took its case that UEFA contravened competition law in seeking to ban a breakaway competition to the Madrid Commercial Court in 2021. The case was referred to the European Court of Justice (ECOJ) in January 2022.

In July 2022, fifteen ECOJ judges heard oral evidence over the course of two days. Evidence was given by member associations and leagues as well as by twenty-one European Union member states.

Gabriele Marcotti, senior writer, ESPN FC, wrote: "The stakes were very high. A win for UEFA and FIFA would quash any real attempt for clubs, many of which are private companies—to organize their own competitions and administer them as they see fit, without governing body approval. A win for the Super League would open the door, potentially, to clubs—not governing bodies—deciding who they wanted to play against, when they wanted to play and how to divide the revenue."

December 21, 2023: The long-awaited final judgment was issued by the ECOJ. It is the most important ruling in the football industry since the Bosman verdict.

The final decision from the ECOJ said that both UEFA and FIFA are "abusing a dominant position" and in breach of competition law: "The FIFA and UEFA rules making any new inter-club football project subject to their prior approval, such as the Super League, and prohibiting clubs and players from playing in those competitions, are unlawful." The ECOJ concluded that FIFA and UEFA are abusing their dominant position. The ECOJ was quick to stress, though, that their ruling does not mean that the Super League must be approved, but that it must be allowed to form based on both the freedom to provide services and the freedom of movement, and that any obstruction of its creation by FIFA and UEFA is unlawful.

Bernd Reichart, A22 chief executive, said, "We've won the right to compete. UEFA's monopoly is over. Football is free. Now the clubs will not suffer threats and punishments. They are free to decide their own future."

How did UEFA and FIFA respond? UEFA president Aleksander Čeferin said, "I personally see this decision as a chance to improve some of the regulations but first, and crucially, football remains united . . . We have national governments and institutions behind us." FIFA said: "FIFA will now analyse the decision in coordination with UEFA, the other confederations, and the member associations before commenting further. In line with its statutes, FIFA firmly believes in the specific nature of sport, including the pyramid structure—which is underpinned by sporting merit—and the principles of competitive balance and financial solidarity."

Florentino Pérez said: "At Real Madrid, we welcome with great satisfaction the decision taken by the Court of Justice of the European Union, which is responsible for guaranteeing our principles, values and freedoms. In the coming days we will study the scope of this ruling in detail, but I would like to anticipate two conclusions of great historical significance. Firstly, that European club football is not and will never again be a monopoly. And secondly, that from today the clubs will be the masters of their destiny. We, the clubs, see our right to propose and promote European competitions that modernise our sport and attract fans from all over the world fully recognised. In short, today the Europe of freedoms has triumphed once again, and today football and its fans have triumphed too."

A22 announced a revamped format for the Super League in February 2023, which would see sixty-four teams competing in a multi-league competition. The new-look Super League would be based only on "sporting merit" with no permanent members. The proposal would see sixty-four teams compete across "Star, Gold, and Blue Leagues," in groups of eight with a guaranteed minimum of fourteen matches per year. There would be promotion and relegation between leagues, and qualification via domestic competition, while all games would be broadcast for free via a new digital streaming platform.

What really changed? The ECJ reaffirmed that UEFA, as a governing body, is a competition organizer, a regulator, and a commercial venture. As such, it has certain obligations to avoid abusing its de facto monopoly power—like having reasonable criteria for clubs that, instead of playing in UEFA competitions, might want to organize their own tournaments.

The ruling gives the big global clubs more of a path to control their own destiny. The real outcome is a further shift in the balance of power toward the global clubs and global fans. Once again, Real Madrid is at the forefront of the evolution of football.

As for oversight—remarkably, it was the U.S. Department of Justice in 2015 that investigated corruption at FIFA, which is based in Switzerland. To prosecute cases that involve foreign nationals, U.S. authorities only need to prove a minor connection to the U.S. Authorities in the U.S. claimed jurisdiction on issues related to the FIFA World Cup because the American television market is impacted, and money is paid by U.S. TV networks. The same could be true for UEFA's Champions League or even the Premier League. In November 2021, U.S. media giant NBC renewed its broadcast partnership deal with the Premier League in a new six-year agreement worth around $2.7 billion.

The Premier League is taking a more active approach in oversight. After an investigation lasting more than four years, the Premier League released a statement in February 2023 saying it had charged Man City with more than one hundred breaches of financial rules from 2009 to 2018.* Man City said it's "surprised by the issuing of these alleged breaches of the Premier League rules, particularly given the extensive engagement and vast number of detailed materials that the EPL has been provided with. The club welcomes the review of this matter by an independent commission, to impartially consider the comprehensive body of irrefutable evidence that exists in support of its position. As such we look forward to this matter being put to rest once and for all."† One accusation is that Man City have artificially inflated the money coming into the

---

* Man City said in a statement: "The club welcomes the review of this matter by an independent commission, to impartially consider the comprehensive body of irrefutable evidence that exists in support of its position. As such we look forward to this matter being put to rest once and for all." Man City are confident in their position, including the charges that were time-barred in their UEFA case. They believe they already provided the relevant evidence around those charges to the Premier League.

† https://www.skysports.com/football/news/11661/12804623/man-city-premier-league-charges-explained-what-are-they-what-could-punishment-be-whats-the-timescale.

club, with particular respect to commercial and sponsorship deals. The Premier League appears to be claiming the money was coming from the club owner, but was being disguised as sponsorship income to circumvent FFP. This is the same issue that went to the CAS, which lifted Man City's two-year ban from European competition.

Another accusation is that Man City have artificially deflated the costs of running the club by having managers on contracts with another company connected to the owners, so that they only put a small element of the true cost of managing the club through their financials.

The case is a Premier League matter that is going to be dealt with domestically via an independent commission. Unlike UEFA's FFP rules, there are no time-barred restrictions. If Man City are found to have breached any rules, there are no restrictions in the penalties that can be imposed. It could be anything from "don't do it again," to a fine, to a points deduction, to stripping them of titles, to even relegating them from the Premier League. After the commission has made its decision, an appeal can be made to a separate judicial appeals body within the Premier League for a final decision.*

While the Premier League had been investigating Man City for years, some critics of the accusations questioned the timing of an announcement—given that a white paper on football governance by the U.K. government was to be published the same month. They feel the Premier League bringing the case is being used as evidence it can deal with governance issues itself rather than the U.K. government's white paper's proposed independent regulator. However, others are criticizing how long the entire process has taken and will take. The Premier League's investigation into Man City is expected to last another two to four years, ending in 2025 to 2027.

Later in February 2023, FIFA said it will examine the U.K. government's proposals to set up an independent football regulator amid concerns that the new body could breach rules on political interference. Legal experts believe there are several areas of concern where the

* The body is headed by a lawyer who reportedly is a member at Arsenal, Man City's closest rival for the 2022–23 season's title.

regulator could breach FIFA's Article 15, which states that national associations must "be independent and avoid any form of political interference." Nothing can happen until the regulator is set up, which is likely to be in 2025.

In September 2023, the U.K. government admitted to *The Athletic* that its embassy in Abu Dhabi and the Foreign Commonwealth & Development Office (FCDO) in London have discussed the charges against Man City by the Premier League. However, the U.K. government refused to disclose the correspondence to *The Athletic*, which had made a freedom of information request.

The Premier League is also considering a ban on loan transfers between clubs under the same ownership. However, many sports law experts believe that regulations on inter-club transfers within MCOs may conflict with EU and U.K. competition laws and will certainly lead to legal challenges. The rules changes seem to be directed to Man City and Newcastle, among others.

While UEFA may have been happy with English fans protesting the European Super League, the public spotlight also caused a U.K. government investigation and recommendation for an independent domestic regulator. UEFA may lose some judicial and disciplinary control to the Premier League—which is becoming its own Super League, or the NBA equivalent of football and a competitor to UEFA itself.

Reportedly, Man City and Newcastle could face an investigation by the European Commission for alleged breaches of new rules that are designed to prevent "state aid" from distorting markets across the continent.* Allegedly, football clubs have complained that Man City and Newcastle have breached the Foreign Subsidies Regulation (FSR), which have been in force since June 2023. The focus will be to what extent the clubs may be controlled "by the state." Man City have always maintained the club are a personal venture of Sheikh Mansour, who is the vice president and deputy prime minister of the UAE. Saudi Arabia's Public Investment Fund (PIF), which controls Newcastle and is chaired

* https://www.dailymail.co.uk/sport/football/article-12449237/Manchester-City-Newcastle-fear-new-probes-European-Commission-official-complaints-owner-state-subsidies-MONEY.html.

by Crown Prince and Saudi prime minister Mohammed bin Salman, has always claimed to be an impartial, independent investment entity.

FRAGILE SYSTEM

Earlier in this book, I explained that while broadcasting revenues have grown in the past but may have peaked, player salaries and infrastructure costs have grown even faster, making the football economic model for the vast majority of clubs even more unsustainable and riskier.

The global pandemic exposed how fragile the system was. In June 2021, The World Economic Forum published a paper titled "COVID-19: How the Pandemic Has Made Football's Structural Problems Worse." The paper stated: "Structurally, football clubs generate little or no cash flows and their equity is limited. At best, as was the case before the COVID crisis, the best-managed clubs made no (or few) losses. This does not exclude the possibility of creating value for investors, but that is predicated on industry revenues growing. If the clubs' revenues are growing, investors may assume that, in the long term, they will get a share of this growth and that they will be in a position to benefit from greater media coverage of football, even though most of the value is captured by the players."

In June 2021, there was an Off The Pitch article titled: "The Football Industry Was About to Destroy Itself Even Before Covid-19 Spread."[*] The article explains that even though the annual revenue growth of the European football industry has been around 8 percent in the last twenty years, expenses (in particular player salaries and transfer fees) have increased even faster. So growth in revenues has not resulted in a significant improvement in financial performance. In fact, the article states: "Losses were a reality for many clubs even before Covid-19 spread." Losses need capital injections. The article articulates, "More than other clubs, two stand out as examples here: Manchester City and Paris Saint Germain. Abu Dhabi and Qatari shareholders invested massive amounts of money to give a boost both to the Cityzens and Les Parisiens. Between

---

[*] https://offthepitch.com/a/football-industry-was-about-destroy-itself-even-covid-19-spread-change-perspective-will-make.

2008/2009 and 2018/2019, Manchester City received capital injections (and due to partners for financing) totaling £1.329 billion . . . From 2011/2012 to 2018/2019, Paris Saint Germain saw €419 million of capital injections and new debts due to partners of €124 million as per June 30th, 2019 . . . That capital, generated from the outside and pumped into the football industry to accelerate growth in some cases and to keep pace in others, made growth possible in the period that was almost in double digits, but at the same time, put stress on the whole process and the entire system."

Most fans generally don't care about all that—they are not responsible for the losses. They push their clubs' owners to spend more and more money to get better and better players to win trophies. But Real Madrid's members do care, because they are the owners. Real Madrid is pushing for changes to make football more sustainable—that's good for football and for Real Madrid.

The Off The Pitch article concluded, "Culturally unacceptable at this point in time, the Super League did partially solve some of the above issues, as well as providing massive new financial resources for the whole system—with the question of how the money would be distributed to other clubs yet to be discussed. Not the best way to guarantee sustainability, but a huge help in keeping football alive."

Don't think that owning a Premier League club is a guarantee of financial success. Vysyble co-founder Roger Bell said: "Owning a top English football club is not a profitable enterprise. Football lacks the merger and acquisition element that we commonly see in general commerce when a sector is performing poorly from a financial standpoint."* Therefore, financial reform must either be operational or structural in nature. The Super League was an obvious and highly predictable expression of structural reform. Bell added: "With numbers as dire as they have been over the last two years, Super League version 2.0 is not at all inconceivable."

---

* https://www.expressandstar.com/sport/football/aston-villa/2022/07/14/premier-league-clubs-rack-up-record-losses-of-more-than-1bn/

The Mythology of the Dream and Leicester City

Yes, yes . . . I know that Leicester City won the Premier League in 2015–16. However, since 2003–04, there has only been one club (Leicester City) not in the Big Six (now Big Seven, with Newcastle, and growing) who have qualified for the Champions League. In 2022–23, Newcastle qualified, after Saudi Arabia's PIF bought control.

In 2022–23, Leicester City were relegated to the Championship. Meanwhile, none of the Big Six (and now Seven with Newcastle) are really under threat of relegation. Not even Chelsea, which had one of their worst seasons in recent memory in 2022–23, finishing twelfth in the league—and that was seen as a complete disaster. The Big Six and Newcastle essentially are "founding, permanent members" of the Premier League—they just don't refer to themselves as that.

As for Leicester City . . . no one wants to talk about this. But Leicester City have reported a record loss of £92.5 million for the 2021–22 financial year, following deficits of £31.2 million in 2020–21, £67.3 million in 2019–20, and £20 million in 2018–19. And the Foxes are often referred to as "the best-run club in England."[*]

Why are Leicester City losing so much money, when they're in the richest league? Leicester City finished ninth in the 2018–2019 Premier League table (just outside European qualification dominated by the Big Six), and their wages-to-turnover ratios were 85 percent, which is not sustainable. (It peaked at 105 percent in 2019–20.) Their wages were €172 million. In contrast, Arsenal and Man U finished fifth and sixth, and they spent €399 million and €267 million, respectively—more than the total *revenues* of Leicester City. This highlights that the Big Six, plus Newcastle and growing, are their own breakaway league.

After five consecutive top 10 finishes in the Premier League, as of July 19, 2022, Leicester were only one of two clubs in Europe's Top 5 Leagues (interestingly, the other was Girona in LaLiga—partially owned by City Football Group) to not register a new player. Why? Finances.[†]

Current Leicester City chairman Aiwayatt Srivaddhanaprabha, and his late (and much loved) father, Vichai, have been very generous owners to the

---

* https://sportskhabri.com/leicester-city-the-correct-model-of-ownership/.
† https://theathletic.com/3431533/2022/07/19/leicester-transfers-rodgers-premier-league/.

Leicester and wider community. Their kindness and sense of giving have made their winning the Premier League all the more endearing. The owners of Leicester City are trying to keep up with the Big Six and Newcastle and new ownership models—they bought OH Leaven in Belgium in 2017.

As I mentioned, Leicester City were relegated at the end of the 2022–23 season. This gets to another point—the real truth about promotion and relegation. Leicester City were promoted to the Premier League in 2013–14. I analyzed the probability of relegation within three seasons of promotion to the Premier League, as well as the number of consecutive seasons a newly promoted club to the Premier League stays without suffering relegation. Most of the time (greater than 95 percent probability), newly promoted clubs stay in the Premier League less than five years. Typically, of the three clubs promoted each season, at least one club will suffer relegation in their first season after achieving promotion. And typically, at least two of the teams will be relegated by the second season, and most of the time (greater than 95 percent probability) within three seasons. Typically, a newly promoted club will not last more than three years in the Premier League. The clubs struggling to be promoted or stay in the Premier League spend almost all their money on players, which is unsustainable. And there is not that much money left for other investments such as youth development academies or fan-friendly stadiums.

THE NBA OF FOOTBALL

In the 2023 Deloitte Football Money League, for the first time ever, more than half of the clubs (eleven of twenty) come from the same country, while 80 percent of the Premier League's current members are represented in the top 30.

The presence of Leeds United illustrates the power of the Premier League. They were in the Championship as recently as 2020, and haven't competed in European competition for twenty years, and yet sit eighteenth in the Money League, above Champions League regulars like Benfica and Ajax.* And eighteen out of the twenty Premier League

* Leeds United were relegated to the Championship at the end of the 2022–23 season. The Yorkshire outfit dropped into the Championship after a two-year stay in the top flight.

teams have players more valuable than any other club outside the Top 5 Leagues. Only Fulham (€296 million squad value) and Bournemouth (€264 million squad value) are topped by FC Porto, Ajax, and Benfica in terms of value.*

The Premier League has double the broadcasting revenues as the other leagues. Many people claim this is because the league is, in their opinion, the most competitive due to "the fairest and most equitable" distribution of broadcasting revenues with a cap of 1.8 times from highest to lowest versus 3 to 3.5 times in the other leagues. But note, if the other leagues didn't pay out a higher ratio to their top finishing clubs, those clubs couldn't be as competitive in European competitions. For example, six Premier League clubs have higher domestic league TV rights than Real Madrid, and the bottom English club earned more in TV rights than the top Italian side. However, I am not convinced that the Premier League is most attractive to a global audience primarily because "it's the most competitive league."

The Bix Six (now Big Seven with Newcastle) can afford to spend much more in salaries than the clubs just outside their group—often more than those clubs' total revenues. So, the Premier League gets the most elite players from around the world—and foreign stars matter not just because they help one win but because they attract global viewers. The fans of players from those nations follow their top players. The Premier League has the highest percentage of foreign players of any European League, by far. There are sixty-five different nationalities represented in the Premier League. French and Spanish players (taking some domestic interest away from Ligue 1 and LaLiga) represent the most common foreign nationalities.

---

* https://offthepitch.com/a/valuation-analysis-fc-porto-boast-highest-valued-squad-outside-big-five -still-worth-less-90?wv_email=sgmandis%40me.com&wv_id=0b33e863-2b87-44e3-82bb-a46dd11bfd 0d&wv_name=.

Premier League vs. LaLiga Results

I often hear that Premier League clubs are "better" than LaLiga clubs—with the exceptions of Real Madrid and Barcelona. So, I looked into LaLiga club (excluding Real Madrid and Barcelona) head-to-head results versus Premier League clubs in knockout rounds of European tournaments. Just looking at the recent finals in the Europa League, we see Villarreal beat Man U in 2020–21 (and beat Arsenal in the semifinals) and Seville beat Liverpool in 2015–16.

Actually, LaLiga teams have dominated the Europa League. In the last twenty years, LaLiga won twelve trophies, while the Premier League won three. In 2022–23, Seville beat Man U in the quarterfinals on the way to winning the tournament. In 2019–20, Seville beat Wolverhampton in the quarterfinals, Man U in the semifinals, and Inter Milan in the finals. In 2018–19, Arsenal beat Valencia in the semifinals before losing to Chelsea.

In the Champions League, in 2021–22 Man City beat Atlético Madrid 1–0 in the quarterfinals before losing to Real Madrid in the semifinals. Liverpool beat Villareal in the semifinals, but after Villareal had beaten Juventus in the Round of 16 and Bayern Munich in the quarterfinals. Of course, Real Madrid beat Chelsea, Man City, and Liverpool in 2021–22.

In 2020–21, Chelsea beat Atlético Madrid and Real Madrid on their way to winning the trophy—but that same year, Real Madrid beat Liverpool.

It is hard to convince me that the Premier League clubs are better than LaLiga clubs at the European tournament level, or at the very least that Premier League clubs are maximizing results with their financial resources. Admittedly, I am very surprised that the Premier League results are not better. I don't really have a good explanation.

What LaLiga doesn't want to talk about is that Real Madrid's success has covered up a recent decline in the performance of LaLiga's clubs overall (excluding Real Madrid). Since 2016, Barcelona and Atlético Madrid have each progressed past the quarterfinals only once—both have two seasons where they did not progress out of the Group Stage. If it wasn't for Real Madrid's Champions League performances, LaLiga would be much lower in the UEFA league coefficient rankings. Not being as competitive with the Premier League is understandable given the gap in TV rights, but LaLiga is being overtaken by Germany and Italy . . . and possibly the Czech Republic or Greece.

Later, I will show how the results for Premier League clubs in the Champions League have dramatically improved since changes in their ownership models—and if it weren't for Real Madrid's results, they would be even better.

However, the real attraction of the Premier League is the fight among the Big Six or Big Seven for the four coveted European Champions League positions. The matches among the Big Seven are "big events" that attract a massive global audience—their own Super League. (Remember, Arsenal versus Man City had a bigger TV audience than a knockout round in the Champions League.) There is enough of a critical mass of evenly matched big clubs filled with international stars to keep a global audience interested. As more closely government-related, private equity, and multi-club ownership models join the Premier League, the number of big clubs and their respective "event" matches will increase. At one time, Man U versus Liverpool was the marquee matchup, like Real Madrid versus Barcelona. Now, arguably, Man City versus Liverpool is bigger, and before Abu Dhabi got involved, a global audience didn't really care that much about Man City. Soon, Saudi Arabia's PIF-controlled Newcastle's supporters won't look to their derby with Sunderland (unless they are bought by a new ownership model), but against their new rival club, which likely will have a government-related, private equity, and/or multi-club ownership model.

And this brings us to the next change.

IMPACT OF GLOBAL BRANDS ON OTHER CLUBS

The few dominant clubs with global brands in the other Top 5 Leagues have further separated themselves, both financially and in performance, from the domestic clubs who primarily rely on league broadcasting revenues (including making matches less exciting and league winners / Champions League qualifiers more predictable), and from most others in the Champions League.

LaLiga has two, maybe three with Atlético Madrid, big clubs that really matter to a global audience and fight for the domestic title, not six or seven as in the Premier League. At a global scale, and simplifying many factors, LaLiga essentially markets El Clásico. In Germany, Bayern Munich have won the last eleven Bundesliga trophies—that can seem boring to a global audience (some believe a lack of a real intense rival or top competition has hurt them in the Champions League). In Italy, there have historically been three clubs with European Cup pedigree that really matter to a global audience: AC Milan, Inter Milan, and Juventus (Juventus won nine titles in a row while Inter Milan and AC Milan had financial issues).* In France, there is PSG and everyone else (some believe a lack of a real intense rival or top competition has hurt them in the Champions League). Real Madrid, Barcelona, Bayern Munich, and PSG—they aren't concerned with promotion or relegation. And neither are the Premier League's Big Six or Seven.

The league to watch with the most big clubs with the best players is the Premier League. It's the "most competitive league" because it has the Big Six and Newcastle, more than any other league. Among that group, it is very competitive and exciting. Instead of El Clásico two times per season, the Premier League has many compelling matches between "Super League clubs" for a global audience two times a season—Man City vs. Liverpool, Man City vs. Man U, Chelsea vs. Arsenal, Arsenal vs. Tottenham, Chelsea vs. Tottenham. Almost every weekend has a "blockbuster match." It is not to say that the Premier League has the best teams at the top, as demonstrated in the sidebar on page 205. However, the financial gap between those big clubs in the Premier League and the other clubs is growing every year—not just the international broadcast revenues but commercial revenues (sponsorships, licensing).

Worrisome for the other leagues in Europe, the mid-table Premier League clubs operate on a completely different financial level than most of the continental clubs. The Premier League spent almost exactly as much as the other four leagues *combined* in the 2021–22 summer offseason

---

* Napoli won Serie A in the 2022–23 season. Lazio, Inter Milan, and AC Milan finished second, third, and fourth, respectively. Juventus were penalized ten points for punishment for false accounting in the club's transfer dealings, which took them out of the top four positions.

(€2.23 billion to €2.25 billion).* The Bundesliga, for example, is becoming a feeder league to the Premier League. However, it's not the Big Six or Seven buying players from Germany; it's even the middle and bottom of the table Premier League clubs. And it's not just the players going to the Premier League; it's the managers, coaches, and scouts. Multi-club owners like Man City owning a stake in Girona will accelerate LaLiga becoming a feeder too.

Look at Real Madrid's recent big player sales—Álvaro Morata to Chelsea in 2017 for €70 million, Ángel Di María to Man U in 2014 for €70 million, Casemiro to Man U in 2022 for €70 million, Mesut Özil to Arsenal in 2013 for €50 million, Mateo Kovačić to Chelsea in 2019 for €47 million, Martin Ødegaard to Arsenal in 2021 for €35 million, and Raphaël Varane to Man U in 2021 for €40 million. With the primary exception of Cristiano Ronaldo to Juventus (which was a special circumstance), the players are sold to Premier League clubs—the only league with clubs that can consistently afford Real Madrid players. (Marco Asensio and Sergio Ramos went to PSG on free transfers. Achraf Hakimi was sold to Inter.)

And the gap can also grow from further investments from new ownership models into these clubs. Since closely government-related or private equity firms can't buy member-controlled big clubs like Real Madrid, Barcelona, and Bayern Munich and the broadcasting revenues gap between the Premier League and the other domestic leagues is increasing, the Premier League will become an even bigger focus for new ownership models—leading to more "big clubs" in the Premier League and/or a larger gap. The primary club of a multi-club owner will be in the Premier League like Man City and Girona. The biggest issue or financial risk for the Big Six or Big Seven owners is that there are only four Champions League positions, and missing a spot is a significant financial hit of potentially tens of millions of Euros (and the difference of keeping or having to sell players)—revenue that was a reason why a European Super

---

* https://www.goal.com/en-us/lists/afraid-game-going-to-die-premier-league-killing-european-football/bltc12ec88eed0c74e9#cs5c9d8c83e6551a22.

League was attractive to them.* This was a reason for the push for UEFA to change the Champions League format in 2024–25 to have two of the four extra places to be awarded on the performance of a country's clubs in Europe over the previous season.

"Maybe That Super League Idea Isn't Such a Bad Thing"

As the gap continues to grow with the Premier League, it will become increasingly difficult for Real Madrid to compete for talent and for the Champions League trophy. In that purely financial context, then, one structural solution to keeping up with the Premier League was the Super League. This isn't just an issue for Real Madrid, but for all the non-big Premier League clubs and fans outside of England. The fans in Europe feel the shift. UEFA president Aleksander Čeferin hit out at Italian and Spanish fans, claiming they didn't help like English fans did during the Super League launch: "The English fans helped us while the Italians and Spaniards did nothing."† In one study 72 percent of fans in Italy, 71 percent of fans in France, and 76 percent of fans in Spain support a European Super League.‡ And the younger they are, the higher the support.

After PSG were knocked out by Bayern Munich in the Round of 16 in the Champions League on March 8, 2023, football journalist and author Gab Marcotti said on ESPN FC:

> I am sure there are going to be people in France and elsewhere who say "Hang on a minute, what happened to that Super League thing? Because we play in Ligue 1, a lot of guys essentially half ass it every week, and we still win the league—do we need more of that motivation to play against tougher competition week in and week out?

---

* It's the same reason golfers who have risks in performance are signing with the Saudi Public Wealth Fund–backed LIV Golf Tour—they have more and guaranteed money. Take a player like Pat Perez, whose highest world ranking was sixteen and his best Masters finish was eighteenth in 2017 and best US Open finish was thirty-sixth in 2008 and 2018. During his twenty-one years on the PGA Tour, he made $29 million; and in eight events on the LIV Tour, he made $8 million.

† https://football-italia.net/ceferin-italian-fans-didnt-fight-help-super-league-fight/.

‡ https://sportsfinding.com/a-survey-endorsed-the-split-plans-of-the-super-league/92967/.

Maybe that Super League idea isn't such a bad thing." I think it will reopen those debates . . . How many top, top opponents has Messi been able to face this season between Ligue 1, the French Cup, and the Champions League? The answer is not many."*

How about the biggest sports market—the U.S.—which is a key part of growth of football? In 2018, the United States accounted for 32.5 percent share of the global sports market valued at $471 billion, with the others in the top five being China (12.5 percent), Japan (4.6 percent), Germany (4.1 percent), and France (3.2 percent).†

UEFA president Aleksander Čeferin said, "Football [soccer] is extremely popular in [the] United States these days. Americans are willing to pay this amount [gestures high with hand] for the best and nothing for the less. So, they will follow European football as basketball lovers in Europe follow NBA. It's a very important promising market for the future. The thing is that we are selling rights very well."

Alexi Lalas, former USMNT player and analyst for Fox Sports, captured the thoughts of many Americans: "If they [the European Super League] produce a better product than the existing competition in the market, then I'll be a customer. I am a consumer of soccer. I want to see exciting, entertaining performances."

Michael Wilbon, a co-host on ESPN's *Pardon the Interruption* TV show (which averages more than one million viewers per day), said, "This new Super League . . . would interest me. Seeing the fabulous world famous teams playing each other home and away . . . I would like to see that . . . We want to see the greatest teams and the greatest players go against each other . . . I know if I lived in one of these places in Europe and grown up with it I'd be a purist to some degree . . . I apologize to people offended by that, but I want to see the new league."

Tony Kornheiser, the other co-host of *PTI*, said, "They [FIFA and UEFA] control European soccer right now and they are fearful they would

---

* https://www.youtube.com/watch?v=2YXExMuiZOw.

† https://www.statista.com/statistics/1087429/global-sports-market-share-by-country/.

not control it . . . You know what, this [the European Super League] is a better idea. This is a better idea, and I hope it works out."

One Everton Fan's Point of View

In 2021, as a result of the proposed European Super League announcement, Everton (which were not invited to be a co-founder) surveyed their fans.* The overwhelming majority of ten thousand Everton fans that completed and submitted the survey didn't support the European Super League. Keep in mind Everton was not a founding member of the Super League, and has more of a "local" fan base than its crosstown rival Liverpool, which has more global fans and sponsors.

However, the survey results showed there is widespread concern from Everton fans over the future of the English game, how English football is regulated, and how the fallout from the ESL proposals could impact Everton as well as the wider footballing pyramid in the future. Only 30 percent of Everton fans in the survey believed the other Premier League clubs strive to maintain the ethos and traditions of the game. Only one in five people believed the current level of regulation in English football is appropriate. So, something seems to be broken, or at the very least needs to be addressed.

Lastly, one Everton fan expressed an interesting sentiment to British talkSport that came up more often from fans of clubs across England that were not invited to participate in the ESL than I would have initially guessed:

> I think this [European Super League] could be a good thing. I think this could be a chance for us to liberate football from the monopoly that is these six [Premier League] clubs that think they think they got hold of football. This is a chance for us to rewrite the rules, whether it be a 51 per cent, whether it be a wage cap . . . whatever it may be . . . For every Man United, there's a Leeds United. For every Arsenal, there's an Aston Villa. For every

---

* After the announcement of the European Super League, Everton sent out surveys to supporters and received almost ten thousand responses. The overwhelming majority did not want an ESL. https://www.evertonfc.com/news/2263658/everton-releases-findings-from-future-of-football-survey.

Tottenham, there's a Huddersfield. These teams could be replaced with teams that have got a rich history and a very big fan base.[*]

LOCAL FANS VS. GLOBAL FANS— FOOTBALL TRIBALISM GOES GLOBAL

In this book's introduction, I questioned what a fan is. This was to high-light the pushback from local, multi-generation, hard-core, season-ticket-holder club fan expectations and preferences against global capitalism and newer, much-larger-in-numbers, global club fan expectations and preferences. The latter are not as tethered to local rivalries, and most have never been to the stadium.

In 2018, then–Liverpool CEO Peter Moore provided a manifesto that captures the essence of Liverpool: "Our pulse is global, our heart is local; and you'll never walk alone is both our anthem and our rallying cry." Local versus global is football's biggest balancing act. Catering to a global fan base is where the revenue growth is. And clubs need to grow reve-nues to afford increasing players' salaries. However, the clubs can't risk upsetting the "authentic" local fans because their "authentic" history, tra-ditions, and values are part of what the global clubs are marketing. The local fans often provide the atmosphere in the stadiums. The local fan feels like they were there first, they are the season ticket holders, and they know the other local fans around their seats—their tribalism is local.

However, football tribalism has gone global with digital technology—broadcasting, the internet, and social media. Most global fans have never even been to the stadium. Instead of season tickets, they have TV sub-scriptions. They are not connected physically, but digitally, via social media. They see the matches as entertainment. The global fan wants to see big club Real Madrid and star Ronaldo play against big club Barcelona and star Messi or big club Liverpool and star Steven Gerrard play against big club Chelsea and star Frank Lampard. "In fact, it is the convergence

---

[*] https://www.sportbible.com/football/news-reactions-everton-fans-argument-for-european-super-league-being-a-good-thing-20210420.

and tension between local and global interests among the actors involved in the Super League project that has hindered its implementation."*

It's not just the clubs. The leagues are also balancing local versus global. In October 2019, LaLiga requested permission from the Spanish Football Federation (RFEF) to move a league match between Villarreal and Atlético Madrid to the Hard Rock Stadium in Miami, Florida. It was the second time LaLiga attempted to move a match to the United States, having previously tried to move Barcelona's match against Girona at the start of 2019. Both times the RFEF and the players' union staunchly objected. In addition, Real Madrid sent a letter to the Spanish Football Federation stating they "utterly oppose" plans to play LaLiga matches in the United States because matches in the U.S. would jeopardize the "integrity and fairness of the competition." And that is what I found Real Madrid most focused on—which is good for football.

There's more to be said about the changes going on more broadly in sports, entertainment, and content. But first, in the next chapter, I'll address a few more football-specific changes:

Calendars/competitions are more congested (including more player injuries because of correlation between number of matches, intensity, and injuries); super-agents have more power and are taking more money (and gaining more influence with clubs).

Players have essentially become global brands, and some have more social media followers than their clubs (including more player recognition from video games) and make more money than the profits of their clubs.

Football media has become immediate news with limited governance (including the public's fascination with transfers and individual players' money and lives, and more people getting their sports news via YouTube, Instagram, and TikTok).

---

* https://www.frontiersin.org/articles/10.3389/fspor.2023.1148624/full#B8.

Chapter 5

CALENDARS, SUPER-AGENTS, PLAYER INC., AND "HERE WE GO!"

M ANY OF THE systemic changes in football are recognized by most stakeholders, but nothing is really being done. Most football stakeholders seem resistant to change, but the sport needs to be thinking about the future. Sadly, the lack urgency for real change, keeping the status quo, may become football's biggest regret. The congested football calendar is a prime example. In this chapter we will also examine the impact of super-agents, players becoming more of a focus than the clubs due to the rise of video games and football media, and the Saudi Pro League signings.

ARE CALENDARS MORE CONGESTED?

A more congested schedule, with more competitions, means, among other things, more player injuries, because of correlation between the number of matches, the intensity of play, and injuries, Real Madrid is concerned with football's governing bodies' decisions to add more games to the schedule. Florentino Pérez said, "We cannot understand that UEFA increases the number of inconsequential games in a new model [i.e., a new Champions League format] that will only serve to further

alienate fans and accelerate the decline of football."* Florentino referenced the NFL's higher revenues than European football even though
they play far fewer games. "The NFL, with 285 games per season, exceeds
the audiovisual revenue of the Champions League, Europa League, and
five major European leagues together with more than 2,000 games per
year. There are no excuses, the data does not admit discussion, football is
clearly losing the battle of entertainment."

Carlo Ancelotti, when asked about the current calendar, said: "What do
you want me to say? There is a calendar here which is absolute nonsense."†

Luka Modrić commented about the number of matches players are
being asked to play: "There are too many games at the moment, we are
playing every three days, in the league, Europe and with our national
teams. We are living in a very complicated time but no one is asking
about the health of the players."‡

While most admit that the calendar is too congested at the top level
of football, organizations and leagues keep adding more games to generate more revenue, instead of planning fewer, more meaningful games.§
The higher the revenues, the more money there is to pay the players too.
But at what cost?

A research report from international insurance company Howden
confirms what leading club managers have been saying for a while now:
injuries are on the rise across European football. Howden claimed that
there were 4,810 total injuries in these big leagues, a 20 percent increase
compared to the previous season.¶ Howden's "Injury Index" calculates the
financial impact of these injuries. In total for European leagues, injury
costs reached a combined $562 million for the 2021–22 season. Injuries
to young players are also alarmingly on the rise. Howden reported that

---

* https://www.archysport.com/2022/10/florentino-perez-attacks-al-khelaifi-for-comments-on-real
-madrid-this-is-how-he-defended-it-football-curiosities/.

† https://www.isspf.com/fixture-congestion-in-football/.

‡ https://www.goalzz.com/?n=977691&o=ns0.

§ Outside the top of football, many agree that there is a lack of playing opportunities. It's only the
very best players who play all these games. Arguably, the rest of the players actually need more.

¶ https://worldsoccertalk.com/2022/09/29/premier-league-clubs-hit-hardest-by-injuries/.

there were 326 total injuries to U21 players last season as compared to thirty reported injuries just three seasons prior.

Earlier, I wrote that the 2022 Champions League final was Real Madrid's fifty-sixth match of the season, and Liverpool's sixty-third. In the Premier League and LaLiga, clubs play thirty-eight matches per season, with each match lasting an average ninety-eight minutes with stoppage time. This means that a player could theoretically play around 3,724 minutes per year in their league, if they played every minute of every match. Real Madrid typically have other matches ranging from Copa del Rey (final in April or May), Supercopa de España (final in January), UEFA Super Cup (final in August), UEFA Champions League (final in May), and FIFA Club World Cup (final in December or February).

In 2021–22, six players from Real Madrid played more than 3,900 minutes during the season (including non-LaLiga matches but excluding international matches): goalkeeper Thibaut Courtois (52 matches, 4,770 minutes), center-back Éder Militão (50 matches, 4,496 minutes), left-winger Vinícius Júnior (52 matches, 4,274 minutes), center-back David Alaba (46 matches, 4,071 minutes), defensive midfielder Casemiro (48 matches, 3,928 minutes), and center-forward Karim Benzema (46 matches, 3,919 minutes).*

Most of their players also star on their national teams and participated in an additional four to eight matches (2022 FIFA World Cup qualification, continental tournaments, and international friendly matches). The six players that played over 3,900 minutes for Real Madrid typically played five to seven international matches and around 400 to 600 minutes.

Interestingly, in 1999–2000, when Real Madrid won the Champions League, they played a similar 65 matches (more than Liverpool in 2021–22). Real Madrid also had six players in 1999–2000 who played more than 3,900 minutes during the season. There were two standouts: Roberto Carlos played 5,162 minutes in 59 matches and Raúl played 4,930 minutes in 57 matches! (Interestingly, Roberto Carlos and Raúl

---

* Liverpool also had six players with more than 3,900 minutes: Allison, Alexander-Arnold, Mané, Robertson, Salah, and van Dijk.

work with the Real Madrid Academy! Also, Liverpool played a total of 53 matches when they won the Champions league in 2004–05.)

I was surprised that the number of matches has not really increased over the last few decades. So, what are all the managers and players complaining about? What has changed? The physical demands in professional football have increased dramatically over the years. There has been an increase both in the distance that players cover in a match and in the intensity at which they sprint. For example, a study that analyzed all Premier League games from the 2006–07 season to the 2012–13 season shows how during these seven seasons the number of sprints increased by 85 percent (31 versus 57) and the distance covered at that intensity increased by 35 percent (232 meters versus 350 meters).[*] The intensity of sprinting reflects changes in the way football is played at the highest level—more managers utilize an aggressive playing style with lots of high intensity running to pressure the opponent. This has resulted both in players getting more tired and in more player injuries.[†] Injuries have a high correlation by position, distance covered, sprinting/velocity, intensity, and ball possession. To illustrate how intensity matters, there are 3.4 injuries per 1,000 hours of training versus 23.8 in matches. This is driven, in part, by the intensity of matches versus practices. It also may be driven by the difference in size of the pitch or distances that need to be run at high intensity.

Fatigue impacts when both goals and injuries happen. Studies show that there is a meaningful drop-off in players' intensity in the final twenty to twenty-five minutes of matches, where they also have the highest risk of injuries. This also explains the trend of an increasing percentage of goals being scored after seventy-five minutes of playing time. This suggests there is a lot to gain from player substitutions during the second half of the match, so a deep bench is a meaningful competitive advantage.

Following a global analysis of the ongoing impact of COVID-19 on football, as well as representations from several key stakeholders from

* Barnes, C., Archer, DT, Hogg, B., Bush, M., Bradley, PS. "The Evolution of Physical and Technical Performance Parameters in the English Premier League." *Int J Sports Med.* 2014.

† https://sciencenordic.com/denmark-football-society--culture/scientists-football-has-changed-dramatically/1440511.

across the football community, in May 2020 FIFA permitted competition organizers the option of allowing teams to use up to five substitutes per match (instead of three). The decision was to support player welfare, in particular where schedules have been disrupted, often leading to competitions being played in a condensed period.

The Week and Season of a Footballer Is Recovery

If a football player at an elite club plays the entire ninety-minute match on Sunday, then on Monday generally he will rest and recover, which can include light physical activity, stretching, and massages. Tuesday, the player will generally practice for about 50 percent of the time they played two days before—so in this case the player will practice with meaningful physical intensity for forty-five minutes (never full speed) and spend time in the film room and going over tactics. On Wednesday, the player may have a Champions League match and play the entire ninety-minute match. Thursday is rest and recovery. Friday is forty-five minutes of practice of meaningful physical intensity. Saturday may be another ninety-minute match.

Over time, week after week, the physical load actually impacts the player over the season. For example, it impacts the biochemistry of the players. Most players are anemic (the blood doesn't have enough red blood cells) at the end of the season. They lose iron through sweat and the physical exertion over the season. It takes the body time to create new red blood cells. There are limits as to what medical staff can do to help players address their low red blood cells, either with supplements or intravenously, because of anti-doping regulations. As the season progresses, the muscles and joints also get more and more tired and susceptible to injury.

By March and April, the players and medical staff are primarily focused on recovery. And this is not just physical; this is mental health and recovery also. The season is a grind for the players with all the travel, especially going to play for their national teams all over the world. The national team matches often have a lot of pressure as well if they are for tournament qualifications—which are both physically and mentally demanding. Typically, the older players who are past their peak ages take more time to recover—so the end of the seasons are particularly challenging for them, just as the physical and mental intensity and pressure is picking up.

Medical staffs use all types of data to help them best keep players at their peak performance. And managers must be able to motivate players for every match and manage the entire squad's rotations. If a player knows they have a difficult Champions League match in a few days, subconsciously they can be less enthusiastic about the match they have to play today in a relatively small stadium with relatively poor facilities. Potentially, they may not have their best performance, especially at the end of the season. But the player needs to play to stay at the highest level. The manager feels pressure to play star players for a variety of reasons (including giving the fans who paid money for tickets what they expect).

According to a new FIFPRO report, the amount of back-to-back matches in elite men's professional football has increased over the last three years, with national-team players spending 70 percent of their playing time in a two-game-a-week rhythm.* The cumulative exposure to matches constitutes a risk for a player's health, performance, and career longevity.

Long-distance travel for national-team players puts pressure on many players' health and performance because of sudden changes in climate and time zones. Some players traveled more than two hundred thousand kilometers over the last three seasons—the equivalent of going around the globe five times.

The changes in the game also mean that to generate a playing rhythm clubs have to navigate key variables such as travel and logistics, training load management, squad rotation, and rest and recovery. For example, coaches and physical trainers design training plans for players to be able to withstand high workloads on a very tight schedule, which in some cases can include up to three matches per week. They vary the training load based on the proximity of the match and the evolution of the season itself—mainly focused on recovery and preparation for the most meaningful matches, because the best players at peak condition are very scarce and valuable assets.

---

* https://fifpro.org/en/supporting-players/health-and-performance/player-workload/rise-in-excessive-back-to-back-matches-in-men-s-football-fifpro-research-shows.

What does the demanding calendar and increase to five substitutions mean for Real Madrid and other big clubs fighting for trophies at the end of long seasons? They need a deeper bench of elite players for late match substitutions and rotations, which costs more money—both transfer fees and salaries. It also means more investment in technology to monitor players' health, performance, and recovery; more investment in fitness, health, and medical staffs; and more investment in training facilities and infrastructure.

A big change is that medical/health, technology, data analytics, and facilities are now viewed as important foundations for sports performance (versus just talent), which is interconnected to commercial success. Directors of football medical / health / science / technology / data analytics are now seen as bridges from the technical on-the-pitch performance to off-the-pitch success. This is because clubs realize they need to perform in the biggest matches, in finals, and in the Champions League—at the end of seasons. It is impossible for the players to perform at their peak for all the minutes of all the matches, especially as they get older. Zidane captured the concern many have about the sport of football being less entertaining to a global audience: "We've reached a point where you start to think that with so many matches and so many injuries, the spectacle is not the same." Former Brighton & Hove Albion striker Maheta Molango, now highly respected chief executive officer of the English Professional Footballers' Association (PFA), said, "I want my kids to see the best version of the players. It's why I fell in love with this game . . . Right now I feel what my kids see on the TV is just a shadow of what they would expect if this person would be able to play a number of games that is sustainable."* (In full disclosure, Maheta and I both serve on an academic board together at FIFA.)

Molango also explained why the calendar hasn't been comprehensively addressed: "What we are seeing is different stakeholders having different interests, trying to protect their own business interests, and the players somehow having to fit within that picture."

---

* https://www.nippon.com/en/news/reu20211007KBN2GW1UQ/.

The players can only play so many high-intensity matches per week and per season—mentally and physically. And they have a limited opportunity (relatively short) to play before they reach peak age, and their skills and fitness diminish. More star players are realizing that, to grow and maximize their earnings per match and season, the matches need to be "events" with the highest global interest. Typically, those higher earning matches are for clubs, whereas national team matches contribute to players' brands.

For Real Madrid, they envision a competition that has more meaningful and entertaining matches for the fans. Since the big clubs pay the player transfer fees and salaries and have the risk when players leave to play for their national teams and have to deal with the player needing rest from travel, they want more input in the calendar.

In a World Cup year, players are unavailable for clubs due to national team duty for up to 22 percent of the season. The ECA broke down a typical elite player calendar in a World Cup year into 104 slots (52 weeks with midweek and weekend match per week). A player can play 38 domestic league matches, 6 domestic cup matches, 19 champions league matches, 12 international qualifier matches, 3 pre–World Cup Camps, 8 World Cup matches, 6 mandatory rest periods, and 12 other. Club football is 75 of the 104 calendar slots or 72 percent of available time while international football is 23 of the 104 calendar slots or 22 percent of player time. The estimated wages of that player's time in Euros is 448 to 585 million, which is essentially paid for by the clubs.

FIFA, the regional governing bodies like UEFA, and the national associations depend on matches to generate revenues (to organize and develop the game)—the more matches, the better. And any changes can impact those revenues.

In the end, the stakeholders have to figure out together how to make the revenue pie bigger—and that inevitably comes down to improving the quality of the entertainment product.

Also worth discussing is the impact of the demanding men's football calendar—not to mention many competing sports and entertainment options—to the coverage and opportunities for women's football. We'll cover this in chapter six.

Arsène Wenger's Proposal to Address
the Congested Calendar

The current FIFA International Match Calendar (IMC) is an outline agreement between FIFA, the six continental football confederations, the European Club Association, and FIFPRO,* which sets out which dates can be used for "official" and "friendly" men's international matches.

The current dates are within five windows: March, May, or June; August or September; October and November. The match calendar also determines the dates of the international windows and when international competitions such as the AFC Asian Cup, Africa Cup of Nations, Copa América, CONCACAF Gold Cup, OFC Nations Cup, UEFA European Championship, and FIFA World Cup can take place.[†]

In September 2021, former Arsenal manager Arsène Wenger, FIFA Chief of Global Football Development, made a proposal to optimize the IMC.

Wenger's proposal was to alter football's annual schedule from 2024 onward. All national team "qualifiers" would take place in a six-week block between October and November, or over two windows in October and March. "Friendly" matches between countries would be eliminated. The rest of the season would be given over to club matches, thus reducing the number of "interruptions" caused by national team football. The changes would create space for a monthlong window for national tournaments in June. Furthermore, FIFA supported the introduction of a mandatory rest period for players.[‡]

Most of July would be reserved as a rest period for players each year. Wenger added: "You have 20 percent national team football and 80 percent club football, and we want to maintain that balance, but we just want to

---

* The Fédération Internationale des Associations de Footballeurs Professionnels, generally referred to as FIFPRO, is the worldwide representative organization for around 65,000 professional football players. FIFPRO, with its global headquarters in Hoofddorp, Netherlands, is made up of sixty-six national players' associations.

† Official matches have a release period of four days, which means that players can take up to four days away from club duties to partake in national team duties. If a player participates in an official match on a different continent from his club's, the release period is five days. Friendly matches are deemed less important and the release period is forty-eight hours. FIFA insist that official and friendly matches take precedence over domestic matches. However, they state that international friendlies that take place outside the designated dates do not.

‡ July would be relevant for European leagues that are August to May, but other leagues are February to November.

reorganize it in a more efficient way . . . This means regrouping and reducing qualifiers in national team football, creating longer periods for players to remain with their clubs, and to establish a guaranteed rest period for players every year."

Then–Chelsea manager Thomas Tuchel's reaction to Wenger's proposal was: "It is a brilliant idea. There are too many windows, too many competitions and too many games for the players. It increases quantity, not quality. Everyone wants their top players to play for them and it's too much."*

Many fans agree there are too many windows and stops and starts of the season and tournaments. However, the issue for the big global clubs is that they often train and travel to other countries during the summer to give their fans an opportunity to see the clubs' players in person, to increase club brand visibility, and for financial incentives.

Wenger has a reputation for being very thoughtful and pragmatic . . . and being an innovator. His FIFA Technical Advisory Group's recommendations deserved serious discussion and consideration. However, the most talked about proposed reform was . . . the recommendation of staging the FIFA World Cup every two years (instead of four). Wenger believes that the World Cup schedule has become "outdated," given fans' apparent desire for more "event matches" and the relative ease of international travel. Unfortunately, the emotional response about having a World Cup every two years drowned out some of the most important problems Wenger and his team were trying to address.

The main point was replacing meaningless games with meaningful ones. The expectation was not to increase the overall number of international games, but rather increase the quality of those games. And one way of doing this was, for instance, using the continental competitions (such as the Euros, the Copa America) as the pathway/qualifiers for the World Cup, which would optimize the qualifiers in each confederation.

---

* https://www.offtheball.com/soccer/it-increases-quantity-over-quality-thomas-tuchel-on-international-breaks-1273604.

SUPER-AGENTS

The so-called super-agents have more power these days, and are taking more money. The results include signing and pushing younger and younger players. Let's look at some prominent examples.

Jorge Mendes

Super-agents are now among the most prominent and well-known figures in the world of football—some are even household names. For example, Jorge Mendes is among the most influential agents in the world, with clients including Cristiano Ronaldo, José Mourinho, Diego Costa, James Rodríguez, and João Félix. He has been named Best Agent of the Year at the Globe Soccer Awards on ten occasions and won Agent of the Century in 2020. He is personally responsible for well over $1 billion in transfers. Sir Alex Ferguson wrote in *My Autobiography*, "Jorge Mendes is the best agent I dealt with, without a doubt. He was responsible, looked after his players in an incredible way and he's very fair with the clubs." He has a reputation for being reliable, honest, passionate, dedicated, and trustworthy.

Benfica president Luís Filipe Vieira told TVI: "[Mendes] has a price, he's a professional, everyone knows he demands 10 percent for every transfer [he conducts]. There isn't a single person in this country who isn't aware of that."* Most high-profile transfers from Portugal are usually put together by Mendes. He is known to be the dominant agent in his native country, often facilitating deals for Benfica, Porto, and Braga. Pippo Russo, author of a book on Mendes, *The Orgy of Power: The Counter Story of Jorge Mendes, the Patron of Global Football*, and a sociologist at the University of Florence who specializes in the business of football, said, "In Portugal he is really the gatekeeper—any transfer involving the big three is mediated by Jorge Mendes. No one moves without him being involved, especially to the Premier League . . . he has been involved

---

* https://bleacherreport.com/articles/2859480-jorge-mendes-how-ronaldos-super-agent-has-built-a -football-empire.

in a lot of transfers. He is really everywhere."* Mendes opened the door
to the English market in 2003 when he transferred Cristiano Ronaldo to
Man U, and in 2004, when José Mourinho, Ricardo Carvalho, and Paulo
Ferreira went to Chelsea. It is important to note that he has an important
role in football, especially Portuguese football, in identifying young talent and giving them opportunities at various European clubs.† It is fair to
write that many Portuguese clubs have benefited financially (some might
say survived) from transfers arranged by Mendes. These clubs have also
been able to invest the transfer proceeds in not only their first team but
in infrastructure and their youth academies.

Some people believe, and are concerned, that Mendes and other
super-agents have excessive influence over certain clubs' transfer business. For example, in early 2016, in front of an audience of football legends, including Mendes's client José Mourinho, Mendes and Chinese
billionaire Guo Guangchang announced a new partnership to expand
football in China and help players build careers. Guo is co-founder of pri-
vately held Fosun International, a Chinese multinational conglomerate
holding company that owns Club Med, Thomas Cook Group, Cirque du
Soleil, and St. John clothing label. As a part of the deal, an entity affiliated with Guo Guangchang acquired a reported 15 to 20 percent stake
in GestiFute, Mendes's football agency.‡

Just a few months later, in July 2016, Fosun bought the English football club Wolverhampton Wanderers for an estimated £45 million. FA
rules prohibit a company or person who owns a club to also own a stake
in a football agency. The FA's rules are aimed at preventing conflicts of
interest. In addition, the rules forbid an agent from being in a position to
exercise any material, managerial, or "any other influence over the affairs
of a club," whether directly or indirectly. The Wolverhampton Wanderers acquisition was approved by the English Football Association even

* https://www.theguardian.com/football/2022/sep/05/another-profitable-window-for-jorge-mendes
-the-gatekeeper-of-portugal.

† Examples include Bernardo Silva (who had limited playing opportunities at Benfica and Mendes
placed him at Monaco and now is in Man City), João Cancelo (almost the same), Diogo Jota (who is
doing very well at Liverpool), and Rafael Leão (Milan).

‡ https://www.dailymail.co.uk/sport/football/article-10268109/Jorge-Mendes-one-footballs
-influential-elusive-super-agents.html.

though the link between Fosun and Mendes raised concerns that the Wolves were in breach of the rules. Remember, reportedly Fosun doesn't directly own a stake in GestiFute, Mendes's football agency—it's an entity affiliated with the majority owner of Fosun.

"Fu-sin" (how it is pronounced) in Chinese means "renaissance." And the Wolves have had a remarkable renaissance—and added to the "break-away Super League" within the Premier League. Arguably that group is becoming the Big Six, Newcastle, and Wolverhampton Wanderers.

The Wolves had spent just four seasons in the Premier League in the previous thirty-two seasons before Fosun acquired them. They had never been higher than fifteenth in the Premier League. After the acquisition was approved, twelve players joined in the next six weeks, and some turned out to be very good. Many of the players or their clubs were close to Mendes. After the 2016–17 season, Nuno Espírito Santo, Mendes's first client and close friend, was brought on as manager because he could work with Mendes on recruitment and a longer-term strategy.[*] In addition, Jeff Shi, executive chairman of the Wolves, moved from Shanghai to Wolverhampton, bringing his family and relocating near the training ground, having previously split his time between China and England. He is focused on the Wolves being a well-run, sustainable business. Lastly, in July 2017, Rúben Neves, a client of GestiFute, signed for €16 million—a club and league record fee at the time. Upon joining, he was reunited with his former Porto manager Nuno.

The Wolves' culture and expectations quickly changed after the Fosun acquisition. Lots of money was invested in the squad, academy, and infrastructure. Under Nuno, the Wolves went on to clinch the 2017–18 EFL Championship title and return to the Premier League after a six-year absence. With the Wolves now in the Premier League, the relationship was reexamined by the EFL.[†]

In 2018, the Wolves' managing director, Laurie Dalrymple, confirmed that Mendes advises the club's owner, has given advice on players, and

---

[*] Nuno became Mendes's first client after a chance meeting in 1996. After Mendes was a Portuguese semiprofessional footballer, he became a DJ, a video shop owner, and then a nightclub owner. At Nuno's request, Mendes helped negotiate a transfer to Deportivo, and the rest is history.

[†] https://www.theguardian.com/football/2018/apr/25/jorge-mendes-wolves-efl-comply.

that players "connected" to Mendes have been signed. A representative of the Wolves said: "Jorge Mendes is available as an adviser to the owners, in the same way as many other agents and influential figures within football are."* Dalrymple maintained that no rules have been broken. Once again, the Wolves were cleared by the EFL. But there is no doubting Mendes' importance to the Wolves' success. Without Mendes, there probably would be no Fosun, no Nuno, no Neves—and no place in the Premier League.

In their first year in the Premier League, the Wolves finished in seventh place. As a result of Man City winning both that season's EFL Cup and FA Cup, they received a spot in the qualification rounds of UEFA Europa League, their first continental competition since 1980–81. They reached the quarterfinals, losing to eventual champions Sevilla. In 2019–20, they replicated their previous season's seventh place in the Premier League. In the difficult pandemic-impacted 2020–21 season, they finished thirteenth and Nuno left the club "by mutual consent." Former Benfica head coach Bruno Lage, a client of GestiFute, was hired as the new manager, and they finished tenth. Eventually he was terminated, and the club hired Julen Lopetegui, who was supposed to manage the Wolves when Fosun acquired them.† Lopetegui and Carlos Bucero, Lopetegui's agent, have a close relationship with Mendes.

According to a January 2019 Reuters article written by Tom Bergin and Cassell Bryan-Low:

What Mendes and Guo didn't publicly reveal then, or since, was that they also envisaged creating a network of clubs and soccer academies in Europe and buying and selling players, emails and internal presentations related to the deal show. Such a network would enable the partners to sidestep a ban on investors buying stakes in players and trading them. With the help of top agents like Mendes, such trading could capture profits that might

* https://www.dailymail.co.uk/sport/football/article-10268109/Jorge-Mendes-one-footballs-influential-elusive-super-agents.html.

† https://www.theguardian.com/football/2022/nov/06/better-late-than-never-lopeteguis-winding-route-back-into-wolves-arms.

otherwise go to assist smaller clubs. Trading and representing players, Fosun believed, according to an internal presentation from 2015, was the only sustainably profitable part of the soccer industry . . . In August [2016], an analyst working for Fosun emailed Mendes' business partner, Luis Correia, saying: "Our goal is to build a complete system in global football world with you, with different levels of clubs and training facilities . . . I believe together we can establish our strong presence in every major league."*

The alleged Fosun presentations and emails show one aim of the new partnership appears to be to create a network for identifying players who could later be sold for profit. A 2016 email from a Fosun executive described investing and trading in players as "the most lucrative part of business in the football industry." Fosun, Guo, Mendes, and Correia did not respond to requests from Reuters for comment. (Note: When partnership studies are conducted, various hypotheses are examined, which can be nothing more than hypotheses and possibilities, and various sections can be taken out of context.)

The alleged ambition of the new partnership comes from Football Leaks that were obtained by the German publication *Der Spiegel*—yes, the same sources as those that exposed confidential Man City and PSG internal information.†

Remember, private equity firm CVC's approach in investing in football seemed to be to make money directly from the increase in the value of TV rights rather than deal with the ownership and risks and potential losses of owning a club. In this case, the alleged aims of the new partnership seemed to be a more direct way to make money from selling/trading football players. Trading in talent can be the most profitable area of football clubs, and a necessary area in order to balance the books. However, any business model that diverts money to agents and financial investors

---

* https://www.reuters.com/investigates/special-report/soccer-files-fosun/.

† Rui Pinto, the creator of the Football Leaks website in 2015, faces ninety charges including unauthorized access to data, violation of correspondence, and attempted extortion. His trial started in September 2020. Pinto acknowledges releasing documents but says he was a whistleblower acting in the public interest.

that would otherwise go to clubs and help sustain the vibrant competition that fans pay to see would probably be criticized and opposed by most fans, governing bodies, and club owners.

The integrity of competition in the sport can be at risk when there are multiple connections between players, agents, and owners of teams. Ivo Belet, a Belgian member of the European parliament who has taken a close interest in football governance, said the relationship between super-agents and clubs is a "big threat to football in Europe and it should be looked into more carefully."[*]

A Cautionary Tale of Relationships Between Agents and Clubs

In a 2017 *New York Times* article, sports reporter Rory Smith wrote about Belgian professional football club Royal Excel Mouscron.[†] In 2015, the club was bought by a Maltese company involving Israeli super-agent Pini Zahavi, then transferred to another Maltese consortium controlled by his nephew Adar. According to *DH Les Sports*, this transfer was allegedly to avoid FIFA's rules on agents owning clubs—an allegation Zahavi has consistently denied.[‡] Pini Zahavi is one of football's most famous and influential agents. He has represented Neymar and Thomas Tuchel.

According to the Smith article, since Zahavi, together with a business associate, the German-Macedonian agent Fali Ramadani, became involved at Mouscron, eight players arrived on loan from Apollon Limassol of Cyprus, another club where Zahavi has strong connections. Smith wrote, "That has triggered concerns that the club is not being run for its own benefit, but for that of Zahavi, Ramadani and their clients, a place where they can showcase players in the hope of earning a move, or a base from which they can loan

---

[*] https://www.reuters.com/investigates/special-report/soccer-files-fosun/.

[†] https://www.nytimes.com/2017/09/09/sports/soccer/belgian-clubs-and-foreign-money-a-modern-soccer-mix.html.

[‡] https://www.dhnet.be/sports/football/2017/08/04/pini-zahavi-lhomme-de-lombre-qui-a-rendu-possible-le-transfert-de-neymar-au-psg-TQQVDVAIN5ABVMVOIYTJDNROIQ/.

them out to other clubs—each time for a fee—in a bid to circumvent FIFA rules on agents' owning the economic rights of players."*

In March 2018, Thai businessman Pairoj Piempongsant of the Carabao Energy Drink bought control of the club.† Eleven months later, the club was put under provisional administration by the Belgian federal judiciary, due to alleged money laundering by Pini Zahavi.‡

In 2021, Belgium's federal prosecutor's office indicted Zahavi for forgery, fraud, and money laundering as a part of an investigation into Mouscron. Zahavi's lawyer said, "He [Zahavi] strongly contests the charges against him," and described the widespread reporting of his indictment as "a clear violation of the secrecy of the investigation and the presumption of innocence." Zahavi has consistently denied any continued involvement in Mouscron.§

Lastly, the multiple relationships may have an impact on grassroots investments. Simon Chadwick, professor of sports enterprise at Salford University in England, expressed concern about the financial effects of close relations between clubs, agents, and investors: "If there is leakage (of money) from the sport, then you potentially have an impact upon the lower reaches of football, into grassroots football."¶

Real Madrid maintain very good relations with Mendes and other super-agents. However, what happened with the Wolves highlights another potential competitive threat to Real Madrid. Real Madrid are not just having to compete with closely government-related, private equity, and multi-club ownership models; they also compete with clubs that can have extraordinarily close relationships with agents. And Real Madrid relies on agents, including Mendes, for talent. While the Wolves are in

---

* Belgian leagues were rewritten so that the ultimate beneficiary of a club is not an agent. However, it is always difficult when dealing with people determined to obscure ownership.

† https://www.lesoir.be/147822/article/2018-03-27/rachat-de-lexcel-contrat-de-5-ans-pour-le-nouveau-patron.

‡ https://www.sudouest.fr/sport/blanchiment-dans-le-football-la-justice-belge-place-mouscron-sous-administration-provisoire-2808561.php.

§ https://www.theguardian.com/football/2021/oct/01/football-agent-pini-zahavi-indicted-in-belgium-as-part-of-mouscron-inquiry.

¶ https://www.reuters.com/investigates/special-report/soccer-files-fosun/.

the Premier League, there is another super agent–related deal closer to Real Madrid's home, in LaLiga.

Pere Guardiola

In 2017, Man City and agent Pere Guardiola acquired 88.6 percent of Catalan club Girona.* Pere Guardiola is the agent for his brother Pep, Luis Suárez, Andrés Iniesta, and many other mostly Spanish players, including a few at Man City. He is a registered agent with the English and Spanish FA. The FA does have regulations that prohibit a club or club official or manager from having any interest in the business or affairs of an intermediary. The purpose is to guard against the very obvious risk that an agent could move players in and out and take fees to suit his/her own opportunities to make money, rather than make recruitment decisions solely in the best interests of the club. Reportedly, the FA and Man City believe Pep, who will be sending players to Girona on loan, to his brother and agent's benefit, and Pere do not have conflicts of interest. However, the FA says that the rule restricts agents from having an interest or influence *only in an English club*. The prohibition does not apply to purchasing a stake in a foreign club. The Spanish FA does not have a similar restriction. Therefore, Pere Guardiola was free to buy his 44.3 percent stake in Girona, with the City Football Group, the parent of Man City, buying an equal 44.3 percent stake.

According to an August 2017 article in *The Guardian* by David Conn:

> [Man] City's Catalan and former Barcelona chief executive, Ferran Soriano, and director of football, Txiki Begiristain, who know and worked closely with the Guardiola brothers during Barça's glory years and lobbied ceaselessly to attract Pep to City, have been central to concluding this deal to buy Girona with Pere. The attractions for their Abu Dhabi employer are said to be that more of the players increasingly accumulated at City from young ages can be loaned for polishing in LaLiga, and that buying the club is an investment. The whole 88.6 percent of Girona,

---

* https://www.theguardian.com/football/2017/aug/29/girona-manchester-city-pep-guardiola -brother-questions.

a small club in a charming ground promoted to LaLiga for the first time in its history last season, is said to have cost €7 million (£6.5 million), which looks like remarkable value. If City's aim is to make money from their stake increasing in value, then they are also helping Pere do the same.[*]

As background, in 2015–16, Girona sold Florian Lejeune to Man City for €300,000, and then Man City immediately loaned Lejeune back to Girona. At the same time, Man City bought another player, Rúben Sobrino, for €550,000 from Ponferradina in LaLiga 2, and immediately loaned him to Girona.

The following season, Man City loaned Girona three players—Pablo Mari, Pablo Maffeo, and Angeliño. Girona then had their best ever season, finishing runners-up and gaining promotion to Spain's top flight for the first time.

Man City's parent, CFG, and Pere Guardiola then acquired 44.3 percent of Girona in the summer of 2017. Girona's debut season, 2017–18, in LaLiga was one of the best in the competition's history, as they finished tenth, abetted by five loanees from Man City. LaLiga president Javier Tebas accused CFG of "financial doping" to bypass the LaLiga spending rules, which applied to Girona. CFG reportedly threatened Tebas with legal action, although they never took it.

Since CFG acquired a stake in Girona, eighteen CFG players have signed for the Spanish club. Five of the 2023–24 squad, including two loanees, originate from CFG clubs.

Girona may be a glimpse into the future, where players are endlessly shifted around multi-club ownership groups (MCOs) and those stables challenge for league titles in multiple countries—and maybe progress to regional or international club competitions.[†]

The deal raises questions about independence and integrity of competition. There are no rules against "dual ownership" in itself. UEFA's

---

[*] https://www.theguardian.com/football/2017/aug/29/girona-manchester-city-pep-guardiola-brother-questions.

[†] There is speculation that the Premier League clubs will vote on banning loan moves between MCO teams to protect the integrity of competition.

rules state: "No individual or legal entity may have control or influence over more than one club participating in a UEFA club competition." One definition of "control," owning a majority of both clubs, will not apply because the City Football Group has structured the deal at 44.3 percent each with their flagship Man City's manager's brother. Control also means "being able to exercise by any means a decisive influence in the decision-making of both clubs." This can be up to interpretation and judgment as much as legal definitions. The UEFA decision to allow Red Bull Salzburg and RB Leipzig to play in the Champions League probably informed the parties' thinking on deal structure.

In March 2024, UEFA declared that City Football Group must reduce its stake in either Man City or Girona. Thanks in part to the super-agent phenomenon, Real Madrid and the rest of football are in a new environment where issues of "integrity of competition" and "independence" are being raised more often.

FIFA Regulations for Agents

As money has infiltrated football, agents have become more and more influential, helping their players earn big-money contracts and moves. Sometimes, the agent represented and/or was paid by both the club and the player—raising potential conflict issues. While there are "super-agents" with increasing power, there also has been a dramatic increase in the number of family members representing players and new agents without the necessary experience coming into the business due to one player. In addition, many believe agents take too much money out of football—and that the money could be better spent on improved facilities, grassroots projects, the women's game, and so on. Fees paid by clubs for the services of football agents were $623 million in 2022, a 24 percent increase in their spending on fees compared to 2021. With all of that in mind, many wanted to cap agents' fees, have some sort of certification, reduce conflicts of interests, and increase transparency.

In January 2023, FIFA announced new rules to help guarantee basic professional and ethical standards for football agents. Under the new rules, football agents, who sometimes charge as high as 5 to 10 percent commissions, can now take a maximum 3 percent commission for any transfer above $200,000 and 5 percent for deals under $200,000. In addition, under the new regulations, agents must also make all transactions public, allowing fans to see how much their clubs paid for deals. The other major changes include the introduction of a mandatory licensing system and the prohibition of multiple representation to avoid conflicts of interest. People wanting to become agents must now follow a strict process, including the need to pass a FIFA exam, and then pay an annual fee to the governing body. FIFA have included a "legacy agent" caveat, which states agents registered before 2015 will not have to take the new exam as they qualified under the old rules.

FIFA is facing a backlash against the new regulations. Leading agents have voiced disapproval and taken legal action. In November 2023, the Commercial Court of Madrid prohibited FIFA and the Spanish Football Federation from applying the new rules in the country. Germany's District Court of Dortmund granted an injunction for the most critical provisions. There are also ongoing actions in other European countries. The provision against dual representation (agents representing both a player and a club in the same transaction), and also the cap on commissions, seem to be two of the biggest sticking points. Others believe the new rules will leave fewer well-paid players unrepresented, force smaller agencies out of business, or require agencies to cut back on services provided to players.

In July 2023, FIFA won an international, multi-case fight by football player agents to block rules that would regulate their industry and cap their fees. The Court of Arbitration for Sport said it "dismissed in their entirety" arguments put forth by the Zurich-based Professional Football Agents Association (PROFAA), which brought the case. FIFA said the ruling "fully confirms the legality, validity and proportionality of the FIFA Football Agent Regulations."*

Many are concerned agents will just find ways to circumvent the regulations. For example, if a star player who is a free agent comes into the market and there's a bidding war, many believe it's unlikely that some

---

* However, it was unclear how the Swiss-based sports court's verdict will weigh on national-level cases in process brought by agents in different countries, plus a complaint filed with the European Commission in Brussels.

clubs will adhere to the rules, including the 3 percent cap. They may be transparent and pay 3 percent, but people fear then the agent will be compensated in another way that doesn't have to be reported. For example, agents have a network of associated companies and associates through which they could accept payments or be paid for "other work" at a later date.

PLAYERS AS GLOBAL BRANDS

Today's athletes can become, essentially, global brands. Some have more social media followers than their clubs (including more player recognition from video games), and make more money than the profits of their clubs.

Traditionally, football fans have chosen "their club" based on locality, familial ties, or perhaps the club's success. Then they would go to watch their club play at the stadium or follow them on television. To many of those traditional fans, the only thing that changed over the years were the kits and players, and possibly the logo.

But slowly a different breed of football fan has emerged. The change began to accelerate with David Beckham, as his global fans (especially in Asia) followed him from Man U to Real Madrid in June 2002. Afterward, Facebook, YouTube, Twitter (now X), Instagram, and TikTok were founded in 2004, 2005, 2006, 2010, and 2015, respectively. And with the growth of each new social media platform there has been a growing number of supporters for whom the color and logo of the shirt is less important than the player wearing it.

Concurrently, the FIFA video game became more and more popular. *FIFA 11* sold over sixteen million units, and *FIFA 18* sold over twenty-six million units. Kids who played the game became familiar with players and their statistics and ratings. These new fans pick their own players, create their own teams in the game, and follow their favorite players in real life—their transfer news, their personal lives, their money, their clothes, their cars, and so on.

For most of these fans, it is the name and number on the back of the shirt that truly counts. The most evident trend from analysis of the social media accounts of the teams that have been most active on the market is related to the orientation of the fans, who are increasingly more interested in the lives and events of individual players compared to those of the clubs. Subconsciously, fans want to be like their heroes and favorite athletes. They want to learn what they do, what they eat, and where they go, so they can do, at least, a few of the things they do.* This makes the fan feel more important and closer to the athlete. The athlete starts to become like a friend. It's a trend that becomes even more central considering Asian audiences and fan bases that make internationality an important social media weapon. There are more and more users who will follow the club where their idol plays only to access content that shows him.

As discussed previously, the higher the number of social media followers an athlete has, the higher their sponsorship value. Fans imitate their idols, buying the same shoes, fragrances, and apparel as they do. This gives them the feeling of being close to their idols and taking part in their fame and success.

Today, many players prefer to have their own social media person or team, or utilize outside services. Real Madrid have over twenty specialized production and publishing employees in social media focused on various platforms (Facebook, Instagram, X, Snap, YouTube, TikTok, and social media platforms in China and Japan) and different forms of storytelling. Because Real Madrid post so much content through so many channels, they have so much data on what works and doesn't work—and even *when* it works or doesn't work. Therefore, Real Madrid prefer that players coordinate with and use Real Madrid resources to maximize effectiveness.

With the rise of social media, the methods used by sports fans to connect and engage with their favorite players and clubs have changed. Fans use real-time data monitoring to track the performance of athletes and different and more social media platforms to follow, engage with, and show their support for their favorite players and teams on a regular

---

* And this can have a serious financial impact. For example, Cristiano Ronaldo's removal of two Coca-Cola bottles at a Euro 2020 news conference coincided with a $4 billion drop in the market value of the American drink giant. Coca-Cola has around two hundred brands worldwide, including different types of water. Without the support of brands like Coca-Cola, many tournaments could not be organized with such success for players and fans, and there would be less investment in the future of football at all levels.

basis. Fans are also looking for clubs and athletes to show authenticity, accessibility, and to provide their own content that a club like Real Madrid republishes or interacts with, strengthening the relationship with its audience. Real Madrid went from a one-to-many relationship to a community-building model, which is the foundation of Real Madrid's digital, content, and Madridistas strategy.

Social Media: The Bad Side

Social media can play a very positive role in sport, widening its audience and connecting fans with their heroes in a way that was never possible before. We are in a society where everybody gives their opinion and wants their opinion to be heard. However, social media can provide an anonymous platform for people to abuse players, managers, referees, officials, and others involved in the game with hateful or racist or bullying or threatening comments without consequences. On social media platforms, it can be extremely difficult to identify the offenders. So social media is a way for "trolls" to express their opinions, get attention, and try to get a response. It is difficult to understand how the bad side of social media will negatively impact how people consume football content and how players and clubs use social media.

In March 2021, former Arsenal and Barcelona forward Thierry Henry quit social media, stating that "the sheer volume of racism, bullying, and resulting mental torture to individuals is too toxic to ignore. There HAS to be some accountability. It is far too easy to create an account, use it to bully and harass without any consequence and still remain anonymous. Until this changes, I will be disabling my accounts across all social platforms. I'm hoping this happens soon."[*]

Accompanied by the hashtag #EnoughisEnough, in April 2021 Swansea announced a club-wide one-week boycott of their official social media channels following repeated incidents of abuse of their players over online platforms including Facebook and X (then Twitter). Many applauded the

---

* https://www.theguardian.com/football/2021/mar/26/thierry-henry-quits-social-media-until
-companies-act-on-racism-and-bullying.

club and their actions." English football and UEFA then also announced a boycott of social media platforms for a week to combat discrimination and online abuse.

During just the final six weeks of the 2022–23 season, a joint PFA and Signify study identified more than three thousand explicitly abusive messages aimed at Premier League players, 56 percent of which were racist. Of the players surveyed, 43 percent said they had experienced targeted racist abuse.[†]

Football is a lightning rod for wider societal issues. And obviously it happens at matches. A 2021 Sky Sports News survey conducted by YouGov revealed 62 percent of match-attending fans fear a player will be racially abused; 60 percent feel racism sanctions aren't harsh enough; 73 percent of ethnically diverse fans planning to visit a stadium are concerned about racist abuse.[‡]

In May 2023, Vinícius Júnior was racially abused by fans when Real Madrid played away to Valencia. He has been the victim of several shocking racism incidents. He wrote on social media: "The championship [LaLiga] that once belonged to Ronaldinho, Ronaldo, Cristiano and Messi today belongs to racists." Real Madrid filed a report with the Attorney General's Office about the events.[§] Some have been critical of LaLiga and its referees for their failure (or ineffective actions and protocols) to address or curtail racism. In September 2022, prior to the incident, Real Madrid issued an official statement condemning all types of racist and xenophobic language and behavior and in particular comments made against Vinícius Júnior and directed its legal team to act against anyone making racist remarks toward their players.

---

* https://www.itv.com/news/wales/2021-04-15/what-impact-has-swansea-citys-social-media-boycott-had-and-what-can-actually-be-done-to-tackle-online-abuse.

† https://www.bbc.com/sport/football/55887106.

‡ https://www.skysports.com/football/news/11661/12383739/racism-in-football-most-fans-worried-about-witnessing-players-receive-abuse-according-to-yougov-survey-for-sky-sports-news.

§ "Real Madrid C. F. strongly condemns the events that took place yesterday against our player Vinícius Junior. These events represent a direct attack on the social and democratic model of coexistence of our State based on the rule of law. Real Madrid believes that such attacks also constitute a hate crime, and has therefore filed the corresponding report with the Attorney General's Office, specifically with the Prosecutor's Office against crimes of hatred and discrimination, in order for the facts to be investigated and for those responsible to be held accountable. Article 124 of the Spanish Constitution stipulates that the role of the Public Prosecutor's Office is to promote the pursuit of justice in defense of legality and the rights of citizens and the public interest. Given the seriousness of the events that took place, Real Madrid has appealed to the Attorney General's Office, without prejudice to its standing as a private prosecutor in any proceedings that may be initiated."

Vinícius Júnior is working with a FIFA task force to make specific recommendations. FIFA president Gianni Infantino has said it is imperative that match officials stop a match when players were subject to abuse.

Real Madrid work with a dedicated social media monitoring platform to identify and remove hateful and violent discourse on their official channels, in order to protect their players and create a safe community for fans to participate. This is an additional effort and investment on top of native social media moderation tools that is critical for the club.

In 2020, five players had more followers on Instagram than the clubs they play for: Cristiano Ronaldo (241 million followers versus Juventus's 44 million), Lionel Messi (168 million followers versus Barcelona's 91 million), Neymar (143 million followers versus PSG's 31 million), Paul Pogba (42 million followers versus Man U's 38 million), and Mohamed Salah (41 million followers versus Liverpool's 28 million).[*] All five of these players also netted more money from their salaries and sponsorships than the profits of any of their clubs. Think about that. They have more followers and make more money than the clubs they play for! They are bigger global brands and companies, with more profits, than the clubs themselves.

As mentioned, the statistics reveal that millions of fans are loyal to superstar players. For example, when Ronaldo was sold to Juventus in 2018, the Serie A champions saw a clear increase in their social media followers. According to Football Benchmark, in the week between rumors of Ronaldo going to Juventus and the announcement in Turin, Juventus gained more than two million social media followers. Part of the commercial rationale for the deal was that Juventus had about one-fifth of Real Madrid's social media followers, and Ronaldo would help increase their social media presence. (When Ronaldo was sold to Juventus in 2018, he sold 520,000 shirts in twenty-four hours, equating to around $60 million.

---

[*] https://www.90min.com/in/posts/5-players-who-have-more-followers-on-instagram-than-the-club-they-represent-01emzmhap89s.

To compare the impact of Ronaldo's brand value, Juventus sold a total of 850,000 shirts throughout the whole season before Ronaldo's arrival.*)

Interestingly, Real Madrid did not see any impact to social media followers when Ronaldo left for Juventus—showing that Real Madrid do an excellent job of retaining fans. When Ronaldo left Juventus for Man U in 2021, Juventus lost a modest three hundred thousand followers and Man U gained almost four million followers.† Messi's move from Barcelona to PSG in 2021 is another example. When Messi left Barcelona for PSG, the Blaugrana didn't see any impact to social media followers, but PSG gained almost seven million followers. Hakimi and Sergio Ramos also added five hundred thousand followers each to PSG. The numbers make it clear that a star player with a global brand can be a precious social media asset for a club, especially those in which the content and social media presence is already highly developed. The data also shows that big clubs like Real Madrid and Barcelona with distinctive global brands have some sort of "stickiness" with fans of players. This was true when Beckham left Real Madrid—generally his fans stayed supporters of the club. Lastly, the numbers show that fans care a lot about star players. They want to watch the best players.

Real Madrid's Impact on a Player's Brand

Five of the world's ten most followed football players on social media played for Real Madrid (indicated by *):

Top 10 Most-Followed Football Players in 2023 (descending order by number of followers)‡
1. Cristiano Ronaldo*
2. Lionel Messi
3. Neymar

---

* https://www.ics-digital.com/blog/which-football-player-has-the-most-valuable-brand.

† https://www.nssmag.com/en/sports/27358/calciomercato-social-ronaldo-messi.

‡ https://www.express.co.uk/sport/football/1741932/Cristiano-Ronaldo-Lionel-Messi-Instagram-followers-Everton-PSG-Premier-League-Neymar.

4. Kylian Mbappé
5. Marcelo*
6. Zlatan Ibrahimović
7. Paul Pogba
8. Sergio Ramos*
9. James Rodríguez*
10. Gareth Bale*

Real Madrid sign many star players, but Real Madrid also provide the players with their global platform and access to their hundreds of millions of fans. It is a symbiotic relationship.

Arda Güler's transfer announcement to Real Madrid was the second most popular signing announcement on social media in history, second only to Messi to PSG.* It highlights the power of the Real Madrid association.

These players are global brands just as much, or more, than their clubs. They have employees or firms that are responsible for branding, social media, sponsorship deals, accounting, and tax—just like a global brand company.

It wasn't just social media that tilted the focus toward star players and big clubs. Video games also enabled the trend. Football video games are accessible across mobile, PC, and console gaming platforms, at any time of day or night, thus offering endless possibilities to satisfy football-obsessed fans. These games have blurred the lines between reality and fantasy. The games' endless customization options allow fans to personalize their own kits, team names, and more, letting fans be a part of the football world through the time they have spent playing the games. The oddity for gaming fans who are new to football is that their virtual footballers exist as real incarnations too. In a uniquely digital twist, some remember players not for their impact on the pitch, but instead their stats on a console. For example, unfortunately, Paul Pogba was injured or unavailable for most of the 2022–23 season. However, he was one of the most popular players in the FIFA video game. In addition, interestingly,

---

* https://medium.com/@melikdemirel/real-izing-the-social-media-goals-with-arda-g%C3%BCler-fad693392189.

many young video game players told me they became more familiar with PSG and their players because the lineup of Mbappé, Messi, and Neymar made PSG one of the best overall teams on the FIFA video game. And when I searched most popular team for *FIFA 23* on the internet . . . the result was PSG.

The *FIFA International Soccer* video game was first released in 1993.[*] By 2010, the FIFA video game series had sold over 100 million copies, making it the best-selling sports video game franchise in the world. And the video game kept getting more popular. *FIFA 12* holds the record for the "fastest-selling sports game ever" with over 3.2 million games sold and over $186 million generated at retail in its first week of release. *FIFA 18* holds the record for units sold, 26.4 million. In 2018, Steve Boxer of *The Guardian* called *FIFA 18* "the slickest, most polished and by far the most popular football game around" and "football [video] games' equivalent of the Premier League." He also praised the game's FIFA Ultimate Team, which "encourages you to purchase Panini-sticker-like player packs to build up a dream team," adding that the series has international superstars, and a mode that lets you control your favorite team on and off the pitch.[†] The Ultimate Team feature on *FIFA* and *Football Manager* allows video gamers to be detached from existing teams, and encourages gamers to create their own lineups. This, in turn, has resulted in a generation of fans who associate with the players as much as the clubs that they play for. This change has brought about a new trend in global fandom, and blends into the way that they consume football offline.

Technological developments have improved footballers' likenesses, expressions, and movements in the game, closing the gap between real life and the virtual world. Football video games have very fluid ball movement, lightning-fast transitions, and an incredible amount of available skill moves—it's almost football fantasy. The games look and sound

---

[*] In May 2022, EA and FIFA announced their partnership of thirty years would come to an end from July 2023 onward (*FIFA 23* is the last entry to the game franchise under the FIFA name); the series will be retitled *EA Sports FC* or *EAFC*. FIFA intended to enter a partnership with a new developer to produce "the real game that has the FIFA name."

[†] https://web.archive.org/web/20180828102658/https://www.theguardian.com/games/2018/aug/28/six-best-football-video-games-fifa-pro-evolution-soccer.

extremely exciting, with outrageous goals and skill moves. These types of moves and matches can only be replicated by the best players and big clubs. The video games immerse fans into football. The video game players pick the star football players and big clubs—and a relationship begins. Once they're there, they become much more educated and have higher expectations of live matches—it isn't good enough to just root for your local team.

Video games and their education of fans about players are becoming more of an entry into football, instead of football leading to interest in the video game. In 2014, an ESPN poll found that 34 percent of Americans became football fans as a result of playing the game, while half of all Americans say that the game has increased their interest in the sport.[*]

It's data and detail in the game simulations that attracts younger fans interested in both video games and data. The series is educating a generation of football supporters to a level even professional coaches couldn't imagine only a decade or two ago. Fans now have knowledge of player statistics, tactics, transfer regulations, and detailed administrative processes in football that they would previously have never known existed. Interestingly, many young fans also know football legends because the game *FIFA* incorporates FIFA Icons—which are legendary players known for outstanding feats or unique play. In many cases, the legendary players take on a larger-than-life image because their ratings may have bias due to nostalgia.

The relationship between fans and football is evolving, and we are seeing far more people interact with football in so many ways. A report by Sky Sports titled "The Football Fandom in 2021" stated that 70 percent of people feel the power of players has enabled the U.K. to advance conversations around discrimination, while 63 percent believe they have a better understanding of social and economic issues because of their love of football.[†] Younger generations are becoming more and more socially

---

* https://www.theguardian.com/technology/2016/dec/21/fifa-video-game-changed-football.

† https://www.skygroup.sky/article/new-sky-sports-report-reveals-how-football-fandom-is-changing-across-the-uk_.

conscious, and that impacts their attachments and support. Commenting on the report, Dr. Martha Newson, Future Leaders Fellow at the University of Kent, said,

> Football is now more representative than ever of the British public. Football is more than what happens on the pitch, it is entrenched in our day-to-day beliefs, embedded in our conversations, and shaping society and community behaviors. Football tends to go far deeper than attending games or keeping up with the fixtures; it's about social connections and how we present ourselves to the world—be it likes on social media, wearing the 'right' trainers, or knowing the words to a song. For some fans, celebrating football manifests in how we shop and the brands we align with.

In this hyper-connected and social media–savvy world, fans aren't satisfied just watching their favorite football stars only during the matches. They also want to get to know them, which is why they love to go behind the scenes, seeing what their favorite players are like off pitch, in their locker rooms, while training, with their families, or even with their pets. Real Madrid provide behind-the-scenes and locker room content.

Players also are building and supporting their brands by giving fans a glimpse into their lives and stories with documentary films. Some examples are *Zidane: A 21st Century Portrait* (2006), *Messi* (2014), *Ronaldo* (2015), *Becoming Zlatan* (2015), *Le K Benzema* (2017), *Kroos* (2019), *Antoine Griezmann: The Making of a Legend* (2019), and *Captains—The Chosen Few: Luka Modrić* (2022). Vinícius Júnior, Sergio Ramos, and Iker Casillas also have had TV documentary series.

Real Madrid also have their own documentaries. *Hala Madrid* (2017) offered behind-the-scenes access to the club in eight episodes. Amazon Prime Video launched the documentary series *Real Madrid, La Leyenda Blanca* (Real Madrid: The White Legend) in 2022. The documentary features Real Madrid's greatest achievements and milestones. The documentary series comprises six 45-minute episodes. *Real Madrid: Until the End* on Apple+ takes you behind the scenes of the iconic football club for a look at their astonishing 2021–2022 season.

Instead of following one club in general, millions of fans are watching and tracking the progress of their favorite players. And as football players switch clubs and fans have several favorite players, the idea of following a second or third team has become far more common in recent years, especially among the younger generation. In 2022, COPA90 did a study and found that 46 percent of sixteen-to-twenty-four-year-olds in the U.K. support at least two football clubs, while 27 percent support three or more teams.[*]

"HERE WE GO": THE CRAZY BUSINESS OF MODERN FOOTBALL MEDIA

It's hard to understate how much football media has changed, becoming immediate news with limited governance. The transformation includes the public's fascination with transfers and individual players' money and lives, and more people getting their sports news via YouTube, Instagram, and TikTok.

Football has long had a limitless hunger for gossip and rumors—these things occupy fans in between matches and seasons. Pick up any Spanish newspaper and there are pages and pages of articles of tittle-tattle and speculation. And with sports radio and TV, it's the same thing. However, these outlets can only talk about a particular match for so long. Their need for content was a limiting factor.

Things changed with social media. Football news (especially transfer leaks) is getting much faster and gets more amplified much more quickly. It is just a click or tweet away (and shared), any time of the day. Also, football news has become more personal. Social media has given journalists a chance to interact with readers and share unfiltered thoughts (without an editor or fact-checker). The line has been blurred between journalist, influencer, intermediary, and participant. Sports reporters can shortcut to reach a global audience. But their popularity highlights that they (and football) are both sports and entertainment. Coverage of the

---

[*] https://www.sportbible.com/football/news-pub-talk-reactions-study-shows-46-of-16-24-year-olds-support-more-than-one-club-20210110.

transfer industry has evolved into a blizzard of social media, pictures, bios, emojis, and trademark slogans.

The most famous example is Italian journalist Fabrizio Romano, who has millions of social media followers—often more followers than the club or players he reports on. He even has more followers than media outlets such as ESPN FC. In July 2023, Romano had the most influential X account in the world, with over four billion impressions. An incredible milestone. The advancement transfer gurus such as Fabrizio Romano have unquestionably even affected Sky Sports News' ability to be first for transfer news. Romano even has his own six-hour deadline day show on YouTube produced by Double Tap, and for much of the time he is literally just scrolling through his phone . . . yet the 1.5 million viewers don't seem to mind. Heineken beer is prominently displayed as a sponsor.

He is *the* journalist covering football's wild multibillion-dollar transfer market. His followers are desperate to be the first to know the players their club is signing. Romano's catchphrase when announcing important, breaking transfer news is "Here we go!" One of the key traits that makes Romano stand out from many other football transfer reporters is his accuracy. He may not be the first to report transfer news, but when he does report a scoop, it is seen as reliable. "Here we go!" means "It's true or it's a done deal."

As transfer sums grew, the public interest grew. Transfer fees are now a $6 billion industry.* Transfers used to involve a player, an agent, and a club representative. Today, whole teams of people are involved to make the transfer signing an event. A player moving clubs creates more hype than a player winning championships. People are as, or even more, interested in transfers than the matches themselves. The most-liked sports team–related post ever on Instagram was a transfer: CR7 returning to Man U. The second most–liked post was Messi joining PSG, another transfer. Fans create boards and chats primarily to discuss transfers. Fans want to interact with/about their clubs throughout the year, and transfers help fill that gap. Traditional media did that. But

---

* https://www.nytimes.com/2022/01/24/sports/soccer/fabrizio-romano-transfer-rumors.html.

social media allows the direct interaction, even with the journalists. It is local tribalism gone global.

Lastly, transfer news matters for video games. Younger fans think about the impact a transfer will have on their teams in the games. For them, it's part of the excitement and fun.

SAUDI ARABIA FOOTBALL ON THE GLOBAL STAGE

A spending spree has thrust Saudi Arabia football onto the global stage. With the Saudi Pro League signing superstar players, the results included an SPL club reaching the 2022 FIFA Club World Cup final, Saudi Arabia beating Argentina in the 2022 World Cup, and Newcastle, controlled by Saudi's Public Investment Fund, finishing fourth in the 2022–23 Premier League standings and qualifying for the European Champions League.

Saudi Arabia has an over century-long history with football. Football is not only the most popular sport in Saudi Arabia, but a point of pride. The country's investments in football since 2016 are a part of a larger strategic framework to reduce Saudi Arabia's dependence on oil, diversify its economy (including in tourism), develop public service sectors, open Saudi Arabia up to the world, and create a healthy and vibrant society (including improving women's rights). And keep in mind, Saudi Arabia's GDP is around twice as much as UAE's and four times as much as Qatar's. In addition, Saudi Arabia has a very young population: over thirty-two million people live in the country and 51 percent of them are under the age of thirty. Most of the population play, attend, or follow football. Football is part of a much broader socioeconomic plan to cater to their younger generation and to promote growth.

Saudi Arabia's national men's and women's teams—the Al-Suqour Al-Khodhur (The Green Falcons)—have shown tremendous progress. The men defeated Argentina in the 2022 World Cup. The women achieved their first FIFA world ranking. A women's professional league was created.

Saudi Pro League teams have been a major force in the AFC and are increasingly competitive globally. In 2023, AFC Champions Al Hilal beat South American champions Flamengo 3–2 in the Club World Cup semifinal. It was the first time a Saudi team has reached the Club World Cup final.

The Saudi Pro League continues to improve and attract top talent such as Cristiano Ronaldo (last with Man U), Karim Benzema (Real Madrid), Neymar (PSG), N'Golo Kanté (Chelsea), Ruben Neves (Wolverhampton), and Kalidou Koulibaly (Chelsea). Reportedly, the SPL is also looking to recruit the best referees from the Premier League and across Europe on a full-time basis.

Saudi Pro League matches can attract huge crowds. For example, Al-Ittihad versus Al Hilal from Riyadh, which is referred to as Saudi El Clasico, fills their sixty-thousand-plus capacity stadiums. The Jeddah Derby between Al-Ittihad and Al-Ahli goes back over seventy years.

The Saudi Pro League wants to be in the top ten football leagues in the world in the next five to ten years. In the 2023 summer window, Saudi clubs spent €827 million on transfer fees on eighty-two different players from European clubs. However, only around a quarter of the players who move to the SPL account for 96 percent of the total transfer fees paid by Saudi clubs. The median squad member in the SPL is still worth less than one million Euros.

In August 2023, the overall value of players on SPL clubs' books was around €1.1 billion, equal to the Turkish Süper Lig, which is ranked seventh in Europe. The English Premier League has players worth a total of more than €10 billion, whereas the other European Top 5 Leagues are around €3–5 billion. Saudi Arabia will have to spend substantially more to build up its football league.

Saudi's Public Investment Fund has very quickly built a leading multi-club ownership model, including a controlling stake in Newcastle and the traditionally top four clubs in Saudi Arabia as well as a minority stake in Chelsea co-owners.* And Newcastle qualified for the Champions League—breaking the Big Six's dominance.

---

* In 2023, the Asian Football Confederation was facing questions about allowing three clubs owned by Saudi Arabia's PIF (Al Hilal, Al-Nassr, and Al-Ittihad) to take part in the Asian Champions League in the same regional zones. City Football Group controls Mumbai City and Melbourne City, which compete in two different regional zones of the competition but also have a chance to meet in the competition.

It's also important to note that Saudi funds have significant investments in video game developers as well. As mentioned, video games are becoming more important in fandom and how it's developed.

With continued proper investment in infrastructure, a savvy focus on human capital, and a long-term, sustainable recruitment strategy, there's no doubt the country and league can be serious global players. Their commitment and resources pose a risk for other leagues and clubs.

In a July 2023 interview with the *Financial Times*, Christian Nourry, managing partner at Retexo Intelligence—a consultancy that advises clubs on their player purchases—said the impact of Saudi spending on the European transfer market had already been "significant" by pushing up wage demands, delaying contract renewals, and forcing clubs to replace players they thought would stay. Nourry said, "The biggest teams in Europe are still trying to understand which players they might lose and how much money they will have to spend to find either short-term or long-term fixes to departures they may not have been expecting."[*] UEFA president Aleksander Čeferin and Major League Soccer commissioner Don Garber have been relatively dismissive so far about the commitment made by the Saudi Public Investment Fund into football.[†, ‡]

The near-billion Euros spent by Saudi clubs has helped elevate the global transfer window to its highest levels since 2019. Only Premier League clubs have spent more on players in the summer 2023 window than Saudi teams. And only the EPL in the top ten spending leagues has, like Saudi, a balance deficit. According to the economist Stefan Legge, who is Head of Tax & Trade Policy at the University of St. Gallen and vice director at its Institute of Law and Economics, the main issue that the Saudis pose to European clubs is an inflationary one, especially on player salaries. He said, "In any market just one player can 'ruin' prices for everyone . . . Saudi Arabia necessarily pays extraordinary salaries and

---

* https://www.ft.com/content/629669b6-e011-49b7-a762-0fa5761d39e9.

† https://www.espn.co.uk/football/story/_/id/37872437/misspent-saudi-money-no-threat-european-clubs-uefa-chief.

‡ https://www.newarab.com/news/mls-commissioner-not-worried-about-emergence-saudi-league.

transfer fees to attract talent. While this generates earnings for European clubs, it also raises costs for the industry as a whole."*

Many believe Saudi Arabia is already too far in to simply stop spending, and that we won't see China 2.0, that is, an ambitious football development program that gets quickly stopped. While it is difficult to predict Saudi Arabia's future policy on football because authorities can quickly shift policies, many believe the Saudis will be patient, long-term investors because football is a part of a larger social and economic development project.

Saudi-Backed LIV Tour Merges with PGA Tour

In 2022, LIV Golf, funded by Saudi Arabia's PIF, debuted a rival golf tour to the PGA Tour and lured several big-name players, including Phil Mickelson, Dustin Johnson, and Brooks Koepka.

LIV (which is the Roman numeral for 54, the number of holes played in each tournament) challenged the traditionalism of the PGA Tour. LIV had music blaring at events, more relaxed dress codes (players could wear shorts), fewer players in the tournaments (normally 48 players versus 132, 144, or 156 players at PGA events), shotgun starts from every hole at the same time (unlike the PGA Tour, starting all players at tees #1 or #10), and team competitions. The tournaments lasted three days instead of four, and had no player cuts. The PGA Tour has around 47 events, while LIV only had 14.

Players including Tiger Woods, Hideki Matsuyama, and Rory McIlroy turned down large guarantees from LIV Golf to remain loyal to the PGA Tour.

The launch of LIV led to a series of lawsuits and caused acrimony between players. The PGA Tour suspended members who competed in LIV tournaments without permission.

By May 2023, there were forty-eight players set to play the whole fourteen-event LIV Tour series, and twelve teams in total. And thirteen

---

* https://offthepitch.com/a/beyond-big-names-unpacking-saudi-pro-leagues-eu800-million-transfer-window?wv_email=sgmandis%40me.com&wv_id=0b33e863-2b87-44e3-82bb-a46dd11bfd0d&wv_name=.

players were major champions (including Phil Mickelson, Bubba Watson, Sergio Garcia, Louis Oosthuizen, and Cameron Smith). Four players—Dustin Johnson, Martin Kaymer, Brooks Koepka, and Lee Westwood—have held the title of World No. 1.

In June 2023, the PGA Tour and LIV Golf (along with the DP World Tour) announced that they will combine operations, and that PIF will make further capital investments to facilitate the new entity's growth and success. Rory McIlroy, previously one of the staunchest critics of LIV Golf, said he thought the deal would secure the financial future of the sport. He also said he had "come to terms [with Saudi money in golf] . . . Honestly, I've just resigned myself to the fact that this is . . . what's going to happen."[*]

The sport of golf and the PGA Tour (see sidebar) with all their history and traditions were resistant to change. The LIV Tour disrupted golf with a new entertainment-and-player-friendly approach and capital.

Many football executives are wondering . . . just as LIV poached a critical mass of the biggest stars from the PGA Tour—which helped force change and lead to a merger—will the Saudi Pro League do the same?

Many football executives are also wondering what Qatar and UAE (or other countries or MCOs or private equity firms or leagues) might do in response to Saudi Arabia's relatively quick emergence on the global football stage.

There was growing speculation that Saudi Arabia clubs were interested in a "wild card entry" to the UEFA Champions League as early as 2025.[†] In an August 2023 interview with Bloomberg, the league's chief operating officer, Carlo Nohra, said the Saudi Pro League is interested in discussing the option of its clubs entering the elite European competition.[‡] He said, "We are trying to be different, so any kind of format-changing or improvements that can be introduced into the league will

---

[*] https://www.nytimes.com/2023/06/07/sports/golf/pga-liv-golf-merger.html.

[†] https://www.corrieredellosport.it/news/calcio/calcio-estero/saudi-league/2023/08/15-111686909/clamoroso_gli_arabi_vogliono_giocare_la_champions_league.

[‡] https://www.bloomberg.com/news/articles/2023-08-27/saudi-arabia-signals-interest-in-champions-league-football-entry.

be welcomed." He added that the SPL is still "completely committed" to being in the AFC Champions League, and that any talks about SPL teams joining the UEFA Champions League would probably be between UEFA and the Saudi Arabian Football Federation. UEFA members include a few non-European countries, including a few transcontinental and Asian countries, whose clubs can participate in the European Champions League.* In August 2023, UEFA president Aleksander Čeferin said, "Only European clubs can participate in the Champions League, Europa League and Conference League . . . Only European clubs can apply [to host] a final, not even clubs . . . We would have to change our rules, and we don't want that."†

But with Čeferin also saying that the Saudi Pro League only appeals to aging players and that "Kylian Mbappé and Erling Haaland don't dream of playing in Saudi Arabia," Liverpool manager Klopp said it is too early to dismiss the threat posed by the emerging Saudi league. He said, "I don't know 100 percent yet but I don't think the Haaland and Mbappé example is a really good one. They are that young and earn already, so that is a different thing . . . I don't know where it will lead to but it feels rather like a threat or a concern than not because I can't see how we really deny it in these moments."‡

Serie A president Lorenzo Casini has called on FIFA and UEFA to address the threat posed to European football's competitiveness by the Saudi Pro League. In an interview, he said, "Of course, the Saudi phenomenon is not entirely new. Other countries have made these sorts of deals [buying star players] in the past. [But] the size of the operation that Saudi football is carrying out is striking. It's moved from phase one, in which Saudi or other Middle Eastern capital was invested in European clubs . . . Now there is phase two, where they want to bring champions

---

* UEFA governs football, futsal, and beach football in Europe and the transcontinental countries of Turkey, Azerbaijan, Georgia, and Kazakhstan, as well as some Asian countries such as Israel, Cyprus, and Armenia.

† https://www.marca.com/en/football/champions-league/2023/08/31/64f06644ca4741c65f8b45e1.html.

‡ https://www.espn.co.uk/football/story/_/id/38303972/liverpool-klopp-warns-saudi-threat-deadline -closes.

to their country and try to establish a real European championship . . .
Clearly, FIFA and UEFA will have to take countermeasures to avoid putting competitiveness at risk."*

FOOTBALL IS CHANGING

The changes in ownership (not to mention the announcement of the
European Super League and subsequent reactions and opinions) led me
to believe some things really have changed, and deserved further investi-
gation. I've shared my unexpected findings in this and previous chapters.
Bottom line: There are serious systemic changes going on in football.
Let's review what we've covered so far:

- **Closely government-related, private equity, and multi-club
  ownership models have proliferated.** This includes how commercial revenues from closely affiliated sponsors can be inflated
  to circumvent Financial Fair Play, and how people/entities with
  many roles can have at least perceived conflicts of interest.
- **While broadcasting revenues have grown in the past but may
  have peaked, player salaries and infrastructure costs have
  grown even faster.** This makes the football economic model for
  the vast majority of clubs even more unsustainable and riskier
  than ever. The pandemic exposed how fragile the system is.
- **The Premier League is becoming "the NBA of football."**
  And the Big Six *and growing* are already effectively in their own
  breakaway league from the other Premier League clubs.
- **The few dominant clubs with global brands in the other (non–
  Premier League) Top 5 Leagues have further separated themselves,** both financially and in performance, from the domestic
  clubs who primarily rely on league broadcasting revenues, and
  from most others in the Champions League. This is making

---

* https://football-italia.net/serie-a-president-urges-fifa-and-uefa-to-take-action-against-saudi-market
-dominance/.

matches less exciting and league winners / Champions League qualifiers more predictable.

- **There is pushback from local, multi-generation, hard-core, season-ticket-holder club fans against global capitalism** and against newer, much-larger-in-number, global club fans who are not as tethered to local rivalries and have never been to the stadium.[*]

- **Calendars and competitions seem more congested as the physical intensity required by players has increased.** This results in more player injuries because of the correlation between number of matches, play intensity, and injuries. The trend is driven in part by FIFA and UEFA continually expanding tournaments.

- **Football's regulation system has been exposed** as a patchwork of rules that often differ by jurisdiction, are inconsistently enforced, and challenged in court (including FIFA and UEFA often having conflicting interests).

- **FIFA and UEFA have been exposed as controlling the multibillion-dollar transnational activity of football** (including the regulatory function over clubs, the moneymaking hosting of tournaments function utilizing clubs, and the judiciary and discipline function over clubs), but being subject to limited regulation or oversight (including over potential conflicts).

- **Super-agents are making more money** with increasing player transfer fees and salaries and have more power, including more influence over clubs.

- **Players have essentially become global brands**, and some have more social media followers than their clubs (including more player recognition from video games), and make more money than the profits of their clubs.

- **Football media has become immediate news** with limited governance. The trend includes fan fascination with transfers and

---

[*] In 2018, Liverpool CEO Peter Moore said, "Our pulse is global, our heart is local." https://leadersinsport.com/sport-business/videos/liverpool-fc-local-heart-global-pulse/.

individual players' money and lives, and more people getting their sports news via YouTube, Instagram, and TikTok.

- **A spending spree has thrust Saudi Arabia football onto the global stage.** Developments have included the Saudi Pro League signing superstar players; an SPL club reaching the 2022 FIFA Club World Cup final; Saudi Arabia beating Argentina in the 2022 World Cup; and Newcastle, controlled by Saudi's Public Investment Fund, finishing fourth in the 2022–23 Premier League standings and qualifying for the European Champions League.

But it's not just changes within the sport that are putting pressure on football clubs to adapt or be left behind. In the next chapter, we'll see that there are also serious systemic changes going on more broadly in sports, entertainment, and content. These include:

- Over-the-top and new platforms to watch entertainment.
- Increasing data capture, analytics, and management (including from on the pitch to off the pitch, and who owns player data).
- Changes in fan engagement, including storytelling, social media, and fan tokens.
- Changes in viewership, including demographics, multiple screens active at one time, and snippet consumption.
- Changes in fan experience expectations, including more sophisticated fans and better stadium experiences.
- An increasingly uncomfortable association with betting companies.
- The increasing popularity and influence of women's sports.

The next chapter will focus on explaining these changes that are going on more broadly in sports, entertainment, and content, and examine how Real Madrid are adapting and innovating while keeping true to their values and identity.

Chapter 6

CHANGES IN SPORTS, ENTERTAINMENT, AND CONTENT

THE CHANGES THAT are going on more broadly in sports, entertainment, and content are happening so fast that it is difficult to keep up. What, why, and how we watch, engage, and experience sports is evolving. In addition, each generation and country is different. Real Madrid are adapting and innovating while keeping true to their values and identity.

OVER-THE-TOP AND NEW PLATFORMS PROVIDE MORE OPTIONS FOR CONSUMERS TO WATCH ENTERTAINMENT, FOOTBALL INCLUDED

According to *Forbes*, in 2019, 52 percent of global sports fans that paid for online video services were planning to "cut the cord" and switch to streaming exclusively by 2024.* Streaming-only services have disrupted the sports TV market by offering a greater variety of content than what's possible on a linear service, coupled with more flexible, cheaper subscriptions.

---

* https://www.forbes.com/sites/stevemccaskill/2021/07/31/sports-fans-are-ready-to-cut-the-cord-if-streaming-service-can-step-up/?sh=60ab731b3eef.

During the global lockdown, people wanted to access more diverse video content of premium quality. Their desire both raised overall digital video consumption and accelerated the switch from traditional cable and satellite services to over-the-top services (OTT) like Amazon Prime, Hulu, Netflix, Now TV (Sky) in U.K., Canal Play (CANAL+) in France, and Movistar Plus in Spain. Also, YouTube, de facto, is a global OTT platform.

OTT platforms can offer the cross-platform and internet-enabled device compatibility desired by most modern sports fans and consumers. In theory, advanced OTT streaming's utilization of 3D technologies, 4K resolution, and virtual reality permit fans to watch sports from different angles just by flicking switches. But in practice there is relatively limited adoption from the broadcasters or league rights holders. It's not a matter that is in the hands of the clubs, because they don't own the broadcasting rights individually. Though there is more innovation happening in the U.S. than in Europe.

In addition, there has been one key issue around 3D (meaning virtual reality or immersive streaming)—the lack of wide adoption of the required hardware. Also, there is a social factor that Apple, for example, is trying to solve with the Vision Pro headset—which is that it's somewhat uncomfortable to view sports in your living room with others while wearing a device on your head.

What is OTT? Simply put, OTT describes a delivery mechanism, in the way that cable and satellite are delivery mechanisms. That is, OTT is an internet protocol that delivers content to devices set up to receive it. This term is used widely in the sports industry, but in fact doesn't really say much because even the traditional broadcasters are delivering content OTT, meaning they deliver via internet connection. The difference is that the cable companies traditionally dominated this space and much of this content was served in a linear format—available at a predetermined time, rather than on demand. The big change is that the platforms that have accelerated are all on-demand platforms, and are driven by the IP rights holders directly to the end user. This (plus the availability of content on mobile devices, not only TV sets) has increased the power of the consumer to choose the content they want to watch. However, the situation has also simultaneously created an overabundance of subscription offers that consumers must select from, which has in fact introduced subscription fatigue.

The direct-to-consumer (DTC) part of OTT is so named because a content owner doesn't go through a cable operator or another intermediary to stream or deliver its content. The owner's content goes directly to the sports fan or the consumer. When most people think of OTT streaming services, they think of Netflix—which goes directly to consumers. When traditional broadcasters, like a TV network, deliver content, they don't necessarily know a lot about the end consumers, or don't necessarily share a lot of information with the content owner. With OTT, the owners of the content get the data on their consumers directly. The content producer can track real-time data, and that information opens an enormous, very valuable set of opportunities to increase revenue.

In 2020, the CEO of the Premier League, Richard Masters, revealed that it's inevitable that the most watched sports league in the world will launch a Netflix-style streaming service—which could result in lower subscription costs for fans and increased revenues for clubs.*

Currently, the league sells its TV rights to traditional broadcasters like Sky and NBC and third-party streaming services like Amazon Prime and DAZN in return for guaranteed annual payments typically over a few years. The 2019 to 2022 TV rights were worth around £3.1 billion per year, of which £1.4 billion comes from foreign buyers.

The value of domestic TV rights for the Premier League has plateaued, but there are two hundred million fans and growing worldwide currently paying to watch live Premier League football. In addition, video-on-demand streaming is growing quickly. So the Premier League has been exploring the possibility of cutting out the "middlemen" of traditional broadcasters and streaming services and going "direct-to-consumer" (DTC) with its own "over-the-top" (OTT) service to make more money.

Smartphones, tablets, smart TVs, and computers are perfect for OTT streaming services, in which sports franchises offer exclusive video content unavailable through the traditional broadcast platforms. The

* https://theathletic.com/1588394/2020/02/08/premier-league-tv-streaming-netflix-rights/.

demand for this is particularly strong in the United Sates where stream-ing services such as NFL Game Pass, NBA League Pass, MLB.TV, UFC Fight Pass, and WWE Network are all ramping up their offerings.

Just as the American NFL got the Big Five thinking about the value of TV rights in 1982, it's the American NBA providing the inspiration this time. The NBA has teamed up with Google to offer basketball fans extra digital content through their mobile phones. Called the Pixel Arena, it allows fans to create their own avatars, watch digital replays, enjoy enhanced statistics, and take part in quizzes. The NBA's "League Pass" streaming service costs about £10 a month in the U.K. If the Pre-mier League were to opt for a similar amount—significantly less than what Sky and BT Sport charge for their bundled packages—its annual income from those two hundred million subscribers could, theoretically, rise to £24 billion, eight times what the Premier League is currently being paid.* And this amount of money would further separate the Premier League from any club in any other league, including LaLiga.

But starting a "Premier League channel" in England, where Sky Sports has around six million subscribers and BT Sport close to two mil-lion, is risky. For example, the Premier League OTT service could make its entertainment content less available to mainstream viewers. Viewers are not abandoning traditional pay TV just yet because they don't feel enough content is available on streaming platforms. The suggestion is that unless content owners ensure their events are shown on a stream-ing service—either in addition to, or instead of, linear broadcasts—they could lose audiences.

Some believe the Premier League is too scared to actually cut out the middleman—the broadcaster—and have their own direct-to-consumer (DTC) internet broadband service. The traditional model is simple. Sell the rights to the highest bidder and you can forecast your P&L for the next five to ten years. In addition, you don't have to worry about distribu-tion because the broadcasters already have it. To go direct-to-consumer means building out your own distribution and building your user base (and even setting up your own billing department). Despite a big shift

---

* https://theathletic.com/1588394/2020/02/08/premier-league-tv-streaming-netflix-rights/.

to streaming content, there are still many people today, probably more than 50 percent, who consume their content through their television and through the traditional networks. This presents a huge risk in the short term of losing revenues, even though the long-term view should look more profitable. What some believe could happen is a big fund (CPP, PIF) underwriting these rights to take a share in the long-term growth. It might take five to ten years to fully transition all fans across to a pure DTC offering, but then the numbers are staggering.

But Masters suggested a two-tiered system with some countries watching matches shown by traditional broadcasting and streaming service providers and others streamed directly by the Premier League will eventually happen. The Premier League would probably start its own OTT service in a few test markets. For example, in Singapore, more than four hundred thousand fans currently subscribe to Singtel's sports offering. Singtel pays £70 million a season to the Premier League, yet it makes £175 million a year from subscribers who pay around £35 a month for live games. A Premier League OTT channel could potentially generate another £100 million in Singapore alone.* Until the Premier League launches its own OTT service, the threat has given them more negotiating leverage with traditional broadcasters.†

To consider one model, Netflix started off as a video rental club, and then got into streaming other production companies' movies and TV shows. Over time, Netflix built an expertise in going direct to consumers, and then started to produce their own content. Sports leagues are looking at Netflix's success and thinking they could have a much more valuable relationship with their consumers if they went direct to consumers. They would know more about them, and they would be able to sell them additional products. However, Netflix and sports are different models. Netflix invests many billions annually into original content and content licensing. Sports, on the other hand, should be a cheaper model and more profitable. But simply offering the matches may not be enough.

---

* https://www.theguardian.com/football/2020/feb/08/premier-league-netflix-tv-sports-rights.

† LaLiga has been streaming a selection of niche sports, such as domestic basketball, futsal, and handball, to subscribers for two years. It now has six hundred thousand subscribers.

The experience should be disruptive due to the additional capabilities offered through DTC channels.

On the other hand, some believe that in Europe it will probably remain more lucrative for the football leagues to sell rights to traditional pay TV platforms rather than distribute their own OTT services. The main reason for this is the very high price paid by these platforms to the leagues, reflecting the role played by football as a subscription driver of their overall pay TV service. Many platforms lose money on the exploitation of football rights, but this is offset by the margin they make on the sale of other content or services (as football is often part of TV bundles including other content and triple/quadruple play packages, along with fixed telephony, broadband, and mobile subscriptions). As a result, independent OTT services such as DAZN, which are pure sports players, have had financial losses. And no relevant independent sports channel (such as ESPN in the U.S.) has been able to operate in any major European market. In addition, many fans typically have access to football matches as part of a subscription offer containing other sports and entertainment content. They may not subscribe to a service that only includes the games of a single league like the Premier League. Content aggregation often leads to a higher number of subscribers.

The NBA's app, which is tied to their League Pass, delivers "moments," which are highlights of games generated in real time, and allows fans to seamlessly drop into the full game at any time through the League Pass integration. This is an example of a sports league delivering content online with the expectations of a younger fan base, and their numbers prove it. Some believe the NBA may receive over a billion impressions on their app, which is unheard of. These are getting close to the number impressions seen in social media. This is in large part due to their design, which borrows many common and familiar elements from popular social platforms.

Not only does the NBA have a direct-to-consumer OTT service, so do the NFL, MLB, PGA, and Formula 1 motor racing. UEFA also launched its own streaming product. F1 TV's (Formula 1's) interface is simple but allows you to follow an individual driver, tune in to the team radio, and see real-time stats such as car position around the track (this is surprisingly interesting, as it's very difficult to get an understanding of the spacing between cars in the traditional format). The PGA Tour gives fans the ability to follow a specific golfer and see AR overlays of shot data.

Madridista Loyalty Program and the Evolution of Content Channels

Real Madrid TV (RMTV) is a digital 24/7 live TV channel operated by Real Madrid. It is available for free via a digital terrestrial signal in Spain and distributed digitally via partners all over the world. It has two signals: English and Spanish. RMTV is also free for those fans that want to join and discover the Real Madrid community and register as a Madridista member at realmadrid.com or madridistas.com. Once a Madridista, a member has a universal Madridista login, which means that the member now has one login to access everything related to Real Madrid. More importantly, Madridistas gain access to all the content on RM Play, the club's OTT platform, where all of the club's video content is available on demand and organized by section, including live access to Real Madrid TV.*

RM Play was created as a value-added service for the entire Real Madrid community, and can be accessed on mobile devices, tablets, and smart TVs (Apple TV, Android TV, Samsung TV, LG, and Amazon Fire TV). Via RM Play, Madridistas have access to news from all sections of the club, highlights, press conferences, interviews, and specials; a historical archive of all sections, including highlights of the last fifteen years of the first team; trailers and first episodes of Real Madrid's original series; the live RMTV signal, in its Spanish and international version; and on-demand news broadcasts of the last fifteen days. In addition, the premium tier of Madridistas get access to premium documentaries and films about the club, produced especially for the club's most engaged and loyal fans and members.

---

* In April 2023, Barcelona announced that it will be shutting down Barça TV due to cost-cutting measures and will focus on its online streaming platform, Barça TV+. According to *Sport*, Barcelona claimed that their channel had €2 million per year in revenues and €14 million in costs, something that was unsustainable. It is very expensive to have a digital TV channel, but Real Madrid see their channel as a part of an integrated digital offering for their fans. https://www.sport.es/es/noticias/barca/barca-tv-funde-negro-89294713.

Real Madrid's digital and content areas have a discipline to speak
the social media platform's native language to be more relevant, and to
unleash the power of storytelling innovation. The use of user-generated
content in Real Madrid's official social media channels honors their community: the best content often comes from Real Madrid's fans (see the
Madridistas Instagram as an example). Real Madrid also experiments
with long-form content monetized via distributors (e.g *Real Madrid Until
the End* on Apple TV) or via RM Play (the Universe Real Madrid series)
to further increase the global footprint of Real Madrid's brand.

When a fan joins, Real Madrid get the fan's basic information and
then can learn what the fan values and likes and how to better provide
engagement. The value of that data is enormous for the club, through
both D2C channels and sponsorship business. Converting fan level
engagement is critically important for revenue growth. Therefore, the
digital TV channel is integrated into and a part of the digital and
OTT platform.

For example, today, Real Madrid have their LED perimeter board
signage, which is used to show sponsor messages during the match (the
LED advertising boards around the pitch). Real Madrid already split this
into ten regions and digitally superimpose (through AR) different sponsor messages per region, depending on the sponsor and the region. Therefore, there are ten different versions of the perimeter signage that you
can see during a game, depending on where you're watching from. The
interesting thing, an idea that is already being worked on, is that if the
matches were delivered over a DTC streaming platform—where each user
receives the feed directly to their device—Real Madrid could individually target an individual IP address. This means that Real Madrid could
generate millions of versions of the sponsorship board, each individually
tailored to the user data tied to that IP address. Again, this speaks to the
power of the Madridistas program enabling Real Madrid to know the fan
directly through an individual digital identity. If the fan has given the
Madridistas program permission, they can use the fan's data to personalize the advertising in the match at a per-fan level, in the same way that
online advertising works. This advertising could even be sold through an
auction process, similar to existing paid media options.

Real Madrid also have a premium membership/subscription model. If a fan pays €35 per year for a premium subscription (€20 per year for a junior subscription, for children under fourteen years old), they get access to what is available for free to Madridista members plus complete, current, and past matches; exclusive content; and all episodes of Real Madrid's original series and films: *Behind the Champions*, *Leyenda Blanca*, the Bernabéu documentary, *Universo Real Madrid*, and *Campo de Estrellas*, among others.

Real Madrid's premium membership is loosely based on the Amazon Prime model: as Real Madrid launch new apps, products, and services, they keep bundling more value into the premium subscription. The goal is to make the subscription valuable enough that, once you have it, you can't consider going back to the basic free membership.

Real Madrid's advantage is that they have one of the largest sports global fan bases: seven hundred million fans, and over 550 million followers on social media (as of October 2024). The first challenge is getting fans to join the free membership. It is easier to first get fans to click "follow" than have them submit information to join the membership. And then if they do join, Real Madrid have to offer enough compelling value for those followers to become premium subscribers. It's not so easy to get even the most passionate Real Madrid fans to upgrade from free to premium.

This is a challenge for any such platform; reportedly, less than 0.2 percent of X subscribers pay for premium services. People have complex prioritization mechanisms for how they distribute their disposable income. For example, someone is sitting in a Starbucks café sipping a €5 latte, yet may refuse to download a €0.50 app on their phone, believing that whatever app they download should be free. But there is huge price elasticity if Real Madrid can continue to make progress. If Real Madrid can provide enough value to their international fans, their loyalty to the club acts as a multiplier.

The math is staggering . . . if Real Madrid can execute. If around 1 percent of Real Madrid's five hundred million global social media followers—five million—subscribed at €35 per year, the annual subscriptions would bring in €175 million, which would exceed the club's pre-COVID 2018–19 matchday revenues. While progress is being made with this endeavor, and success will make global fans even more important, executing it is easier said than done. While a global brand like Real Madrid now has the technology to deliver content directly to the end user without going through intermediaries (increasing their ability to deliver a more tailored experience to their fans), doing so also means that Real Madrid must compete for wallet share with HBO, Disney+, Apple TV+, Netflix, Hulu, and all the other subscription-based services that compete for consumers' disposable income.

INCREASING DATA CAPTURE, ANALYTICS, AND MANAGEMENT

Data and data analytics are fundamentally changing sports.[*] Clubs, leagues, broadcasters, stadium operators, and athletes are increasingly capturing data and using data analytics to make better decisions. Most big clubs now employ data analysts who provide a raft of metrics for coaches to digest. Slowly, their work is growing ever more sophisticated, and ever more important to the clubs they advise.

High-speed video and wearables such as "sports bras" (GPS tracker vests) or special soles in shoes are capturing all types of data to be analyzed to improve performance. And advancements in computer power, cloud technology, and machine learning algorithms are increasing the amount and quality of data analysis capabilities. The analytics of the data have transformed everything from how talent is identified to how athletes are trained to how matches are played. Every big club, including Real Madrid, has data analytics experts on staff to crunch the numbers on behavior, tactics, and fitness.

Data analytics can even change a team's tactics. In basketball, data analytics (along with Steph Curry's success) convinced NBA teams to attempt more 3-pointers. Data has also persuaded many football managers to have their players attempt *fewer* long-range shots, because they

---

[*] https://www2.deloitte.com/xe/en/insights/industry/technology/technology-media-and-telecom-predictions/2021/athlete-data-analytics.html.

connect so infrequently. The distance from where players have taken shots was much higher ten years ago, because data analysts noticed the risk/reward ratio was not attractive.

Real Madrid focus on two main types of data from athletes: positional and biometric. Positional data includes a player's position, acceleration, lateral motion, distance covered, and speed. Biometric data includes a player's pulse rate, oxygen levels, sweat rate, and sleep rhythms.

Today, most biometric data collection and analysis happens during training or postgame. Typically, leagues prohibit in-game collection and use of biometrics unless explicitly approved by the league.

Both Real Madrid and their players want to predict when conditions may heighten the risk of injury. For clubs, fewer injured players mean more wins and more revenue; for athletes, it means having information that can help them stay available for matches, extend their careers, and increase their earnings potential. Predicting injuries more effectively requires measures that help balance exertion and strain with the proper amount of recovery time and sleep—and each player is different.

Data and data analytics help on-the-pitch and off-the-pitch performance—they are codependent. More efficient training, and increasing the likelihood that star athletes stay healthy, is linked to more matches star athletes can play and play at peak performance. Which is linked to more wins, which is linked to higher attendance, more sponsorships, and greater broadcast viewership.

The use of wearables and other in-game technology can provide enhanced broadcasts, differentiated fan experiences, and revenue generation. Of course, players, clubs, and leagues are trying to figure out how all the data collected and analyzed can create new revenue. Revenue can come from licensing the player data to video game developers, betting companies, and health and fitness companies. Revenue can also come from better fan engagement, due to broadcasters providing more data and insights to viewers—the heart rate of a player during a match, their top speed in a sprint, the total distance they ran during a match, the number of touches they had of the ball, the height they jumped for the header, and so forth. A recently launched chess league called Armageddon is using heart-rate monitors to show spectators how players' stress levels fluctuate during matches. And an Israeli company called MindFly has developed a chest-mounted camera that can be worn by athletes in any sport, and used to capture video footage from the field of play.

Sports fans are looking for more and detailed data related to performance and surrounding events and conditions of the match. The goal is to give fans a better understanding of the athleticism and skill of the players. This is leading to a blurring of the lines between the physical and digital experiences—making the real-world experience more like video games. Video games and "gamification" are common themes because of the influence and impact video games have had on how young people view, interact with, and consume sports—from big clubs to star players. The increasing use of data and analytics has begun to blur the boundaries between many disparate areas of sports, including e-sports, virtual sports, gaming, broadcasting, fantasy sports, betting, and the live-venue experience. Society and sports have been transformed into data. Athletes are almost ceasing to be humans to the viewer, and are becoming a series of data points.

New revenue streams from player data also lead to issues such as equitable revenue distribution, player protection policies, and data-ownership policies. The questions ultimately become who owns the data and how can it be used . . . and if you are a player—how is that data used by, for, and against me? Some players are not comfortable about others possessing their biometric data. They are concerned that biometric data collection could bias contract negotiations. Some are worried that data collection is going beyond their "workplace" of matches and training, and encroaching on areas of their private lives outside of work, including family activities, sleeping, and vacation.

Another issue is the use of player data for betting. An example of this is Project Red Card, the claims brought by more than 850 current and former Premier League, English Football League, National League, and Scottish Premier League players over the allegedly unlawful collection and use of their performance data by gaming, betting, and data-processing companies. The complaint is that under U.K. and EU data protection laws, player performance data is "personal data" concerning health. And these third-party firms have been using players' personal performance data without consent or compensation—and therefore unlawfully and invading the privacy of the players. The lawsuit also claims that betting companies and video game developers create player profiles based on health data they have collected and processed without consent, which promotes hate and abuse of players, especially through social media. Project Red Card seeks to recover lost income going back six years, which could be worth hundreds of millions of pounds. Project Red Card is a pivotal lawsuit. The impact of a successful claim would not only be felt domestically, but would have an effect across the world, in numerous sports and leagues, and would represent a huge shift in athletes taking ownership of their performance data.

Fan databases—derived from a combination of the quantity of fans in a club's client relationship management (CRM) system, and the depth of information that a team knows about their fans—are valuable assets. Clubs are getting a better understanding of the value of the data, and of who is prepared to pay for it and how it will be used (in a privacy-compliant way) to connect to subsets of a club's fan base. Slowly, a fan's data is being linked to the revenues they generate.

Football clubs have many opportunities to collect data from and about their fans.* Legislation is trying to keep up to ensure that fan data can only be collected, held, processed, and used for purposes that the fan overtly consents to. Football clubs try to use customer data to offer more personal and better deals, better access, better content, better experiences, and better recognition to fans.

Data provides intelligence about what the fan consumes in terms of experiences, content, and products. Acting upon better intelligence leads to deeper and more meaningful fan engagement. And an engaged fan is a spending fan. Data collection opportunities happen at all interfaces in the team–fan relationship: ticketing, in-stadium, official events, point of sale, membership/travel clubs, loyalty programs, social media, web engagement, and others.

---

* https://www.linkedin.com/pulse/collecting-fan-data-opportunities-sports-clubs-bodies-karl-mulligan/.

Digital technologies, for example at the renovated Santiago Bernabéu Stadium, will play a key role in accumulating data to provide more personal and meaningful fan engagement and experience. Wi-Fi access, stadium apps, cashless (and/or mobile) point-of-sale systems, and social activity tracking will all be deployed to great effect in gathering contact, engagement, and behavioral data. Importantly, all of these will also significantly transform the in-person game day experience. The renovated stadium is not only about engaging fans.[*] It's also about creating more revenue opportunities.

Real Madrid Next

In 2020, Real Madrid, with the aim of remaining sports industry leaders as well as social and economic leaders, launched Real Madrid Next (RMNext). RMNext is the new brand for innovation at Real Madrid, collaborating with startups and companies looking for better performance, features, and the sporting and economic strength of Real Madrid, as well as hoping to make the most of what those involved with the club have to offer.

RMNext looks at six key areas: e-health, performance, fan engagement, audiovisual, cybersecurity and technology, and social. They look for excellence and the best technological advances possible, which helps to create Real Madrid's own, exclusive tools adapted to their way of working. The club wants better results in every area. And, in particular, they look to improve performance in the sporting area, in digital transformation, and in globalization of the entire organization.

For example, in the e-health space, RMNext is collaborating on the development of smart insoles connected with the Spanish company Podoactiva to prevent and detect possible injuries while analyzing the daily footprint of an athlete. Likewise, they have carried out various tests to improve decision-making using infrared muscle cameras. They have also started a project to link sports performance with the physical load of training, to develop evaluation and comparison indices. And these efforts are not

---

[*] https://www.statsperform.com/resource/how-data-can-transform-the-fan-experience-in-sports-stadiums/.

confined to the physical. RMNext is also working on cognitive methods to improve decision-making on the field for the athletes. They have the possibility of having almost five hundred permanent athletes at the training center of Real Madrid, La Ciudad Deportiva Real Madrid, that allow them to manage new developments with the squads and associated staff and coaches.

In addition to the direct developments promoted by RMNext, collaborations with partners of the club have led to the creation of an Innovation Lab with Abbott Laboratories, focused on the field of e-health. This laboratory is a space where Real Madrid Medical Services and Abbott scientists collaborate to generate innovative ideas and explore the future of sports nutrition and physiology. The center is located in the Real Madrid first team facilities and is designed to improve the performance of the players.

In the cybersecurity area, to give another example, RMNext participates in a pioneering European program (called Safe Stadium) to define an efficient protocol against possible NRBC (nuclear, radiological, biological, and chemical) threats. The Real Madrid club and its Santiago Bernabéu Stadium are a key pilot stadium in this three-year project, which includes European experts from Poland, Germany, Slovakia, Italy, and Spain. It will allow European experts (including the Spanish entity INTA, Instituto Nacional de Tecnica Aeroespacial) to evaluate and analyze the management of the security operation in a large-capacity football stadium and the security regulations applied.

RMNext will follow up the continuity of its growth of various programs and collaboration agreements with new projects, including the launch of several open call programs that will allow some startups to enter the Real Madrid ecosystem. Once selected, these companies have the opportunity to carry out pilots in collaboration with Real Madrid's internal teams, with the aim of supporting faster growth for these companies, and for Real Madrid to benefit from the cutting edge of innovation in all areas of Real Madrid Next. In the last four years, RMNext has reviewed more than eight hundred startups, and has launched forty-five of them into the Real Madrid ecosystem.

CHANGING ENGAGEMENT

Only about 1 percent of sports fans ever actually attend a game. The rest watch from their homes. That hasn't changed. However, sports teams and leagues are now trying to digitally engage that 99 percent who are watching from the comfort of their couch.[*]

The web provided a kind of democratization of content—more people are able to create, and more people are able to consume. Those creators can go directly to their fans and to consumers. The whole process is just continuing to accelerate and expand and make new inroads that were once unimaginable. Now, there is a "creator economy"—driven by Gen Z and their obsession with digital storytelling and content creation—which reflects the changing engagement with, and experience of, fans.

Real Madrid are very sophisticated users of various channels and platforms like X, YouTube, Instagram, TikTok, and Facebook. Many clubs have social media editors responsible for all social media channels and online content creation. In addition, many clubs have likeable "insider" hosts and personalities who connect so much deeper with their younger fan bases and give new and younger fans perspectives and experiences that interest them—and in a language and on a platform that they connect with.

However, now the fan is the content creator too. Social media changed the nature of how highlights are produced and distributed. Fans now post their own highlights from their seats in the stadium based on what they want to share socially.

The survey research data firm Morning Consult found that 45 percent of Gen Zers said they've purchased clothing because an influencer or celebrity sponsored it—game tickets and sports subscriptions won't be far behind.

Sports and entertainment are more interactive than ever. TikTok's journey from karaoke-esque app to global obsession to Real Madrid having TikTok specialists tells a story of convergence between social media, streaming, entertainment, content—and sports. Snapchat's rise is partially linked to its groundbreaking Stories format, now copied by almost everyone. Justin.tv's morphing into e-sports-centric Twitch proves how

---

[*] https://www.techtarget.com/searchbusinessanalytics/news/252489982/Pandemic-speeds-up-digital-transformation-in-sports.

seemingly niche ideas can, over time, be transformed into community-building interactive powerhouses.

Outside entertainment and sport, we're witnessing the gamification of . . . almost everything. Apple Health, Fitbit, Peloton, Strava—all incentivize physical activity with elements borrowed from games.

Back to the world of entertainment and sport consumption of today: audiences notoriously have shortened attention spans. Yet the same people will binge-play FIFA video games or short clips on Real Madrid TikTok when captivated. Within some sports, an acute drop-off of younger fans is motivating traditional broadcast and streaming companies to reconsider the nature of their core streaming products.

Many experts believe there are several interconnected elements that will form part of the next-generation streaming services—which applies to sports and entertainment fan engagement. Tom McDonnell, CEO of technology company Monterosa, focuses on four interconnected ingredients to create interactive experiences for passionate fans: participation, community and togetherness, gamification and rewards, and real-time data visualization.* All of these elements transcend any specific technology or screen or UI.

Participation has the goal of motivating interactivity to make the outcome meaningful and visible. Examples include voting for Player of the Match, or rating the players. Even feelings about a goal or a referee decision can be the basis of a participatory interaction. Viewers can vote, their vote counts, and they can see the results. One can enhance the interactive-ness with clips or stats before viewers make their decision. One can take this even further, bringing participation to player selection or even the match itself. Imagine inviting football fans to vote on starting lineups or formations using fan tokens—and monetizing the right to have a say in the decision. In such scenarios the club becomes a hybrid of e-sports and reality.

Community and togetherness can be a conversational experience, as in X, Reddit, and YouTube comments, but this type of involvement has

---

* https://tommcdonnell.medium.com/how-interactive-fan-engagement-will-transform-the-next-generation-of-streaming-service-2547c83c5818.

moved to "watch parties." Groups of friends, family, or fans can stream themselves while watching a match! To demonstrate community and togetherness, one can see a live counter of how many people are watching and participating. Combining this with participation, people can see how many people voted in various polls and games.

Gamification and rewards refers to the concept of adding points, progress, and leaderboards to give viewers satisfaction. Can you imagine getting some sort of recognition for watching every Real Madrid match this season? Participation can also be made into a game—fans can get special badges or points, for example, the more they interact and vote. And that can lead to something valuable to the fan.

Real-time data visualization is the utilization of sophisticated data visualization tools that rely on optical tracking technology and computer vision. For example, viewers can see how the players are linked in triangles or a back line. One can combine real-time data visualization with participation. For example, imagine a player about to take a penalty kick. One could see the percentage odds of where the player has kicked the ball in the past, and then fans can vote before the outcome. Imagine that being extended to live betting.

All these forms of interactive fan engagement will play an increasing part in how we consume sport and entertainment. There are many new startups focused on consolidating interactive, personalized content to differentiate user experiences and add value that can be monetized.

Major players are merging fan engagement, participation, community and togetherness, and gamification and rewards. For example, Socios.com is a creator of fan tokens (sometimes referred to as digital currencies) and works with many European football clubs, including Arsenal, Atlético Madrid, Barcelona, Juventus, Man City, PSG—and UEFA. Fan tokens are digital assets created using blockchain that give their owners the right to vote on official team polls that can help a club make fan-related decisions. Token holders can also get perks, exclusive promotions, rewards, VIP experiences, and engage with a community of like-minded fans. Typically, fan tokens do not require subscription or renewal—you only pay once. You can then buy and sell your token on selected crypto exchanges.

Some critics believe digital currency partnerships in sports commonly imply an offer of influence in sports for supporters, without properly explaining the risks—for example, fan tokens are prone to rising and falling in value, meaning people's investment in the token is at risk. In addition, the extent of the influence that becomes available once buying in is often relatively minor. Lastly, some critics raise serious ethical questions as to what extent supporters' commitment to their clubs is being taken advantage of.

While Real Madrid are seriously investigating the application of tokenization, blockchain technologies, and digital ownership to new models of fan engagement and community building, the club decided not to move forward with the first-generation fan tokens due, among other things, to the potential and significant financial risks it posed to fans of the club until the technology further matures.

CHANGING VIEWERSHIP

There are rapid changes happening in sports viewership and experience expectations—especially among younger generations. Some define Millennials as being born beginning anywhere from 1978 to 1981. Similarly, the post-Millennial generation, known to most as Generation Z, begins with a birth year roughly around 1997. They were about a decade old during the deepest and most protracted global recession. And they began entering high school, pursuing post-secondary education, or entering the workforce during the disruptions of the global pandemic in 2020. While the Millennials were children of the peace and prosperity of the 1990s, Gen Z are children of the wars, uncertainty, recession, and pandemic of the 2000s.

They are the first true digital natives who grew up in an environment defined by wireless internet, technology integration, infinite content, and immediacy. "They are totally plugged in—whether through social media, search engines, or instant messaging—to each other as well as to an infinite array of answers to any questions at any time."* They have been indelibly

---

* https://www.forbes.com/sites/brucetulgan/2023/02/23/what-makes-gen-z-different-and-not-so-different-from-older-employees/?sh=325bd15524bc.

shaped by an era of profound change with rapidly advancing technology and perpetual anxiety. Their "new normal" is the accelerating pace of everything, infinite information, remote and hybrid work, and permanently constrained resources. Making money on the side is popular for the youngest generation entering the workforce. Nearly 65 percent of Gen Zers, ages eighteen to twenty-five, have a side hustle, according to a LendingTree survey.[*] So they have more money to spend, but less time to spend it. Therefore, they focus on premium entertainment that matters to them—in sports terms, think "blockbuster matches" or "matches with meaning."

Gen Z's overall interest in sports remains significantly below that of older generations. Their appetites for attending live games and watching them on TV are lower.[†] These are trends that worry Real Madrid management. The future of football depends on its fans, so as those fans change their behaviors, it is essential that football responds and innovates. The Morning Consult surveyed one thousand U.S. Gen Zers between the ages of thirteen and twenty-five and found that 33 percent do not watch live sporting events, compared with 24 percent of U.S. adults and 22 percent of Millennials in a corresponding survey.[‡]

Morning Consult's survey results revealed that about 38 percent of Gen Zers said they have watched a professional sporting event on TV in the past four months, while 53 percent said they had done the same at least once in 2022. About 18 percent said they have attended a professional game this year, compared with 25 percent of Millennials.

People across generations are consuming sports and entertainment very differently. Gen Zers who watch live sports are doing so more often via digital platforms. Around 32 percent of Morning Consult's survey respondents said they utilize streaming services, compared with 28 percent who said they consume through traditional broadcast or cable TV. This is a change. In 2020, traditional broadcast or cable was still the preferred viewing method. Gen Z is the only generation that said it streams more live sports than it watches on traditional TV.

---

[*] https://www.gobankingrates.com/money/jobs/8-best-side-hustles-for-gen-z/.

[†] https://morningconsult.com/2022/12/13/gen-z-interest-in-watching-sports/.

[‡] https://morningconsult.com/2022/12/13/gen-z-interest-in-watching-sports/.

According to Morning Consult, almost half of Millennials and adults overall said they watch live sporting events on a weekly basis, compared with just around a quarter of Gen Zers.* The young generation's relative lack of interest in sports was also reflected in how infrequently they watch their own favorite teams—if they even have one. And this is a big change. In the Morning Consult survey, almost 40 percent of Gen Zers said they don't cheer for a favorite team, 13 percentage points fewer compared with all adults. Almost 40 percent of adults said they watch "all" or "most" of their favorite sports team's games in a season, as compared to only around a quarter of Gen Zers.

Despite what the data suggests, Gen Z is immersed with sports 24/7. Sports are a constant part of their life, but how they interact with sports has changed dramatically. Sports leads social media platforms in views. Gen Z are obsessed with the digital storytelling and content creation of sports. Athletes are some of the most influential public figures on the planet. However, Instagram attention isn't equating to ticket sales. Roughly half of Gen Zers said they have never attended a professional sporting event. The most often cited reasons for the challenges with engaging with the younger generation are the many other readily accessible entertainment options; the ability for spectators to be connected to a community during a match without being at the match; the popularity of established and emerging social media platforms; the fragmented nature of sports media rights distribution; accessibility to games; and ticket affordability.

However, the Morning Consult survey found that almost 60 percent of Gen Zers who have not watched a sporting event on TV in a few years said a "major reason" was because they just aren't interested in sports, followed by 20 percent who said games are too long. So, while fandom of athletes, teams, and leagues may exist, it exists on social media platforms. And the top three media platforms where Gen Z gets their sports news are YouTube, Instagram, and TikTok (in that order). Adults overall, meanwhile, preferred traditional outlets like ESPN and Sky. The top social media platforms for adults to obtain sports information are Facebook and

* https://www.immersiv.io/blog/gen-z-sports-media-innovation/.

YouTube. In addition, engaging with gaming will be viewed in a similar manner to being active on TikTok or other social media platforms. They are both platforms hosting fans that clubs are trying to reach.

Gen Xers are the demographic cohort following the Baby Boomers and preceding Millennials. Researchers have generally defined Gen Xers as people born from 1965 to 1980. Many Gen Xers consider themselves football fans, but they may really be an athlete's fan. And they may not necessarily be paying fans—just following the athlete. So clubs must convert them into passionate and consuming fans. In addition, soon leagues and clubs will start to welcome, and worry about, Generation Alpha, the new age group starting at fourteen years old in 2024. This is mainly due to their impact on decision-making in most multi-generation homes for the next decade for TV, audio, social media, gaming, and . . . football.

Multiple Screens Active at One Time

In recent years, changes have taken place in TV viewing patterns during live broadcasts of major sports events. One of the biggest changes is the use of "second screens" during viewing the event, also known as "media multitasking." In a Nielsen survey, around 46 percent of smartphone users and 43 percent of tablet users reported using mobile devices as a second screen while watching TV.[*] In most cases the audience can interact with a TV program in a different way by using a second screen, which can be referred to as a "companion device" for "social television."

The use of a second screen offers new opportunities for interaction and sharing data, additional touch points with audiences, direct transactions, and data gathering. Academic research shows that most viewers prefer to watch the broadcast of a major football match with other people, though co-viewing is not necessarily done in the physical presence of others. Viewers are using technology to connect with others in order to create remotely shared experiences around TV content.[†] Findings also reveal a connection between the viewer's engagement with a game and the enjoyment of watching the broadcast. Further, this relationship is

---

[*] https://core.ac.uk/download/pdf/76357116.pdf.

[†] https://journals.sagepub.com/doi/10.1177/2167479518821913.

mediated through the use of a smartphone or tablet as a second screen, accompanied with the use of social media platforms and texting services.

Researchers have found that sports programming allows for more communication between viewers than any other content on television. According to Nielsen, sports events comprise somewhere between 2 and 3 percent of TV programming in any given month but generate close to half of X activity. Studies show most fans watch sports to gain knowledge about their favorite teams and players so they can discuss what they know with friends and fellow fans.[*] Fans use mobile apps, social media, and websites to fill the gaps of information and interaction not provided in live TV commentary.

Many TV rights experts predict that companies like Facebook, Amazon, Apple, Netflix, and Google will be even more serious players in broadcast media because they have the expertise to offer their customers a flexibility in viewing that traditional broadcasters cannot—including incorporating the second device. It's possible that live sport will be sold by delivery devices (TV versus smartphone). Also, there will be a greater focus over time on the quality of the viewing experience on a single smaller screen if social media platforms buy up more sports rights. For now, social media is a complement to TV, but that can change.

Snippet Video Consumption

From trending TikTok videos to Instagram Reels and Stories to YouTube Shorts, the sports and entertainment industries are focused on snippet video consumption—that is, the viewing and sharing of very short videos. Attention spans are shrinking, and video represents an entertaining, passive way to consume information. Around 60 percent of internet traffic revolves around video, and video content gets 48 percent more views on social media than other content types.

The concept of the "viral video" exists because of how easy short videos are to consume and share. People tend to share videos like crazy and, versus any other type of content, videos are most likely to spread.

---

[*] https://core.ac.uk/download/pdf/76357116.pdf.

Sports entertainment embodies more than just the professional games or matches found on broadcast TV. Trick shots might not be what you'd consider a traditional sport—it doesn't have a league or a championship. But one of the most popular videos at Real Madrid is when the players do something spectacular during training. Real Madrid's fans enjoy the entertainment, and the video also highlights a reason why fans support Real Madrid—the best players doing amazing things. Locker room access via video also brings fans closer to the action and humanizes the players, manager, and coaches. No matter what the nature of the content is or the platform you watch it on, Real Madrid are engaging with the audience and telling stories that build real connections with their fans.

Until recently, fans pretty much watched sports live, as they happened. But with online video, fans are watching sports on their own terms. And with short attention spans and a multitude of entertainment options, some of the most popular videos are highlights. Fans really seem to crave content that makes them feel like they're reliving these big moments without having to watch an entire match. In other words, online video gives sports fans control of the timing, and of what they want to watch. This is a concern for broadcasters, leagues, and clubs as it could limit revenues. So they are all working together to increase the engagement of fans during the match by offering interactive features. They are also trying to expand the match event time (to more than ninety minutes) with compelling pre- and post-match shows that offer more data analysis and insights, more replays utilizing technology to highlight strategic intricacies, more access on the pitch and in the locker room, more player and manager interviews, and more entertainment.

CHANGING EXPERIENCE EXPECTATIONS

Technology is changing rapidly, all around us—and consumer expectations are ramping up because of it.* If a consumer has an experience that costs Netflix billions of dollars to develop, that in their mind becomes the baseline standard of a high-quality premium experience. Every time

---

* https://cxmtoday.com/leadership/sports-viewership-is-changing-in-todays-consumer-landscape/.

a sports league utilizes new camera angles they previously couldn't, that becomes the expectation for other leagues and sports. And the consumers expect that new normal to be available everywhere, and on all devices. This impacts football because global fans see the best players in the world at the best clubs—and they expect that quality all the time. Even what is happening in the FIFA video game starts to set expectations for what fans expect to see from players on TV. And vice versa; video gamers expect as realistic an experience as a live match. The more visually appealing a club or team can make their product, the more people they can get to watch or play at home, the more they can attract and keep viewers. And the more leagues and clubs can charge advertisers for commercials to increase ad revenue.

However, there will be a limit to the fixed number of subscriptions any consumer will take on—it's like any other choice and expense. If it's worthwhile to you, you will spend on it. And this is a big problem in football. As options proliferate, consumers will start to make hard choices and not subscribe to every league and tournament. They will want to watch the big clubs with the best players playing meaningful matches. Consumers may have to choose on margin to pay to subscribe to watch the Premier League or the Champions League. Content providers need to prove value—with each match. You must show consumers it's worth paying for your content.

This is the key to engagement: making it worthwhile for subscribers to continue to engage and value their subscriptions. And to do that, appealing to subscribers is becoming more about personalization. In essence, one's audience is asking, "When I come to consume your content on the device of my choice, are you giving me what I had in mind?" So you need quality content, delivered in a quality way, and with the personalization that comes from using the data of consumer behavior. One of the keys is discovering who the fans are and directly marketing to them. Multi-club ownership models are gathering data on who buys tickets to a match. OTT providers are gathering data to know who is watching at home.

As previously discussed, Real Madrid must provide an experience that compares favorably to watching a match sitting in your specially designed and equipped media room with a high-definition big-screen

TV. Fans can watch a match originating from anywhere and view it in the comfort of their own home, eating and drinking what and when they like, with the company of their choosing. And as they watch on their spectacular TV, having reliable Wi-Fi enables them to use a second screen to search for player stats and interact with others on social media to enhance the experience.

The renovated Santiago Bernabéu Stadium is equipped to cater to Gen Z's digital-first habits, including fast Wi-Fi, reliable mobile ordering, and communal spaces to gather with friends where users can show off their experiences. Fans want to share these moments via Instagram, Snapchat, and their other social media accounts. Gen Z then converts that experience into content, into social currency, that ultimately influences their peers to say, "Wow, look at that. I need to go to a live Real Madrid match in the Santiago Bernabéu."

Real Madrid believe fans need better reasons than that to leave the comfort and conveniences of their homes, though. To get fans closer to the match, the new stadium will have a huge screen wrapped around the top of the stadium to amplify the spectacle. Rather than simply showing the current score, the boards will provide lots of sports data, offering unique insights to spectators. For example, fans will be able to see match and player statistics that reveal match narratives, engaging fans in new ways. When the game is slow, the stadium can still capture fans' attention by engaging and gamifying them on their smartphones via data-powered interactive quizzes, competitions, and fan challenges. Real Madrid will be providing a data-rich, personal stadium experience that football fans can't get watching a TV or device at home.

But the renovated stadium is not only about engaging fans.[*] It's also about creating more revenue opportunities. Data collected can be used to drive additional advertising revenue from brands and sponsors. The additional sponsorship space available on stadium screens provides new and improved opportunities for brand promotion and for connecting commercial partners with on-field action and fans. Through electronic

---

* https://www.statsperform.com/resource/how-data-can-transform-the-fan-experience-in-sports -stadiums/.

advertising boards, concourse screens, and external signage, the stadium will attract new and existing commercial partners looking to get exposure in front of more engaged fans.

AN INCREASINGLY UNCOMFORTABLE ASSOCIATION WITH, AND REVENUES FROM, BETTING COMPANIES

The sports betting industry has a size of about $66.8 billion as of late 2020, and is expected to rise to $106.25 billion by 2025.[*] Football is the biggest sports betting market in Europe and all over the world. Several European countries rank among the top countries with the highest gross gambling revenue. The European sports betting market grew in 2021 by almost 8 percent.

Middle Eastern countries and entities have helped grow European football with investment and sponsorship, and the same is true for sports betting companies. According to KPMG Football Benchmark, in 2020 sports betting had twenty shirt sponsorships in the Top 5 Leagues.[†] The next highest sector was banking and finance with eleven. In 2021, nine clubs in the Premier League had sports-betting companies as front-of-shirt sponsors, bringing in an estimated £54 million in annual revenue. In the EFL sports, betting sponsorships generate club revenues of over £40 million annually and over half of the clubs have commercial partnerships with brands in the sector, including fifteen front-of-shirt sponsors in the Championship. (Middle East Airlines sponsorship, after automotive, is second in terms of value because of their association with big clubs.)

In the Premier League and EFL, a few of the gambling sponsors who directly hold a license with the U.K. Gambling Commission (William Hill and Bet365) are familiar names to the U.K. audience. However, many more are Asian companies trying to get brand exposure in Asian markets where gambling advertising is banned or heavily restricted.

---

[*] https://breakingthelines.com/opinion/how-sports-betting-is-contributing-to-the-growth-of-soccer-across-europe-and-beyond/.

[†] https://www.footballbenchmark.com/library/the_changing_face_of_football_sponsorship_key_players.

Frequently, they are using Premier League and EFL as a billboard to reach gamblers in China and circumvent Chinese rules. Yet often the U.K. clubs and regulators know little about the Asian companies—their ownership and funding—or if they are alleged to be associated with any criminal activity.

Middle East and Kit Sponsors

The involvement of Middle East sponsors plays a key part in driving the commercial growth at many of Europe's biggest football clubs. According to KPMG Football Benchmark, Middle East brands represent the largest sponsors and investors into Top 5 League football, with close to €200 million in sponsorship per year.[*]

Some of the big European clubs are sponsored by the three Middle East airlines:

1. Emirates: Real Madrid, AC Milan, Arsenal, and Benfica
2. Etihad Airways: Man City
3. Qatar Airways:[†] PSG, Bayern Munich,[‡] Roma

Middle East brands account for over 30 percent of the value of shirt sponsorships in the Brand Finance Football 50 league table, with Emirates supporting more clubs than any other sponsor.[§]

Interestingly, the Bundesliga's clubs are typically sponsored by German-owned brands. Fourteen of the twenty Bundesliga club shirt sponsorships are from Germany-based companies.

According to KPMG, kit sponsorship across the Top 5 Leagues is dominated by adidas and Nike—with combined total annual sponsorship investment of €679 million per year across twenty-nine clubs, they represent

---

[*] https://www.footballbenchmark.com/library/the_changing_face_of_football_sponsorship_key _players.

[†] Qatar Airways has been one of the main partners of FIFA. Qatar Airways was one of the main sponsors of Euro 2020 and the 2021 CONCACAF Gold Cup.

[‡] After fan protests, Bayern Munich didn't renew their sponsorship from Qatar Airways in June 2023. In August 2023, Bayern Munich and Visit Rwanda signed a five-year "platinum" deal.

[§] https://acornstrategy.com/a-renewed-middle-eastern-interest-in-football-sponsorships/.

68 percent of the total kit deal spend. Puma and New Balance spend €194 million per year across sixteen clubs.

People have become more interested in football matches, in part, thanks to betting. Sports betting has contributed to the growth of football. Fans who bet on a particular match have a different, unique match-day experience than fans who don't. Betting on a match increases one's interest in it and makes one more invested in watching the entire game.

Like in any other sport, football's global appeal thrives on fan engagement, interactions, discussions, analysis, and unending debates. As a result, football betting platforms are beginning to incorporate social elements, like live chat sessions, to foster customer engagement. These tools allow fans all over the world to interact with each other to share their experiences, discuss games, and place wagers. Online sports betting also lets football followers access real-time information on their devices and bet on games without having to visit a physical location. Some sports betting sites provide streaming services to sports bettors, allowing customers to watch live games and make in-play wagering on different betting metrics, like the first team/player to score, the number of goals scored before halftime, and free kick conversions. Sports betting combines many key aspects of fan engagement, including participation, community and togetherness, gamification and rewards, and real-time data visualization.

Typically, sports bettors do some research before wagering, raising their level of football, team, and player knowledge and expectations. This ties into increasing data capture, analytics, and management (including from on the pitch to off the pitch) and who owns player data. It's important to be aware of how well a team and player are playing, winning and losing streaks, head-to-head matchups, and other critical factors that can affect the outcome of a game. That means you have to stay current with transfer news, injury updates, club management, and other important information. This feeds into the football media becoming immediate news, including the fascination with transfers and more people getting their sports news via YouTube, Instagram, and TikTok. As a result, bettors become highly invested in football, thus increasing fan engagement. It's a positive reinforcing loop.

The Italian government implemented new regulations in 2019, including a blanket ban on all sports betting–related sponsorships and advertising partnerships for Italian sports organizations domestically. However, the Italian Football Federation (FIGC) wanted the ban suspended to help clubs recover financially from the losses incurred during the global pandemic. The Spanish government implemented a ban ahead of the 2021–22 LaLiga season. Prior to its enforcement, gambling companies made up seven of twenty principal shirt sponsors in LaLiga in the 2020–21 season. The 2020–21 betting sponsorship agreements were worth an estimated €16.5 million collectively.*

Real Madrid have some betting partnerships, but only in markets where it is still legal to do so. For example, the deal Real Madrid had with Codere in Spain is now focused on Latin America. All the current betting deals are regional in nature—they are geo-targeted to specific territories.

English clubs could be forced to drop sports betting sponsors from their shirts soon because of the U.K. government's ongoing review of the 2005 Gambling Act. Also under examination is a loophole that currently allows overseas betting brands without a U.K. license to partner with "white label" companies, often based in territories such as the Isle of Man or Malta, effectively to "rent" the license and benefit from the global popularity of English football to advertise to consumers in markets where the promotion of betting services is illegal.

Football bettors are typically younger, male, and higher income fans who believe they have a special skill or expertise in football and in betting on football matches. They are looking to spice up both their interest in a match and their conversations with their friends. To them, betting is a way to be rewarded for their perceived investment in following football and their skill, as well as being a form of entertainment. Gambling researchers and addiction specialists believe the booming sports betting industry, lawmakers, and even the professional sports leagues themselves are making it easier, faster, and more tempting for

---

* https://www.tifosy.com/en/insights/what-would-a-ban-on-sports-betting-sponsorship-mean-3521.

people to bet on games—and potentially develop gambling additions, disorders, and problems.

As an interesting aside related to OTT/DTC, the betting platform LiveScore has bought the EPL rights for Ireland, and they're currently the only region that offers the matches through a DTC platform for free. They upsell users through their betting products. Reportedly, they've seen that by offering the matches for free they've increased the overall viewership of the Premier League by around ten times in Ireland.

Lastly, the next frontier for the in-stadium fan experience may be dictated by how much governments and leagues will allow sports venues to adapt to accommodate the availability of sports betting. This may be less likely in Spain or most of Europe, which is generally restricting sports betting, but may be more likely in the U.S., which is generally more open to sports betting.

WOMEN'S SPORTS ARE INCREASING IN POPULARITY, VALUE, AND INFLUENCE

Recently fans witnessed the best-attended and most-watched women's World Cup in history, and where football leads, other women's sports - are rapidly following. The FIFA 2023 Women's World Cup reached an estimated two billion viewers, almost double those who watched the 2019 tournament. Swiss star Alisha Lehmann saw her follower count go over 14 million on Instagram. According to Nielsen Sports, a single Instagram post by Lehmann is worth over $300,000 in value to a sponsor. Viewership for the 2022 WNBA playoffs was up 22 percent over 2021; in 2023, the NCAA Women's Final Four averaged 4.5 million television viewers, a 32 percent increase over 2022.

In September 2020, USWNT players Tobin Heath and Christen Press signed with Man U of the FA Women's Super League. Their jerseys outsold all of the players on the men's side—including surpassing Paul Pogba's, Bruno Fernandes's, and Marcus Rashford's jersey sales for the three days following their historic signings.

In 2021, viewership for the regular season of Major League Soccer (MLS) averaged 276,000 viewers across ESPN channels. That was an improvement to 2020's average of 233,000 viewers. Only nine National Women Soccer League (NWSL) games were broadcast in 2020, with the average viewership at 434,000. As of April 2022, aired NWSL matches attracted over 450,000 viewers, while MLS matches recorded an average of 283,000 viewers per game. Only one MLS game drew more viewers than NWSL games, which led some experts to believe that NWSL's current media rights deal of $1.5 million annually is undervalued.*

The Angel City FC ownership group paid a $2 million fee to join the National Women's Soccer League in 2020; in 2023, a group led by private equity firm Sixth Street committed to a record $53 million expansion fee to place an NWSL team in San Francisco. In 2023, the WNBA's Seattle Storm sold a 14 percent stake in the team at a $151 million valuation—more than ten times the prior record for a WNBA team. In India, five new women's cricket franchises were recently sold at auction for a combined $572.4 million. In 2023, the private equity firm CVC made a $150 million investment in the Women's Tennis Association (WTA) for a 20 percent stake in a commercial subsidiary, as the tour seeks to expand its marketing of events and players (creating media programming that will raise the profiles of players and tournaments) and increase prize money.

Women's professional sports sponsorships grew 20 percent year-over-year in 2022.† In 2023, Ally Financial Inc. made a multimillion-dollar ad buy across ESPN properties that will send 90 percent of the money to women's sports. Justin Nicolette, director of public relations for Ally's sports and entertainment division, explained the buy to *Fast Company*, saying, "People are so driven to support the brands that are supporting women's sports."

Over the last few years, a confluence of factors has begun to accelerate the popularity, value, and influence of women's sports. A younger generation of sports fans is embracing the social activism that comes along with women's sports. Women's sport inherently stands for issues like gender equality. The popularity of women's soccer in the U.S. stems from the

---

* https://askwonder.com/research/comparison-women-s-men-s-professional-sports-tv-viewership-rating-ng0c0h7p7.

† https://www.cnbc.com/2023/03/04/for-womens-sports-the-media-buys-are-becoming-a-big-deal.html.

USWNT players being such great advocates and fighting for equality. In addition, thanks to the growth of streaming, online highlights, and social media, women's sports have become more accessible than ever, which is driving growth. A social media user who followed a player for her LGBTQ or equal-pay advocacy might decide to watch her play. Women's FIFA video games have gone from depicting national teams to including women's club football too. A gamer can even have men play against women in *FIFA 23*. Sam Kerr, of Chelsea and Australia, graced FIFA's global cover (women have previously appeared on regional covers). With video games, fans are becoming more educated about women's players.

Women athletes drive higher volume social media engagement with fans, and at a deeper value, than their male counterparts, potentially boosting their appeal to advertisers. Women's sports and female athletes will continue to benefit from technology and direct-to-consumer opportunities.

The dramatic growth of women's sports is a hugely positive development—for fans, the sports, and the athletes themselves . . . and also for the betting market. It is creating very significant and untapped opportunities for sports betting. The dramatic increase in women's sport has been accompanied by a similar growth in betting on women's sport. Football is leading the way in terms of the number of people betting and placing bets on women's sport, with an annual market growth rate of approximately 20 percent since 2020.* This is followed by tennis, basketball, and cricket, with growth rates of over 10 percent during the period 2017–2022.

According to a study conducted by Purdue University in March 2021, coverage of women's sports in the media has barely changed since the 1980s.† The study found that, in 2019, women's sports coverage only totaled 5.4 percent of airtime, compared to 5 percent in 1989 and 5.1 percent in 1993—quite a small change. The Women's World Cup accounted for a large part of that percentage, as it drops to 3.5 percent

---

* https://www.entaingroup.com/news-insights/latest-news/2023/groundbreaking-study-into-growth-in -women-s-sports/.

† https://journals.sagepub.com/doi/full/10.1177/21674795211003524?_ga=2.239005058.326479783.167 8094105-2093098057.1678094105.

when removed in 2019. This goes back to the point that global fans want to see the highest-intensity and -interest matches. They want a spectacle that brings excitement to viewers. One needs to offer fans top-level games between the strongest teams, with the best players competing.

The study also found that digital media coverage had the same disparity, despite the lack of time constraints. Without equal media coverage, it is difficult to say whether or not interest in women's sports would otherwise be the same or closer to interest in men's sports, but trends show that it certainly would help. The most common reason people gave for not watching female sports was the lack of coverage. And as it relates to football, as previously discussed, there are so many matches—not to mention other sports and entertainment options. The congested international calendar of men's football takes opportunities and coverage away from women's football.

Obviously, there is still a big disparity in pay. Though prize money is equal for men and women at the four Grand Slam tennis events, the gap in prize money for many stand-alone men's and women's tennis events has widened in recent years. The chasm reached the highest levels in twenty years in 2022, with the men earning on average about 70 percent more than the women outside the majors.

The Women's World Cup is getting $150 million in prize money, a 300 percent increase over 2019. But while the $150 million for the first thirty-two-team tournament is a huge boost from the $30 million for the twenty-four-team edition in 2019, and ten times what it was in 2015, it is still considerably lower than the $440 million total prize money awarded at the thirty-two-team men's World Cup in Qatar in 2022. FIFA said it is aiming for parity between the men's and women's tournaments by 2027.

Real Madrid Femenino

Real Madrid started their Femenino section and began to compete under the Real Madrid brand in the 2020–21 season. They have a senior team; reserve side similar to Castilla, known as Real Madrid Femenino B; an under-19 team, Juvenil; and a Cadete for under-15s and below.

One of Real Madrid's objectives is to promote women's football in Spain. In total, eight players from the Real Madrid Femenino first team were 2023 Women's World Cup champions, including Spain's goal-scoring hero Olga Carmona (who was also the captain). Five of Real Madrid's junior players were on the U-17 World Cup Champions in 2022. In July 2023, the Spain Women's team ranked sixth in the Coca-Cola FIFA world rankings, and the Spain Men's team ranked tenth.

Real Madrid Femenino play at the Di Stéfano Stadium, which has a capacity of 5,900 seats. The average attendance per match is around two thousand people. They have virtually identical facilities to the men's team—natural grass training and playing fields, gym, physiotherapy area, locker rooms, medical areas, and technical rooms.

The Real Madrid Femenino fan profile is around 59 percent male and 41 percent female (compared to 68 percent male for the men's fans). The majority of the Femenino fans are under thirty-four years old (same with the men's). Real Madrid invested in dedicated content production and publishing resources for Femenino, and the fan base doubled in eighteen months. Real Madrid Femenino have around 6.2 million Instagram followers (compared to 150 million for the men's). Real Madrid Femenino have more Instagram followers than every men's club in LaLiga except Real Madrid, Barcelona, and Atlético Madrid.

The women's team gets exposure via Madridistas and RM Play. Many of the men's team sponsors are also sponsors of the women's. The kit looks like the men's, with Emirates as the main shirt sponsor and Adidas the kit sponsor.

The Femenino section is slightly loss-making because, despite increasing revenues (especially in sponsorship), the other areas of income, such as broadcasting, ticketing, and income from competitions, are relatively small. Broadly speaking, the main expenses of the section are salaries, which are around €4.5 million, and travel, which is around €1 million.

In our closing chapter, we'll discuss Real Madrid's success on the pitch, including how Real Madrid do against Premier League teams in the Champions League. I try to explain how Real Madrid support their culture on the pitch, and some unique characteristics about their star players.

Chapter 7

REAL MADRID'S SUCCESS ON THE PITCH

REAL MADRID HAVE won the Champions League six times in the last eleven years. Pundits and Real Madrid fans ask me why Real Madrid are pushing for changes in football when they have had so much success under the current system. Ironically, their success is obscuring the serious systemic changes in football. Real Madrid are concerned that football is not innovating enough or fast enough, and is losing its leadership as a global sport—that's not good for football, or for Real Madrid as a leader in the sport. That's why they believe European competitions must change, to offer fans top-level games year-round between the strongest teams, with the best players competing. In addition, they believe that, without professional, modern, and transparent governance, the sport of football can't prosper and remain the most universal sport in the world. What's good for football—and Real Madrid—are more intertwined than you think.

There are many reasons behind Real Madrid's success in the Champions League. Florentino Pérez believes culture is the most important ingredient to winning on and off the pitch. For the media and pundits, culture is hard to define, let alone analyze, measure, and compare—so they seem reluctant to attribute success to culture, although now there are more and more references to "Real Madrid's DNA." It's much easier to reference and compare transfer values and total salaries or performance data and statistics for insights.

Maybe our fascination with fantasy league sports has made us lose sight of the fact that, at the end of the day, a real team must work together and sacrifice for each other. Football is a highly improvised and team-oriented sport, even more so than basketball, for example. Eleven soccer players form a team on the pitch, interacting in a fluid, rapidly unfolding manner. In football, a team's probability of scoring goes up as it strings together more and more successful passes. There is no shot clock like in basketball, so a team can possess the ball as long as it would like, and limit scoring opportunities for their opponents. However, football teams do face the pressure of a timed game. Star players like Cristiano Ronaldo and Lionel Messi can significantly impact a game, as can NBA stars. But a football star's scoring is much more dependent on the player receiving passes from teammates at exactly the right time and place. Therefore, the stars who score need teammates willing to pass and sacrifice themselves for the team. They need team culture and chemistry.

Sixty Seconds

On average, when Ronaldo and Messi were at Real Madrid and Barcelona, respectively, they possessed the ball twenty times a game, three seconds each time, for a total of merely sixty seconds per ninety-minute game. You read that right! Ronaldo and Messi touched the ball for around sixty seconds per game, around 1 percent of the game time. Both stars must work for their shots, as they are often fouled three to four times per game, reducing their twenty possessions to sixteen or seventeen. Goals mean a lot more in football than points do in most sports. Quality shot opportunities in football are very scarce, so making the most of them is critical. Within those sixteen to seventeen non-fouled possessions, Ronaldo and Messi typically attempt four to six shots per game.

Of Ronaldo's and Messi's four to six shots, 40 to 50 percent would be on goal, and 40 to 50 percent of shots on goal (about 25 percent of all shots) will actually result in a goal, which is ridiculously high compared to most other football players. Ronaldo and Messi were responsible for around 50 to 60 percent of their teams' total shot attempts when including assists.

Football stars get no guarantee of possessions or shots. Because of the interdependence required in football, the entire team needs a culture and team chemistry of trust and sacrifice to work together without hesitation.

I remember watching the highlights of PSG beating Olympique Lyon in September 2017—memorable not for the goals, but the surprising sight of Neymar and Edinson Cavani fighting over taking a penalty kick. Cavani had been the penalty taker in the 2016–17 season; however, it appeared that Neymar assumed that he would now hold that responsibility following his €222 million transfer. Both players moved to the ball and had what appeared to be an awkward discussion. Cavani converted the penalty. However, in Unai Emery's post-match press conference, the manager explained, "I have asked both players to settle this between them. I hope they are able to reach an agreement—otherwise, I will decide. I do not want this to become a problem for us." To me, Emery's response indicated that maybe something was missing.

Later during that 2017–18 season, Real Madrid played PSG in the Round of 16 in the Champions League. Pundits were talking about PSG's talent and domination in Ligue 1 and the goal scoring of Cavani, Mbappé, and Neymar. (In the 2017–18 season, PSG would win Ligue 1 by thirteen points, and win the Coupe de France, Coupe de la Ligue, and Trophée des Champions.) However, Real Madrid beat PSG 5–2 on aggregate. (Neymar was injured and did not play the second match at home, but PSG were already down 1–3.) Real Madrid would go on to beat Juventus in the quarterfinals, Bayern Munich in the semifinals, and Liverpool in the final.

It's not easy to win the Champions League even if you have the best team on paper. There are too many factors and elements. However, I couldn't help but think Real Madrid's culture helped them.

Too-Much-Talent Effect

One of the questions I asked in my research was whether having too much talent may have contributed to some clubs' underperformance on the pitch. One of my former colleagues at Columbia Business School, Adam Galinsky, who co-authored an academic study with Roderick I. Swaab and Michael Schaerer of INSEAD Business School, Richard Ronay of VU University Amsterdam, and doctoral student Eric Anicich of Columbia Business School, looked into this effect for an academic paper published in *Psychological Science* in June 2014. They used it as the basis for their study of individual and team data from regular season NBA play from 2002 to 2012. They specifically analyzed the Estimated Wins Added, or EWA, which estimates the victories that any given player adds over and above what a replacement player would contribute. They used play-by-play metrics, such as total assists and defensive rebounds, to quantify team coordination. For overall team performance, they simply calculated the percentage of the season's games that were wins. The business school researchers discovered that adding more talent only improved team performance to a certain point, after which it became a liability due to diminished team coordination. Apparently, having too many stars is not a good idea in basketball.

When Galinksy and Swaab conducted a similar study for football, based on data from FIFA, their conclusion was the same. Loading a football team with star players doesn't guarantee a winning season because, at some point, the too-much-talent effect kicks in (pun intended). In football, even more than in basketball, scoring requires a team to get the ball to the right person, in the right position, at the right time, which typically involves a number of complex moves performed quickly under time pressure. Remember, Ronaldo typically possesses the ball only a few times a match and a few seconds at a time.

"If you have too many people and they all want to be stars, coordination goes down," Galinsky says.* Unfortunately, there is no way to predict when a

---

* Adam Galinsky, "Is Your Team Too Talented?" *Columbia Ideas at Work*. http://www8.gsb.columbia.edu/ideas-at-work/publication/1700/is-your-team-too-talented.

particular team is nearing the too-much-talent effect threshold. Most teams need people with different skills to accomplish various tasks—a basketball team, for example, needs players who can rebound and excel at defense in addition to star shooters. Galinsky says, "Having a range of skills is critical . . . When you have interdependence, you need role differentiation."

A warning sign exists when a team is nearing the tipping point: too many team members are competing to perform the same tasks, while other tasks—those that aren't in the spotlight—aren't getting done. Many managers and team members have observed the too-much-talent effect personally. Galinsky asks, "Have you seen a situation where many people on a team are suspicious of each other and they're not integrating their behavior very well?" In general, Galinsky says, it is better not to model your basketball team after the All-Stars—in which every player wants the ball, and no one wants to play defense.

Galinsky and Swaab's research findings support the existence of a too-much-talent effect and explain why it occurs. However, as the professors explained in a final study, people intuitively believe that their favorite team will get better by piling on more and more top talent. This is true in baseball, where a pitcher's or batter's individual performance has more impact on the final score. Baseball teams spending as much money as they can to get as much talent as possible will have positive results more often than in basketball and football, which also explains why some lessons of Michael Lewis's book *Moneyball*, which is about a baseball team, may not be applicable to organizations that require interdependence.

When I followed up with Galinsky and Anicich in person to talk about Real Madrid, they told me that a strong culture and shared values can minimize or possibly even eliminate the too-much-talent problem. A shared culture and values may serve to direct attention away from status conflict and toward an overarching group goal. They think that when that group goal is salient and status conflict is minimized, coordination becomes easier because stars will be less focused on their own standing within the group (and on the need for individual glory that comes with that self-focus). They believe that an organization's commitment, manifested in mutual values, to channeling focus toward a common purpose and a common vision for the group's future increases the likelihood of stability and success.

PILLARS THAT SUPPORT REAL MADRID'S CULTURE ON THE PITCH

After reading *Moneyball* and watching the film of the same name, I wanted to answer the question: *What are the secrets to building a successful sport team?* One of the biggest, unexpected surprises I had from my discussions with the Real Madrid executives was how much they talked about supporting the culture. I call them "pillars" of support—as a pillar is constructed as a vertical support of a building or structure. On the pitch, Real Madrid's leaders are concerned that without pillars of support a sporting team's success can quickly deteriorate, especially when a key leader or manager or player(s) leave the club.

I learned a few key pillars that support Real Madrid's culture on the pitch:

"Codified" Mission and Values Statement

One of the first things Florentino did when he took over as president was to "codify" Real Madrid's authentic culture by writing down a mission and values statement that was derived from the fans. The statement creates outstanding clarity and serves as a North Star or GPS for the club. The fact that it is written down means that the statement can be referred to and passed down.

The mission and values statement helps with player selection. If a player, for example, had made racist comments in the past, then it is challenging for Real Madrid to sign the player no matter how talented the player is or what the data analytics say because of Real Madrid's mission statement, which includes:

> To be a multicultural club that is both appreciated and respected throughout the world both for its sporting successes and for the values it disseminates, which, based on the search for excellence both on and off the field of play, contribute toward fulfilling the expectations of its members and followers.

Real Madrid want to be a multicultural club that's respected and has values. The hypothetical player who had made racist comments would not fit.

Captains

Typically, a manager/coach appoints the captains of a sports team, or the players elect a captain. Many times, it is the star player. At Real Madrid, the two most senior players on the squad are automatically named captains—they are not elected by the players or appointed by the coach. This is for several reasons. The players would have been at the club a long time, and know the history, traditions, and values of Real Madrid very well. The process rewards seniority and loyalty—the role is earned over time. In addition, the process supports the idea that all players are equal and a star player doesn't automatically become a captain or leader—you have to earn it. Captains at Real Madrid hold a unique position of respect on the squad because the other players know how difficult it is to be on the squad for that long—it takes an extremely high level of football skill combined with dedication and commitment.

Homegrown Academy Graduates

Statistically, Real Madrid's academy is the most successful in Europe. There are more Real Madrid academy graduates playing in the Top 5 Leagues than graduates of any other academy.[*]

Since 2000, typically around five to eight of the twenty-two to twenty-five players (around 25 percent) on Real Madrid's first team were developed by the club's own academy. For context, during Bernabéu's era, between 1955 and 1960, the rate of academy graduates on the team was around 10 to 15 percent.

Real Madrid executives value academy graduates on the first team because these players have grown up with Real Madrid's history, traditions, and values. In an interview, Florentino explained: "Real Madrid constantly devotes a great deal of effort to the instilling of values. This involves channeling the necessary attention and resources into the youth clubs and nurturing not only the sporting development of its youth players but also their social, ethical, and civic education."

The academy graduates bring such love, passion, and enthusiasm to being on the first team because for many this has been their life's dream.

---

[*] https://onefootball.com/en/news/real-madrids-youth-academy-contributes-the-most-players-to-the-five-big-leagues-38454643.

They are the "culture carriers" reinforcing the club's culture and values. Their presence alongside imported star players yields the greatest benefits. According to Florentino, "The world-class players we have signed have increased our prestige in world football, but we will combine them with our own players from Real Madrid in what can be an explosive mix."* Like the experienced captains who know and exemplify what Real Madrid means, the academy players promote the values that unify the club, set examples, and create the right atmosphere to achieve the club's goals and mission. Many times, it is the academy graduates who do many of the little things that don't show up in the stat sheets to make the team better.

In addition, members and supporters very much like to see academy players on the first team and especially as starters. It creates a sense of pride, enhancing the passion of the fans. This was part of the special allure of the legendary *Quinta del Buitre* in the 1980s and the community's love for former academy graduates and captains Raúl and Casillas.

"First Among Equals"

Real Madrid executives believe the best player on the team ("first among equals") must be the hardest working and most dedicated in both practice and matches. This first among equals player sets the tone for the rest of the players and supports the culture.

When doing research for *The Real Madrid Way*, my first Real Madrid book, in 2014–15, I attended a practice and Ancelotti had the players do a team running drill. When the whistle blew, Cristiano Ronaldo took off first and started sprinting as hard as he could. Of course, the other players followed and tried to catch up. Ancelotti didn't have to scream at the players to pick up the intensity—Ronaldo brought the intensity. When I spoke to the trainers, they told me incredible tales of Ronaldo's commitment to performance. He didn't go out late to clubs. He didn't

---

* "Perez Works a Quiet Revolution at Real Madrid." Rediff. http://www.rediff.com/sports/2001/oct/17foot1.htm.

have "cheat day" meals. The entire world could see his dedication and commitment. And so could his teammates.

Similar to extremely competitive champions like Michael Jordan and Kobe Bryant, Ronaldo did not need a coach to tell him to work hard. He shows up for practice and training ready to compete with the same intensity as he would for a game. He is self-motivated and driven, and he doesn't want to be outworked or beaten in anything. This intensity and work ethic drives the other star players in a way that the coach can't. The younger players mimic his good habits.

The first among equals, captains, and homegrown academy graduates all work together as leaders. All must work symbiotically with the coach.

Certain Characteristics of the Coach

Real Madrid executives believe that the most successful managers of the club who won Champions League trophies typically had certain helpful characteristics. Being manager of Real Madrid is very unique, because Real Madrid are very unique. The squad is filled with some of the best players in the world who are highly competitive. They all want to play and believe they can contribute to success. They all have different personalities and are at different stages of their careers. As manager, you also have lots of media obligations, public scrutiny, and constant rumors to navigate.

One characteristic that seems to work best for Real Madrid's recent managers is being a former elite player, such as Ancelotti or Zidane. Ancelotti was a key part of the Milan squad that won consecutive European Cups in 1989 and 1990. Before coaching Madrid, he had won two Champions League trophies as manager of Milan. As a player, Zidane was named FIFA World Player of the Year several times and won the 1998 Ballon d'Or. In the 2002 Champions League final, he scored a left-foot volleyed winner for Real Madrid that is considered one of the greatest goals in the competition's history. Before coaching the Real Madrid senior team, Zidane was the coach of Real Madrid's second team, Real Madrid Castilla. After Zidane took over the senior team, remarkably, he accumulated eight trophies before he had eight losses. Zidane was the second former Real Madrid senior player (after Miguel Muñoz) to win the European Cup / Champions League as both a Real Madrid player and Real Madrid manager.

Muñoz won two European Cups as a player (1956 and 1957) before retiring. And after a brief apprenticeship as coach for the Real Madrid reserve team, he led Real Madrid to two European Cup wins (1960 and 1966). Zidane won three Champions League trophies in a row (2016, 2017, 2018)—the only manager to have accomplished this—and one as an assistant manager to Ancelotti in 2014. Vicente del Bosque won five LaLiga and four Copa del Rey titles with Real Madrid. He was also a starter on the Real Madrid team that lost to Liverpool in the 1981 European Cup final. After retiring, he coached Real Madrid Castilla and was a caretaker for the senior team two times when managers were fired. He won two Champions League titles as Real Madrid manager (2000 and 2002) before coaching Spain to the World Cup title in 2010, not to mention Euro titles in 2008 and 2012.

The manager being a former elite player helps facilitate the manager having a special relationship with star players, because the manager understands what they're going through, while the players respect the manager's success as a player. When Ancelotti or Zidane tells a star player something, it has more gravitas. And this is important when it comes to rotation and substitution decisions.

Another characteristic of a successful manager is a calm demeanor. Some clubs need a hard-driving, intense coach to squeeze the maximum talent from each player and the team, or to set the tone because things have gotten stale or athletes are too complacent and comfortable. At Real Madrid, there is a lot of scrutiny, stress, and pressure, with lots of ups and downs. Frequently, the manager being calm helps the overall environment. Ancelotti, Del Bosque, and Zidane are not only calm, they are patient, humble, and unassuming.

Lastly, the manager knowing the culture of the club (having been a former player or academy player) can be a big factor in success. Real Madrid academy graduate Vicente del Bosque is a perfect example of this.

Zidane also played at Real Madrid. However, being a former Real Madrid player hasn't always proved advantageous.

Ramos in 90+3; Rodrygo in 90 and 90+1; Bellingham in 90+

Think about all the late-game player heroics in El Clásicos or the Champions League. And how important these moments are in the history, traditions, and shared community experiences of Real Madrid. The names and numbers in the title above speak for themselves. No explanation is necessary for anyone in the Real Madrid community.

Real Madrid are known for never giving up until the referee blows the whistle—which is a key value of the club and expectation of the community. A large, sophisticated medical staff and manager's rotations and motivation are required to support the players and that value of the club, especially at the end of the season.

Fair and Equal Treatment

Fair and equal treatment is a key element of the Real Madrid culture that supports Real Madrid's leadership roles and success. The club philosophy, published along with Real Madrid's mission and values, emphasizes the good of the whole over that of the individual. Equal treatment for all has been a guiding principle since the days of Bernabéu. With a firm grasp of this principle, Florentino and his management team have made difficult and potentially unpopular decisions with confidence that they are acting for the good of the entire community.

Real Madrid go to great pains to treat players as equally and consistently as possible. Every member of the team must feel important, especially when superstars are involved, and the best way to convey that is by treating all of them in exactly the same way. In the Real Madrid locker room, for example, all players have the same exact lockers and are strictly

ordered by number. If all the players sat down simultaneously on the
wooden bench in front of their lockers, they would be shoulder to shoulder. In the U.S., in contrast, teams commonly provide star players with
special, larger lockers and cushioned chairs or preferred locations in the
locker room. Similarly, no Real Madrid player receives special or different
travel accommodations. In the U.S., on the other hand, teams commonly
provide star players with larger hotel rooms and other amenities. Also,
no Real Madrid player receives special seating for family members for
matches. A player who wishes special seats or box seats must pay for the
difference in cost. In the U.S., however, star players' families are often
provided VIP seating as a part of their contract. Real Madrid's players'
contracts are standardized, each including the same provisions and codes
of conduct.* The only real difference between one contract and another
is the Euro amount. Real Madrid management found that sticking to this
policy removes any unfair disadvantage or treatment when negotiating
contracts with different players, reducing negotiating time and confrontation because "it is what it is."†

Of course, every player knows compensation will differ depending
on demand, technical skills, and performance, but Real Madrid believe
treatment outside of that must be consistent. Real Madrid management
believes exceptions can negatively impact teamwork and team spirit and
create future challenges and distractions. Over time, the managers have
learned to be even more focused on making sure they do not rationalize

---

* The Code of Conduct requires the players to adhere to and support the club in its commitments
with sponsors, advertisers, social actions, etc., providing the players a proper and adequate image.
In any public appearances of the club, the players represent the same need to respect agreements
with sponsors while transmitting an image of Real Madrid according to their sport and institutional
values. They must show respect to the institution they represent, through both verbal and nonverbal
communication, an essential part of which is the dress and behavior.

† Research by organizational culture expert Vega Factor and shared in *Primed to Perform* by Neel
Doshi and Lindsay McGregor has proven that *why* people participate in an activity determines how
well they perform. When people are motivated by emotional pressure (such as prestige chasing) or
economic pressure (the desire to win a reward or avoid a punishment), their performance declines.
Policies like this keep players focused on the motives that have been proven to truly drive performance: play (love of the game), purpose, and potential. Athletes driven by these last three have been
proven to have higher levels of grit and lower burnout.

incremental exceptions. Real Madrid's strategy means that talented employees may leave the organization because leadership is unwilling to compromise the community's goals and core values. Players who put their personal or professional aspirations first (going against the stated team philosophy, including economic responsibility or fairness) may choose to leave if their contract demands are not met. Management may be criticized by the press and fans for letting players walk, when management is actually acting in concert with the community's values and expectations. Determining which players to sign, or re-sign, and which to let go, and even how much to pay each player, is part art and part science, balancing financial considerations with cultural ones, economic responsibility with talent needed to win, all with relative fairness and in alignment with the organization's core values. Making tough decisions regarding beloved players and managers seemed to be one of the most challenging aspects for Real Madrid executives.

REAL MADRID VS. THE PREMIER LEAGUE IN THE CHAMPIONS LEAGUE

If you talk to players and managers, winning the Champions League is very different than winning the domestic league. The intensity and pressure are much higher. Any mistakes are magnified by the knockout format—that is, elimination of the losing team of each match. The home/away and knockout formats also impact strategy. The knockout rounds are at the end of the season, when players tend to be mentally and physically tired or dealing with injuries. Experience is often an advantage for players and coaches, allowing them to remain calm. Typically, a club's history can provide inspiration and belief, or intimidation and doubt.

Real Madrid focus on elements to intensify and sustain the club's culture, such as equality and the incorporation of academy players to improve their chances. However, in the end, they can't control the outcome on the field, just as a casino manager can't control the outcomes of randomness and luck in the casino.

The Impact of Luck

Man City CEO Ferran Soriano stated that Real Madrid winning the Champions League in 2021–22 should be accredited to luck more than anything else. Soriano said, "People now talk about the success of Real Madrid in the Champions League, and I think it's fair to say that there has been a bit of luck. Maybe I could say that they deserved to lose against PSG, Chelsea, Manchester City, and Liverpool . . . People no longer remember that at the end of the 1980s Madrid had a fantastic team, one of the best in history, with Emilio Butragueño, and that they failed to win the Champions League."*

At the outset, it is important to mention that it is actually very frightening how much luck impacts football results and the narrative. Around 50 percent of goals in soccer are a result of some sort of lucky incident (e.g., a ball redirection, or a lucky bounce or block to a goal scorer). Goals typically happen in situations that can't easily be replicated, many times even when the players are in exactly the same position (e.g., a fluke 1-in-100 shot by an unheralded player, or a defender slipping at a crucial moment). The game can be significantly impacted by a refereeing error or judgment (e.g., if the referee sees or judges a hand ball, or believes a foul was made in the box or not, or the referee believes an infraction merits a yellow or red card). Also, referees are human, and can be influenced by crowd reaction and noise (part of the "home field advantage"). Players can be missed through injury or suspensions for red cards and accumulation of yellow cards, or not play at peak performance because of mental and physical fatigue.

All of this is magnified by a low average total goals per game in football (around 2.7). A lower-ranked team can "park the bus" in front of the goal and limit opportunities for their higher-ranked opponent to score. Then the lower-ranked team can capitalize on one mistake, score, and win the game.

---

* https://psgtalk.com/2022/06/deserved-to-lose-exec-says-one-factor-helped-real-madrid-win-the-ucl-this-season/.

In basketball there is a shot clock to ensure many opportunities to score and defend. In baseball, there are a minimum number of opportunities to bat. The team favored by bettors wins just half the time in football, whereas the favorite wins three-fifths of the time in baseball and two-thirds of the time in basketball.

A team can have a favorable or unfavorable Group or draw in the Champions League. Even the timing of when a team plays their match can have a significant impact, as teams must decide when to prioritize rest and recovery of players for domestic leagues and other tournaments that could impact their qualification for the following year.

Sports are supposed to reward determination, skill, and hard work. The existence or acknowledgment of luck undermines merit—luck rewards the undeserving. Paradoxically, luck is both an ugly truth about the game and an essential part of the beauty of the game.

While luck has an impact, many factors matter such as culture, history, experience, traditions, money, and talent.

Real Madrid's recent success in the Champions League has obscured what has been going on with Premier League clubs. In the six seasons from 2011–12 to 2016–17, LaLiga with Real Madrid, Atlético Madrid, and Barcelona had the most finalists (five) and winners (four). The Premier League had one finalist and winner—Chelsea. The Premier League only had five quarterfinalists compared to LaLiga's seventeen and Bundesliga's ten.

In the six seasons since 2017–18, the Premier League has the most finalists (seven) and winners (three). LaLiga has two with Real Madrid. The Bundesliga has one with Bayern. The Premier League has fifteen quarterfinalists compared to LaLiga's eleven and Bundesliga's seven. Going deeper, Barcelona and Atlético Madrid have each only been to the semifinals once since 2016/17—while Real Madrid won four times since then. Meanwhile, since then, four clubs from the Premier League have reached the finals—Chelsea, Liverpool, Man City, and Tottenham.

Table 7.1: Clubs from Various Leagues in the Quarterfinals
of the Champions League Since 2011–2012

	2022–23	2021–22	2020–21	2019–20	2018–19	2017–18	Total	Winners	Finalists
Premier League	2	3	3	1	4	2	15	3	7
LaLiga	1	3	1	2	1	3	11	2	2
Bundesliga	1	1	2	2		1	7	1	1
Serie A	3			1	1	2	7		2
Ligue 1			1	2			3		
Other	1	1	1		2		5		
Total	8	8	8	8	8	8	48	6	12
Finals	Man City	**Real Madrid**	Chelsea	Bayern	Liver-pool	**Real Madrid**			
	Inter Milan	Liver-pool	Man City	PSG	Totten-ham	Liver-pool			

	2016–17	2015–16	2014–15	2013–14	2012–13	2011–12	Total	Winners	Finalists
Premier League	1	1	0	2	0	1	5	1	1
LaLiga	3	3	3	3	3	2	17	4	5
Bundesliga	2	2	1	2	2	1	10	1	3
Serie A	1		1		1	1	4		1
Ligue 1	1	1	2	1	1	1	7		
Other		1	1		1	2	5		
Total	8	8	8	8	8	8	48	6	10
Finals	**Real Madrid**	**Real Madrid**	Barcelona	**Real Madrid**	Bayern	Chelsea			
	Juventus	Atlético	Juventus	Atlético	Dort-mund	Bayern			

Premier League dominance would be even more pronounced in the last six seasons (2017–18 through 2022–23) if it weren't for Real Madrid. In the last seven seasons, Real Madrid have faced Premier League teams eleven times in Champions League knockout rounds and have eight wins to three losses (two of the losses were to Man City).

PLAYERS FOR THE CHAMPIONS LEAGUE (AND WORLD SERIES)

After speaking to Real Madrid executives for my first book, they explained some things to me that, upon reflection, if applied to other sports, seemed to identify some potential oversights in some baseball data analytics closely associated with Billy Beane and *Moneyball*.

Obviously, Billy Beane is one of the most respected sports executives in the world—and for good reason. Having never met Beane, I "cold called" his office to explain that I was writing a book about Real Madrid, and as a part of my research I had done some analysis that showed there may be some potential oversights in some "Moneyball" ideas. I said that out of professional courtesy I wanted to send him a draft of the book in advance of its publication for him to be able to comment. Remarkably, and showing the type of person that he is, Billy Beane read a draft of *The Real Madrid Way*, called me back, gave me comments, and even wrote an endorsement.

When we spoke, I could immediately tell his mind was focused on innovation, in part supported by the environment and culture he was in—close to Silicon Valley. He wasn't defensive at all; actually, he was the opposite and wanted to be challenged. (His approach reminded me of several Real Madrid executives.) But what surprised me the most was how important he thought culture was to the Oakland Athletics' success—the easy-to-digest data analytics headlines generated by his story obscured a lot of nuances of what he had helped build.

In the appendix of *The Real Madrid Way*, I provided data and analysis to show that there were certain baseball players who had higher batting averages in the playoffs than the regular season, like Reggie Jackson (often referred to as Mr. October for hitting home runs in the October playoffs). Until my book, most of the top baseball data analytics experts said this was because these players didn't have a large enough data set—more at bats in the playoffs would eventually bring the batters to their historical season batting averages. But I showed that certain batters like Reggie Jackson had higher batting averages against the best two pitchers of the opposing team during the regular season, and worse batting averages against the bottom three pitchers. My hypothesis is that certain players preferred to hit pitches with more speed, and the two best pitchers typically threw the ball faster than the bottom three pitchers on the team. And in the baseball playoffs, most of the pitches are thrown by a team's best two pitchers. The media called Reggie Jackson a "clutch" hitter. But Reggie Jackson was simply doing what he did in the regular season—it's just that absence of the bottom three pitchers during the playoffs obscured what was happening.

The inspiration for my baseball analysis was my examination of selected Real Madrid player performances during their time in LaLiga and the Champions League. I selected certain players who played at least fifty games for Real Madrid in the European Cup / Champions League. I did not examine players' statistics before or after they played at Real Madrid, because they could have played in a different system with a different caliber of players. The Champions League games should have higher quality opponents than a typical LaLiga game, since teams must qualify. The analysis shows that Di Stéfano and Gento, Figo, and Raúl, and Benzema averaged higher goals per game in the Champions League than in LaLiga. Emilio Butragueño was an amazing player and legend for Real Madrid. His average goals per match for his 341-match LaLiga career was 0.36. While he didn't have over fifty matches in the European Cup competition to be included in the analysis, he did have twenty-nine appearances, and he had seventeen goals (0.58 goals per match).

They were all like Reggie Jackson—they did better against better competition.

Table 7.2: Goals per Game in LaLiga and Champions League

	Goals per Game*		
	LaLiga	Champions League	% Change
Di Stéfano	0.76	0.84	+10%
Gento	0.30	0.35	+19%
Figo	0.23	0.27	+15%
Raúl	0.41	0.50	+21%
Benzema	0.53	0.60	+13%

* Butragueño, Puskás, and Zidane didn't have more than fifty games in the European Cup / Champions League for Real Madrid.

Examining Cristiano Ronaldo and Messi, while they were both in Spain, illustrates how dominant both players really were in LaLiga, averaging around a goal per game, which is absolutely remarkable. Comparing their goal-per-game numbers with the Real Madrid legends above highlights how amazing they both are to average that rate. This is especially true if one considers that the average goals per game have gone down from around 3.5 overall during the 1950s and 1960s to just above 2.5 over the last several decades. Both of Ronaldo's and Messi's Champions League goals per game are lower than in LaLiga, but that can be attributed somewhat to the numbers moving from simply ridiculous to merely obscene (and moving closer to the mean).

Table 7.3: Goals per Game in LaLiga and Champions League (Ronaldo and Messi)

	Goals per Game*		
	LaLiga	Champions League	% Change
Ronaldo	1.06	1.03	-3%
Messi	0.91	0.80	-12%

* Since Ronaldo joined Real Madrid. Data from Opta Sports Data.

Examining the median for the top fifty scorers in Champions League history in the tournament, we find what we expected: on average, most players, even the best ones, have slightly lower performance in the Champions League, probably due to more competitive teams and/or teams playing more conservatively. Ronaldo's and Messi's goals per game in the Champions League are two times the average of the top fifty players, demonstrating how truly incredible they are. The percentage change in goals per game is -5 percent for the best players in the Champions League, while Real Madrid's players over history are 10 to 20 percent higher.

Table 7.4: Median Goals per Game for the Top Fifty
Scorers in Champions League History

Reg. Season	Champions	% Change
0.48	0.46	-5%

Real Madrid are trying to find special players (like Reggie Jackson) who will help them win Champions Leagues titles, not just domestic trophies. Sometimes certain players who are great at helping a team qualify for the Champions League or win domestic titles don't perform as well in the Champions League. When I speak to players, they explain that the Champions League and domestic leagues are very different—the format, pressure, atmosphere, level of competition, intensity, approach, and so on.

As for baseball, after my analysis became public, some MLB data analytics teams started to emphasize high school batting statistics from away games on Friday nights. Typically, the home team puts their best starting pitcher on the mound in front of the larger home crowd on the weekend.

With more information and context, I hope that now when you look back at the recent Champions League tournaments that Real Madrid won, you have a greater appreciation of some of the important on- and off-the-pitch elements about Real Madrid and football.

There are many reasons behind Real Madrid's success in the Champions League. But Florentino Pérez believes culture is the most important ingredient to winning on and off the pitch. The Real Madrid Revolution is really a story about the continuation of Real Madrid's culture.

Rodrygo's header in stoppage time, to tie Manchester City in the semi-finals of the 2022 Champions League at the Santiago Bernabéu stadium.

FINAL WHISTLE

IN CASE YOU FORGOT . . .

Real Madrid are the most successful football club in history—fifteen European Cup / Champions League titles to date. They have won the Champions League six times since 2013–14. Real Madrid have been in all twenty-four Champions League tournaments since reforms were implemented in 1999–2000 to include up to four clubs per country and won seven of them since (2000, '02, '14, '16, '17, '18, '22, '24).

Real Madrid have always been owned by socios, members who vote on the president every four years, and on other key matters, including the budget. Real Madrid talk about fans owning football because—steeped into their history, ethos, and legal organizational structure—they do.

Real Madrid helped create FIFA and the European Cup and promoted many necessary reforms for the good of the sport. Their accomplishments have been good for both football and Real Madrid.

Ironically, their success is obscuring the serious systemic changes in football. In September 2023, Rory Smith of the *New York Times* wrote, "Perhaps, then, it is time to concede that the UEFA Champions League is not the most interesting continental tournament this season. It is not even the most interesting tournament of that name." Real Madrid recognize the problems in football that need to be resolved and will be a leader in resolving them.

Uninformed pundits say that Real Madrid need a European Super League because they are in financial trouble or have too much debt. This is absolutely ridiculous. Real Madrid were the only club in the Top 5 Leagues to report profits each year during the pandemic. Real Madrid have negative net debt (meaning more cash than debt), excluding financing of the stadium remodeling project. Real Madrid have a sustainable economic-sport model. They have to because they are owned by socios, not billionaires or closely government-related, private equity, and multi-club ownership models.

The truth is that the sustainable economic-sport model for the industry is broken. Even though the annual revenue growth of the European football industry has been around 8 percent in the last twenty years, expenses (in particular player salaries and transfer fees) have increased even faster—meanwhile broadcasting revenue growth may have peaked. Therefore, growth in revenues has not resulted in a significant improvement in financial performance. Losses were a reality for many clubs even before COVID-19 spread, but not Real Madrid. Losses need capital injections.

Closely government-related, private equity, and multi-club ownership models have pumped serious money into their clubs and the football industry to accelerate growth, but at the same time, this has put stress on the entire system. Many fans generally don't care and will push their club's owners to spend even more to get better and better players. But Real Madrid's members do care, because they are the owners. As a result, Real Madrid are pushing for changes to make football more sustainable. That's good for Real Madrid, and that's good for football.

Real Madrid are concerned that football is not innovating enough, or fast enough, and is losing its leadership as a global sport—that's *not* good for football or Real Madrid as a leader in the sport. That's why they believe European competitions must change, to offer fans top-level games year-round between the strongest teams, with the best players competing. The data clearly shows that young people are less and less interested in football, and Real Madrid believe that football has to change before it becomes too late. Young people are interested in online platforms, video games, and social networks. They demand a quality product that football does not presently offer with most of its competitions and stadiums. As for the competitions, as they are currently designed, they do not attract the interest of the global viewer except in their final phases. The proof: The combined new TV rights for the NFL and NBA are expected to bring their total revenues to around €50 billion, and yet European football as a whole makes €30 billion, despite having a much larger fan base across the world. In fact, the domestic value of most European football league's TV rights has stagnated. To compensate for this, many are raising the prices of subscriptions. This may lead to losing fans in the long term.

Obviously, the internet, social media, video games, and even gambling are having an effect on the way that fans interact with the game. At what point, for a global audience, does watching a full match become such a tedious inconvenience that fans would rather absorb the highlights on X and other social media channels? Could the very omnipresence of football, its endless number of meaningless matches, eventually start to eat away at the excitement that powered its growth? Over time, it's likely fans will only make an "appointment to view" for the biggest matches, with the best players—with another device open as they watch.[*]

A more congested schedule, with more competitions, means among other things more player injuries, because of the correlation between the number of matches, the intensity of play, and injuries. In addition, the congested international calendar of men's football also takes opportunities and coverage away from women's football. Many stakeholders are concerned with football's governing bodies' decisions to add more games to the schedule. For Real Madrid, they envision competitions that have more meaningful and entertaining matches for the fans.

At the World Football Summit (WFS) in 2018, Andrea Agnelli, in the context of characterizing one of the debates within football, stated: "The clubs are the only ones taking risks; it used to be true when people said it was only a game, but now it's a business and this needs to be taken into account [. . .] When I look at the cluster of football stakeholders, I see leagues, federations and players that don't take risks, while we are the ones who invest in stadiums, training centres, the development of young players."

When UEFA hosts the Champions League, they are essentially marketing and leveraging the big clubs' global brands and their star players. However, the big global clubs have limited input and there is limited oversight. For as long as the competition organizers are doing both the

---

[*] https://www.theguardian.com/football/2016/oct/24/sky-sports-bt-sport-people-switching-football-off.

commercializing and regulating, there are potential conflicts of interest. In addition, with too many uninteresting matches and entertainment trends, football risks losing some of its global audience and the next generation of fans.

Real Madrid believe that without professional, modern, and transparent governance, the sport of football can't prosper and remain the most universal sport in the world. Football's regulation system has been exposed as a patchwork of rules that often differ by jurisdiction, are inconsistently enforced, and get challenged in court. UEFA is making the rules, and enforcing them, and at the same time UEFA is organizing the competitions with a clear business interest. A separation of these roles would make football more transparent. At the very least, full transparency and consistency in its decision-making processes would strengthen legitimacy and acceptance of UEFA's regulations. While closely government-related owners may be willing to continue to spend, new institutional investors in football won't necessarily accept continued losses at their clubs. If UEFA doesn't consistently punish clubs breaching financial regulations, they will feel more pressure to leave or restructure the current governance.

After the Bosman ruling in 1995, the money in European football moved to the biggest economies in Europe. The few dominant clubs with global brands in the Top 5 Leagues, which are also the top five economies, have further separated themselves, both financially and in performance, from the domestic clubs who primarily rely on league broadcasting revenues and from most others in the Champions League.* However, the threat is the Premier League is becoming "the NBA of football"—with

---

* According to Jordi Badia Perea, who conducted a longitudinal analysis of results between 1996 and 1997 to the 2020–21 seasons, after the Bosman ruling and the rise of satellite televisions (pay TV) between 1994 and 1995, the economic inequality among the clubs is a progressive and unstoppable trend. Hence, economic inequality increases the difference in sport performance among clubs. "This difference in sport performance affects the competitiveness of the domestic leagues. It is only a matter of time, therefore, that this loss of competitiveness ends up affecting the interest of the spectators and, consequently, the commercial value of both, domestic leagues and their clubs, decreases." Badia J. "Cap a una superlliga europea? La desigualtat econòmica i mediàtica i el desequilibri competitiu en l'era del futbol global," PhD thesis. Bellaterra, Cerdanyola del Vallès: Autonomous University of Barcelona (2022).

a critical mass of global clubs with the Big Six (and Newcastle) already effectively in their own breakaway "Super League." The leagues compete against each other for things like time slots; they all play on the weekends, and therefore they compete in the media markets for rights— and the Premier League are the premier TV rights. To compete against the "blockbuster match each weekend" from the Premier League, European and other leagues and clubs are already starting to discuss strategic alternatives, including the joint sales of international broadcast rights— which could be a first step to multi-country leagues.

If trends continue, most of the star football players will play in the Premier League (where the "parent" club of an MCO model is). And the other leagues will essentially become development leagues with feeder clubs.

In the 2023 summer transfer window, the Premier League clubs spent more money on transfer fees than all of Europe's four other major football leagues . . . *combined*. The net spend of the Premier League, transfer fees paid minus transfer fees received, was an over £1 billion *loss*. In comparison, combined, the Bundesliga, Serie A, LaLiga, and Ligue 1 teams made a £531 million *profit* from the transfer market. Bournemouth had a higher net spend during the 2023 summer window than every team outside of the Premier League other than PSG. The spending gap between the Premier League and everyone else will only get wider.

Even the UEFA Champions League should fear the power of the Premier League. The Premier League has more and better match slots for TV. For example, the Premier League can sell a 12:30 PM weekend kickoff to Asia (9:30 PM in Tokyo and 8:30 PM in Beijing) and afternoon and evening weekend games to the US (New York is six hours behind London), which UEFA can't really do with midweek night matches. Because of the midweek night match times, many fans around the world couldn't watch Real Madrid's thrilling comeback victories against PSG, Chelsea, and Man City in the Champions League.

With the proliferation of MCO models, it is not inconceivable that many of the big clubs with the best players essentially will be controlled (maybe not on paper, or officially) by a few people who are closely related to governments or private equity firms.

The players can only play so many matches—mentally and physically. And their professional careers are relatively short. More elite players will realize that to grow and maximize their earnings per match with a fixed limit on matches they can play in a season and their lifetimes, the matches need to be as many global "events" of quality as possible to maximize revenues. Typically, those higher-earning matches are for clubs. Therefore, elite players will be more conscious that their club matches also need to be more meaningful.

The sport of golf and the PGA Tour, with all their history and traditions, were resistant to change. The LIV Tour disrupted golf with a lot of capital and a new entertainment- and player-friendly approach. There were fewer players playing at tournaments, fewer tournaments, and fewer tournament days of golf—the opposite of what's happening in football. The critical mass of star players that left the PGA and joined the LIV Tour forced change. Can a new or existing league get a critical mass of players and disrupt football? Can a new competition excite current fans and attract a new generation of fans?

A new FIFA Club World Cup can offer more opportunities for clubs and players from leagues around the world to compete to be world champions—not just champions of Europe or another continent. It could have more global interest. Can it be as, or more, prestigious than the UEFA European Champions League? Could global fans, sponsors, and broadcasters like the tournament so much they will think it should be held every two years (instead of every four)? A FIFA World Cup every two years may not have had some support because of history and tradition, but a FIFA Club World Cup may be viewed differently. Currently, Real Madrid have the most FIFA Club World Cup titles with five (Barcelona is second with three).

Remember what I wrote at the beginning of the book about the founding of the Premier League and Liverpool: the histories and traditions of all big football leagues and clubs were built with many motivations—including money and power.

A brilliant Apple TV+ documentary entitled *Super League: The War for Football* is different from others in that it listens to, and presents arguments from, all sides rather than just the backlash and victory for fans. Film director Jeff Zimbalist said, "The problems underlying the industry that led to this [European Super League] proposal have not been addressed . . . Everyone we speak to in the series, which is over thirty different experts, agrees that there's another crisis facing the sport . . . One way or another, football will have to reckon with some of the challenges it's facing."

Football has an inbuilt, reflexive aversion to change, but the sport should be thinking about the future. Football, and especially European football, requires reforms. It's obvious. It's not a sustainable industry. There are people trying to protect either something that already disappeared, or themselves. The myth of football is that it belongs to the working-class, local fan. But rightly or wrongly, capitalism got its hands on football and made it entertainment, and it's not going to let go. Football is becoming more about entertainment with each TikTok highlight, transfer update tweet, video game release, premium subscription, new tech-enabled stadium, and DTC docuseries. If the sport is to continue its position, evolution is inevitable—toward more entertaining, competitive, and attractive football for fans all over the world.

The Super League debate exposed the hypocrisy within contemporary football. Professor Paul Widdop, from Manchester University, in an interview in the *Yorkshire Post* in 2021, explained that at a time when investors from the U.S. have taken control of some English teams, it is logical for football to explore financial models similar to that of the NBA or NFL. Investment requires stability, leading to the near certainty that "a Super League would be huge, it would rival the NBA, the NFL, there's no doubt about it. We are so outraged now, and yet you, me, every fan that has watched Sky Sports and paid money for replica shirts is complicit in this move towards where we are going."[*]

It's hard to see a happy ending for everyone because you'd need every stakeholder to come together, and work together, for the greater good. It would take everyone to essentially compromise, and that just doesn't look

* Westby N. (2021). "European Super League Idea Arose Because Global Fans Not Interested in Tradition." *Yorkshire Post*, April 27. Available at: https://www.yorkshirepost.co.uk/sport/football/european-super-league-idea-arose-because-global-fans-not-interested-in-tradition-3212637. (Accessed April 27, 2021.)

like it will happen at the moment.* And sadly, no urgency for real change may become football's biggest regret. What can the consequences be? Remember that baseball was once America's pastime.

Real Madrid don't want to take football's current position as the world's most popular sport for granted and are keen to innovate for the future. They recognize entertainment is more competitive and behaviors are changing. Fans are less resistant to change than commonly assumed. New generations are more informed and have higher expectations. You also have globalization, technology, and a new mindset. Global fans deserve the right to watch the top-quality matches more frequently, which requires top players having enough recovery time and rest to perform at the highest level.

Real Madrid are doing what they have done since their founding, taking leadership and innovating to protect football and themselves. What's good for football—and Real Madrid—are more intertwined than you think.

---

* In Europe, the stakeholders include: Domestic Leagues (World Leagues Forum, European Leagues), National Associations / Governing Bodies (FIFA, UEFA), Clubs (ECA), Players (FIFAPRO), Agents (The Football Forum, EFAA), Supporters (Football Supporters Europe), and EU/Government (European Commission).

ACKNOWLEDGMENTS

I WOULD LIKE to thank BenBella and their editors and staff. Thank you for believing in the importance of this project.

I would like to thank my family for their support and a few friends for reviewing the book and giving me feedback: Simon Amselem, Borja Arteaga, Tim Cahill, Thomas Lombardi, Peter Maguire, Federico Mari, and Stefan Szymanski.

I would also like to thank my 2023 and 2024 Summer Research Analysts: Bruno Arteaga Barreiros (The Global College, Madrid), Miguel Báez Herrera (Runnymede College, Madrid), Tommaso de Donato (Boston College), Thomas Garity (Harvard University), Charlie Pliner (Brown University), Arabella Titley (St. Mary's Calne, England), Franz Vacca (Bocconi University), and Jamie Weymouth (Yale University).

In addition, for information about the history of the Premier League, in particular, I utilized the works of Joshua Robinson and Jonathan Clegg, including their book *The Club: How the English Premier League Became the Wildest, Richest, Most Disruptive Force in Sports*.

Finally, I want to thank a few special places and their staff that inspired, supported, and encouraged me writing this book: El Landò Restaurant Madrid, Don Giovanni Restaurant Madrid, Salmon Guru Bar Madrid, Matador Club Madrid, Mandarin Oriental Ritz Madrid, Avra Restaurant New York, and Rao's Restaurant New York.

INDEX

ABOUT THE AUTHOR

STEVEN G. MANDIS has been an adjunct professor at Columbia Business School and has taught at Columbia's Masters of Sports Management Program. While writing his award-winning book *The Real Madrid Way: How Values Created the Most Successful Sports Team on the Planet* (BenBella, 2016), he was the first researcher to be given unprecedented behind-the-scenes access to analyze both the on-the-field and business aspects of a global sports team. Mandis worked at Goldman Sachs in the investment banking, private equity, and proprietary trading areas; his previous award-winning book, *What Happened*

The author (center) with Emilio Butragueño and Raúl, Real Madrid gentlemen, champions, and legends.

to Goldman Sachs: An Insider's Story of Organizational Drift and Its Unin-tended Consequences (Harvard Business Review Press, 2013), is a rigorous analysis of if, why, and how the culture of Goldman Sachs changed. After leaving Goldman, he co-founded a multibillion-dollar global alternative asset management firm that was a trading and investment banking client of Goldman's. During the financial crisis, Mandis was a senior adviser to McKinsey before becoming chief of staff to the president and COO of Citigroup, and serving on executive, management, and risk committees at the firm.

Mandis is Chairman and Senior Partner of Kalamata Holdings, an investment company. He holds a BA from the University of Chicago and an MA, MPhil, and PhD from Columbia University. Mandis was a two-sport varsity athlete in college and currently competes in triathlons and ultramarathons, including the IRONMAN World Championships in Kailua-Kona, Hawaii; IRONMAN 70.3 World Championships in Zell Am See-Kaprun, Austria; Escape from Alcatraz in San Francisco, Cali-fornia; and Marathon des Sables in the Sahara Desert, Morocco. He was awarded the Ellis Island Medal of Honor, given to children of immigrants who exemplify a life dedicated to community service.